D0082722

CLINTON JR. COLLEGE LIBRARY

Legalizing Marijuana
Drug Policy Reform and
Prohibition Politics

RUDOLPH J. GERBER

FOREWORD BY
JOHN SPERLING

PRAEGER

Westport, Connecticut
London

Library of Congress Cataloging-in-Publication Data

Gerber, Rudolph Joseph, 1938–
    Legalizing marijuana : drug policy reform and prohibition politics / Rudolph J. Gerber ;
foreword by John Sperling.
        p. cm.
    Includes bibliographical references and index.
    ISBN 0–275–97448–0 (alk. paper)
        1. Marijuana—Government policy—United States.   2. Narcotics, Control of—History—
United States.   3. Marijuana—Therapeutic use—United States.   4. Drug legalization—
United States.   I. Title.
    HV5822.M3G47   2004
    364.1′77—dc22   2003068715

British Library Cataloguing in Publication Data is available.

Copyright © 2004 by Rudolph J. Gerber

All rights reserved. No portion of this book may be
reproduced, by any process or technique, without the
express written consent of the publisher.

Library of Congress Catalog Card Number: 2003068715
ISBN: 0–275–97448–0

First published in 2004

Praeger Publishers, 88 Post Road West, Westport, CT 06881
An imprint of Greenwood Publishing Group, Inc.
www.praeger.com

Printed in the United States of America

∞™

The paper used in this book complies with the
Permanent Paper Standard issued by the National
Information Standards Organization (Z39.48–1984).

10 9 8 7 6 5 4 3 2

Copyright Acknowledgment

The author and publisher gratefully acknowledge permission to reprint material from "Dope
Fiends," *Harper's* (November 2000), 23–26. Copyright © 2000 by *Harper's Magazine*. All rights
reserved. Reproduced from the November 2000 issue by special permission.

To my wife, Kathleen

Integer vitae, sclerisque purus
—Horace

CONTENTS

FOREWORD

In *Legalizing Marijuana: Drug Policy Reform and Prohibition Politics,* Judge Rudy Gerber recounts the sorry history of how criminalizing the use of a medically useful and essentially harmless plant has justified the erosion of our constitutionally guaranteed liberties: the suppression of political dissent, the oppression of the races, the condemnation of non-white art and artists, and the denial of a life-enhancing medicine to the ill and infirm.

It is a tale of sociopolitical pathology in which a solid core of conservative voters and their political representatives support policies that lack any rational social or economic justification. As Judge Gerber points out, every legitimate study of marijuana's physical and mental effects on humans has shown that it is the drug of choice for alleviating the symptoms of a host of illnesses, especially the treatment of pain and nausea. It is impossible to overdose on marijuana, it is not addictive, one does not develop a tolerance, so dosages do not need to be increased, and no deaths can be attributed to marijuana as are linked to alcohol and tobacco—deaths by accident or by respiratory ailments. Reported deaths from tobacco average 400,000 a year, from alcohol 50,000, and from marijuana, zero.

The political pathology has been particularly marked in the three presidents before the millennium—Reagan, Bush the elder, and Clinton, who shared a drug-induced ethical poverty. In spite of the fact that four presidential commissions convened to study marijuana and found it a relatively harmless narcotic and the drug of choice for several ailments, each of them declared it a dangerous drug requiring Schedule I status. By dint of a clever advertising campaign to sell Nancy Reagan's "Just Say NO to Drugs," Reagan and Bush managed to scam Americans into believing that drugs were the number one problem our society faced—beating out the economy, violent crime, poverty, illiteracy, spousal abuse, and TV violence. Clinton seemed the most unethical. Not only did he cravenly assert that he did "not inhale," once out of office he said that marijuana should be decriminalized, cold comfort to the thousands charged, convicted, and incarcerated for marijuana use during his two administrations.

The drug war is essentially a war against marijuana. If one removes the number of pot users, only about two million hard-core addicts are left. Federal, state, and local direct expenditures on the drug war now total around $60 million annually. If we add to this the millions spent on incarcerating people for drug-related crimes, we reach a sum that, if diverted from the drug war, could pay for the college education of the entire country.

Marijuana, one of the early drugs to be criminalized, has remained the bedrock of a drug war that has wasted billions in tax dollars, incarcerated millions of people for victimless crimes, destabilized and pauperized a half-dozen Andean nations, spawned an international criminal class, and elected countless numbers of witless politicians on a "get tough on drugs" platform. While the drug warriors can rail against the drug lords of the Andes for cultivating poison, marijuana, now homegrown, constitutes the most valuable cash crop in a dozen states. Perhaps the only things that could bring the horrors of the war on drugs home to the voters would be Air Force fighters shooting down private planes suspected of drug trafficking and Army helicopters spraying defoliants over the fields and forests of America. It is ironic that the most fervent supporters of the war on drugs are those who cry loudest for small government.

Even more ironic is the effect the drug war has had on marijuana itself. In *The Botany of Desire*, Michael Pollan writes:

> Operating in the shadow of a ferocious drug war, global pot growers have literally been forced underground into modern, scientifically managed marijuana cellars, where crossbreeding and improved growing methods have turned pot into a more potent, benign high while removing the noxious side effects of the old. The result? Cannabis has been transformed into what is today the most prized and expensive flower in the world.

Since a recent Supreme Court ruling that police can no longer use heat sensors to detect indoor marijuana growers, it is possible that, across the nation, millions of people, including a high percentage of teenagers, will be safely growing hundreds of tons of this prized flower.

So why do the drug war supporters find drugs to be so abhorrent? As Judge Gerber sets forth the case, they believe that undesirable members of the community use drugs—blacks, foreigners, social dissidents, and political radicals. It matters little to these citizens and their legislative representatives that the overwhelming number of drug users are members of the middle class who use drugs in the privacy of their homes and thus are invisible to the moralists and safe from the law. It matters not that the most visible users are addicts whose addiction is most often a product of racial discrimination, poverty, untreated mental illness, and other pathologies of the ghetto. If they are visible, they are to be condemned. The only effective treatment for them is incarceration.

Not only do the supporters of the drug war vote against any politician who is in favor of reform, they also vote in favor of any politician who is "tough on drugs." Unfortunately, a majority of the politicians who inhabit Washington, D.C., and most of the state legislatures are either fearful of these voters if they support drug reform or they ensure their support by being tough on drugs. The ability of these voters to influence legislative behavior is the main reason legislative reform of the drug laws is difficult to the point of impossibility.

The obverse of the question of why there are solid votes to elect legislators who are tough on drugs is this question: Why is there no equally solid block of voters who are prepared to vote for a reformer and against a candidate who favors the drug war? That is a puzzle, because we know that in most states, when given a chance, a majority of voters will vote for reform. The only explanation that can be given is that illegal drugs lack a supportive social context equivalent to the social context that supports alcohol and tobacco. The American culture, for all the talk about multiculturalism, is part of Western civilization, and alcohol has been its major drug of choice for at least 3,000 years; it is used ceremonially as a social fuel and, through the nineteenth century, was the most widely used painkiller. Tobacco, the second drug of choice, has been with us for some 400 years, since the arrival of the first Europeans in the sixteenth century.

There are no widely accepted American social practices that place illegal drugs in contexts that support their use to promote conviviality and social cohesion. How can marijuana, cocaine, and heroin compete with alcohol served in bars and restaurants, at cocktail parties, or before dinners graced with fine wine? Not only are illegal drugs used by "the other," they do not promote a conviviality equal to that promoted by alcohol. With the exception of uppers, such as cocaine and methamphetamine, whose use is not associated with any common ceremony, the other drugs are downers. Although marijuana used socially sometimes leads to group risibility and munchies, it more often leads to quiet and deeply personal calm. It would be difficult to imagine any of these drugs being effective as the social fuel for the gatherings at Thanksgiving or Christmas, at weddings, or at large social functions such as political fundraisers.

Realizing that drug reform through legislation was impossible, Judge Gerber in 1994 was a member of a group of prominent Arizonans who began a campaign to reform Arizona's drug laws through the initiative and referendum process. This effort culminated in 1996 with the passage of Proposition 200, the nation's first initiative dedicated to drug law reform. The initiative was drafted as a referendum on the war on drugs. Not only did the initiative medicalize marijuana, it medicalized all illegal drugs, including cocaine, heroin, methamphetamines, and LSD. In preparation for the initiative campaign, focus groups and poll results showed that nearly 90 percent of likely voters believed that the war on drugs was not only a failure but a fraud as well, and the election results proved the predictability of the work of the focus groups.

Proposition 200 was opposed by all public officials who could make their voices heard—President Clinton, the three former presidents Ford, Carter, and Bush the drug czar, the Arizona congressional delegation, the Arizona legislature, the International Chiefs of Police, and the editorial writers of the major statewide newspaper. It was, they all declared, a cynical attempt to exploit the chronically and terminally ill, well beyond any attempt just to legalize pot. Not one official in Arizona voiced support, and all who spoke predicted its defeat. The voters spoke otherwise by nearly 60 percent.

What was the postelection response of these public officials? Universal denunciation. The voters had been "duped" by slick advertising paid for by out-of-state billionaires while responsible public officials were unfortunately "asleep at the switch." President Clinton, cabinet secretaries, the drug czar, and outraged senators demanded corrective action. In order to prove its own members were not duped, the Arizona legislature immediately passed bills nullifying Proposition 200. Fortunately, the Arizona constitution provided a remedy. By gaining the signatures needed to place Proposition 200 on the 1998 ballot, it remained in effect. In 1998, it once again won overwhelmingly, as did a companion proposition that removed the power of the legislature to amend a voter-approved initiative, thus preventing further legislative tampering with Proposition 200.

The vote in the Arizona legislature to overturn Proposition 200 could have been predicted. The social conservatives would always vote against any form of reform. The social liberals voted for repeal because they feared that the pro–drug war vote would be a large-enough block to defeat them either in the next primary or in a general election. Because social liberals, even when they have a majority, are afraid to vote for reform, the only effective voices for reform are the voters who have voted in favor of seventeen state initiatives modeled on one or more parts of Proposition 200.

As of the date of publication of this book, millions of Americans have voted in favor of some form of drug law reform. By the time initiatives have passed in all of the states allowing initiatives, the majority of voters in nine states and the District of Columbia have cast ballots in favor of reform. With these millions of votes for reform piling up, the drive for reform will finally reach a tipping point, and politicians will then calculate that a vote in favor of drug law reform will not be fatal. Only then can the nation move away from the stupidities of the war on drugs. The change might well begin as it did when Americans forced the politicians to end another stupid war, Vietnam. A U.S. senator might rise in the Senate and recommend that we declare victory in the war on drugs, send the warriors home, and release the prisoners.

Although the drug reform initiatives are made possible by contributions from wealthy reformers, money cannot buy votes in favor of drug law reform. None of the seventeen successful reform initiatives could have won large majorities except for the fact that these voters had a latent disposition to vote against the obvious failures of that war. The function of the campaigns for reform is to trigger that latent disposition.

As one would expect from a distinguished jurist, *Legalizing Marijuana* is a carefully reasoned indictment of the laws against medical marijuana and the slow process of reform. It will help to drive another nail in the coffin of the war on drugs and provide a unique addition to the literature of reform that, taken together, constitutes the intellectual foundation for the war against the war on drugs.

John Sperling, President (ret.)
University of Phoenix, Chair, the Apollo Group

INTRODUCTION

Pot causes insanity—not in its users but in politicians.

Anonymous

"The abuse of tea has taken on the characteristics of a plague—it is not only confined to men but has even spread to women and children. The situation is becoming very dangerous. Tea abuse . . . takes the form of an imperious and irresistible craving." This was the reaction of a Tunisian physician in the 1930s, horrified by the British habit of afternoon tea being adopted in his country.

This book is about a similar horror—our politicians' addiction to the war on drugs and particularly to marijuana that, as of 2004, costs the average American $380 per person per year to wage. While these pages focus on the war against marijuana, their thesis addresses its ramifications for political science, particularly its implications for how to govern well. This war against drugs and marijuana in particular rests on governmental exaggerations no less far-fetched than the Tunisian doctor's misguided alarms about a habitual afternoon cup of English tea.

Lest readers view this topic only as a selfish herbal indulgence, these pages have germinated not in a private marijuana garden but from twenty-two years of judging on the trial and appellate courts of Arizona. Our courts both in Arizona and throughout the nation continue to witness the financial and human boomerang involved in prosecuting people for marijuana use. In the process, they witness how government policy alienates its own citizens by teaching counterproductive lessons about how to govern.

In the 1920s, our nation's prohibition of alcohol divided our country, like Caesar's Gaul, into three parts: the wets, the drys, and the hypocrites. The last group quickly became the most populous and most vocal. Dominated by politicians, this group found that prohibition could offer the best of both worlds: they could inveigh against the evils of alcohol to preserve national virtue while criticizing the overreach of governmental paternalism that was interfering with their right to enjoy a drink of their choice.

Cannabis has achieved a status similar to that of alcohol in the waning days of Prohibition. One in three adult Americans admits to having tried pot. All have survived. Several have even gone on to run for president. Some of the most prolific users have been elected to that or other high offices. Notwithstanding its political triumphs, our government spends billions of dollars through its penal law to deny ordinary nonpolitical folk access to pot, with pot-using officials sometimes leading the assault.

This new prohibition entails substantial costs in lives. In 2000, 734,497 people faced arrest on marijuana charges, twice the number arrested for the same conduct in 1991. Nine in ten of the arrestees were guilty only of simple possession. As of 2003, it cost $1.2 billion annually to keep 60,000 people in our prisons for their marijuana misconduct alone.

The scale of this campaign against marijuana makes pot prohibition the worst injustice perpetrated by our frayed criminal justice policy in the twenty-first century. Instead of more grease for oiling our expanding criminal justice machinery, judges, lawyers, and politicians need more hard questioning about whether this reefer war against our fellow citizens reflects anything more than an expensive, bullheaded, and myopic panic exceeding even the Tunisian doctor's hysteria over English tea.

Our war against pot continues to breed ironies beyond a novelist's dream. Former President Clinton, our first president to publicly confess to the use of marijuana, excused his conduct by "not inhaling." That defense helped him to avoid the prosecution regularly visited during his two terms upon millions of his pot-using fellow citizens disadvantaged only by being less glib or more respiratory than he was.

With varying degrees of candor, three of the four major presidential candidates in the 2000 campaign admitted directly or by pregnant evasions to past illegal drug use, including long lapses into marijuana. On the campaign trail, George Bush pointedly evaded all drug questions about his college years, tacitly suggesting at least some early indulgence. While Bill Bradley's flirtation with pot may have been short-lived, Al Gore's pot use apparently extended over the many years he was in the army, studying in college, working as a reporter, and running for Congress. His sister's use of marijuana under a prescription to combat cancer made her an early poster child for the nation's medical marijuana movement, the same movement repeatedly denounced by her brother's administration as a "hoax."

Among its many other ironies, our war against marijuana betrays a class distinction between the escapees and the arrestees. In government circles, this war regularly generates high-level—but safe—confessions of youthful pot indulgence by those now immune from prosecution. In 1980, when President Ronald Reagan withdrew the name of Douglas Ginsburg for appointment to the United States Supreme Court, the reason given was nothing other than pot: Ginsburg admitted he had smoked marijuana as a student in the 1960s plus a few times in the following decade. Immediately after his *mea culpa*, then-Senator Al Gore, Arizona Governor Bruce Babbitt, and Congressman Newt Gingrich announced that they too had smoked the evil weed in their wayward youth, all without political or penal consequences.

The saga continues. In 2002, New York City Mayor Michael Bloomberg, asked by a reporter if he ever had smoked pot, responded enthusiastically, "You bet I did. And I enjoyed it." Quickly thereafter, the city's billboards featured his larger-than-life picture with this cheerful admission as part of a drug liberalization campaign.

Like lightning, the pot thunderbolt strikes its users with a selectivity revealing this respect for rank and disrespect for equal treatment. While none of the prominent politicians in the preceding paragraphs ever answered criminally for their pot violations, millions of their fellow citizens of lesser political pedigree have shuffled through courts and prisons for the very same conduct overlooked for well-placed politicians. Since 1970, over 13 million lesser-known Americans have faced arrest on marijuana-related charges. Some 52,000 people were arrested and jailed in New York City for smoking marijuana the same year that Mayor Bloomberg made his grinning confession on the city's billboards.

In 1970, before the marijuana panic arrived, 188,903 persons were arrested for marijuana use. By 2000, that number had multiplied seven times. While late-night comedians entertain us with laughs at the expense of Clinton, Gore, Bush, Bloomberg, and others, those not laughing include thousands of less notable users busted for behaviors those in the limelight successfully shrug off as mere youthful indiscretions. In some politicians' minds, marijuana laws apply to The Other, not to oneself.

Political science questions lurk beneath these policies gone awry, but most unscathed politicians have learned how to avoid the questions—indeed, some know the answers but not the questions. Some of the same lawmakers who offhandedly dismiss their personal pot indiscretions become divinely self-righteous in enforcing pot and hard-drug prohibitions against others. Youthful indiscretions appear as felonies on the records of less fortunate persons lacking the protection of college, politics, and high office.

The striking ironies between how our drug law criminalizes ordinary citizens while exempting prominent politicians raise questions not only about hypocrisy but also about the integrity of our government's continuing war against marijuana. Why should such a policy be politically popular? The pot campaign offers subtle advantages for the campaigners. The prospect of personal aggrandizement extends well beyond policy myopia and arbitrary enforcement to larger governmental issues of credibility, inconsistency, cost-benefit analyses, balance of evils, wasteful spending and, not least, legislative paralysis regarding reform. Most elected officials gain from maintaining the status quo no matter how unwise because votes tend to endorse rather than change the status quo.

One of the messages of the following pages is how candor and careful distinctions could produce a more prudent governmental policy. Someday, for a modest beginning, a candid member of our political cabal may acknowledge to the rest of our citizens a meaningful distinction between differing kinds of drugs and differing kinds of users, between the prosecuted and the exempt, between marijuana and hard drugs, and between marijuana, on one hand, and alcohol, cigarettes, and prescription drugs on the other, the latter far more harmful than the former. We may then begin to debate with more honesty whether our current war against pot produces any social effects beyond hysteria and any government lessons beyond hypocrisy and failed political science policies. The realization of these political science prospects regarding marijuana is the subject of the following pages.

Chapter 1 begins with some early history of our nation's campaign against marijuana. Chapter 2 looks at presidential policies regarding pot from presidents Nixon to George W. Bush. Chapter 3 deals broadly with law enforcement and cultivation practices, including patterns of caprice in pursuing marijuana users with creative growing habits. Chapter 4 addresses pot's health issues. Chapters 5 and 6 focus on the burgeoning medical marijuana movement, and Chapter 7 addresses federal responses to these and other liberalization movements. The conclusion evaluates our reefer war on a scale of effective political science policy. It may come as no surprise that these pages conclude that our nation's pot policy teaches repeated lessons on how to govern poorly.

Given the topic, a personal note is probably in order. I have neither inhaled nor otherwise used marijuana in any form. My firsthand knowledge comes from sensory perception of evidence in courtrooms and from witnessing hundreds of pot defendants wending their tortured way through our court labyrinths. As with any other mind-altering drug, I do not advocate its use and would dissuade my family members from using it unless their health would benefit, as from aspirin or green tea, in which case I would have no hesitation in recommending it. I write not to spread the pot gospel but instead to highlight an inconsistent and counter-productive national policy hurting not only our citizens but also our government's credibility.

Rudolph J. Gerber, Judge
Arizona Court of Appeals (ret.)
Adjunct Professor of Justice Studies, Arizona State University
Shughart, Thomson and Kilroy, P.C.
Phoenix, AZ

HISTORY OF DEMONIZING DRUGS

DEMONIZING BEGINS

On Christmas Day, 1998, on a visit to a British charity hospital, Prince Charles of England advised a multiple sclerosis patient to use marijuana to relieve her pain, advice violating British law. Like the pot admissions of former President Clinton and New York Mayor Bloomberg, such stories about pot's illegal under-the-counter benefits are numerous, even amusing apart from personal tragedy. Not all the stories amuse.

In March 2000, at 3:30 A.M., Mondovi, Wisconsin, police raided the home of Jacki Rickert, forty-nine years old, wheelchair-bound, and weighing ninety pounds. Rickert's Ehlers-Danlos syndrome kept her in constant pain and made eating difficult. She smoked marijuana to ease her pain and to stimulate her appetite. She was the last patient excluded from the federal government's shrunken Investigative New Drug Program that, as of 2001, still permitted the therapeutic distribution of 300 prerolled marijuana cigarettes each month to eight previously authorized patients. The police who searched her home until 10 A.M. found a small amount of marijuana and pressed charges against her. According to her daughter, her mother was only trying for "some semblance of a quality of life." Rickert's marijuana, which the government "pretty much told her she could use, helps a little. The whole thing is unbelievable."[1]

As these pages are written, the local Arizona press carries a story about a woman from northern Arizona, Deborah Lynn Quinn, thirty-nine years old, born without arms and legs, and sentenced to eighteen months in prison for illegally using marijuana to mitigate her physical plight.[2] State

Corrections director Terry Stewart, not known for softness on drug crime, expressed his frustration:

> I simply cannot understand how a judge can sentence a disabled woman to prison who presents absolutely no escape risk, no physical danger to the public, and who will be an extremely difficult and expensive person to care for at $345 per day, without exploring any alternative sentence measures such as intensive probation.[3]

WHAT IS IT?

Green leafy *cannabis sativa* grows in almost any climate, spreads like milkweed, reaches great heights, and offers several valuable uses. Its woody nine-foot stalks—"hemp"—contain fibers usable for rope, canvas, and paper. Its flowering buds and leaves secrete yellow resin rich with delta-9-tetrahydrocannabinol or THC,[4] its potent ingredient.

In England, like some of her subjects, Queen Victoria took marijuana for medical problems related to persistent menstrual cramps. English royalty's interest in hemp and in the medicinal values of cannabis was shared by its American colonies. America's first law on marijuana, dating from 1619 in Virginia, required farmers to grow hemp. Its stalks were useful for sails, riggings, and caulking, products the colonists badly needed, and its oil could be used for food and fuel. Colonies like Maryland exchanged hemp as legal tender. George Washington, Ben Franklin, and Thomas Jefferson grew hemp on their lands, conduct for which they could be prosecuted as drug felons today.[5] Like Queen Victoria, Washington used the cannabis from his hemp production for occasional medicinal purposes, also a crime in many states today. Jefferson probably wrote the Declaration of Independence on hemp paper. Betsy Ross made her first American flag of hemp fabric.

A century ago when pharmacies legally sold marijuana in small packages as a cure for migraines, rheumatism, and insomnia, hemp products were widely available.[6] The townships of East and West Hempfield in Lancaster County, Pennsylvania, acquired their names to honor their prodigious hemp productivity. Physicians recognized pot for medicinal use as early as 1840. The weed appeared in the nation's official list of acceptable drugs from 1850 through 1942 in the *United States Pharmacopoeia*.

THE RISE OF PROHIBITION

Our nation's pot picture has not always been so bucolic. Our prohibition of pot reveals a history rooted in racism and hysteria. When the Mexican Revolution of 1910 prompted immigration to the American

Southwest, establishment prejudices against immigrants and the hatred of doper Pancho Villa generated biases against their marijuana habits, including their little bags of "motas"—marijuana cigarettes. Texas and California officials claimed marijuana incited Mexican immigrants to violent crimes, aroused a "lust for blood" and generated superhuman strength. Mexicans supposedly rolled dried cannabis leaves into cigarettes and distributed this "killer weed" to unsuspecting schoolchildren.

Similar stories arose when sailors and West Indian immigrants introduced marijuana to the Deep South. New Orleans newspapers and prosecutors tagged it to African-Americans, jazz musicians, prostitutes, and the underworld. By 1926, New Orleans sported many lower-class cannabis users in its riverfront barrios. River crews took reefer from New Orleans and spread it to riverfront towns along the Mississippi River. Law enforcement's ensuing campaign against this "marijuana menace" targeted foreigners, inferior races, sexual deviants and social misfits working rivers, daydreaming on wharves, and making unconventional music.[7]

As alcohol prohibition waned, a new moral crusade helped fill the void. Government agents shifted energies from alcohol to cannabis. Pot, they claimed, caused "reefer madness"; other officials claimed it caused the exact opposite behavior known as "amotivational syndrome," thus ascribing to marijuana exactly contradictory reactions.

The Eighteenth Amendment and the 1920 Volstead Act, banning alcohol, prompted an increase in marijuana use for recreational purposes. As alcohol prohibition inspired the search for other euphoriants, it gave birth to marijuana "tea pads," low-priced speakeasies and opium dens where the weed could be bought, sold, and shared. By the early twenties, the number of tea pads had risen to 500 in New York City.

By the late twenties, cannabis demand in the South and Southwest became so strong that Mexican and West Indian importers could not meet market requirements. With shipments arriving from Havana, Tampico, and Vera Cruz, marijuana importation offered full-time work for many new immigrants. The price of pot jumped from ten dollars a kilo (2.2 pounds) to nearly fifty dollars.

In the wake of the Roaring Twenties' reports about marijuana's spread throughout the genteel South, a New Orleans newspaper and its district attorney reported sensational stories about its behavioral effects. The newspaper campaigns resulted in Louisiana passing a law prohibiting possession and sale of marijuana. Colorado passed a similar law in 1927 after an exposé on its evils appeared in a Denver paper. Around the same time another Colorado newspaper claimed that schoolchildren from forty-four public schools regularly smoked "motas" obtainable as readily as sandwiches and much more cheaply—a quarter for two. In this account lies an early foreshadowing of the economic relationship between law enforcement and pot prices: strict enforcement and big profits directly correlate.

THE ANSLINGER ERA

Harry J. Anslinger, a drug czar well before his successors inherited that title, founded and headed the Federal Bureau of Narcotics from 1932 through five presidential administrations to 1962. President Hoover appointed him in 1930 at the recommendation of Andrew Mellon, the Treasury secretary and banker to the DuPont chemical firm, whose synthetic fiber market competed with hemp sales. Almost single-handedly, Anslinger planted the seeds of our nation's legal pot jungle.

Distrusting any public health approach to drug addiction, including marijuana, Anslinger dismissed treatment clinics as "morphine barrooms." He saw the only solutions to pot as dogged enforcement, legislation, condemnatory rhetoric, and suppression of the new foreign music known as jazz. His bulging office files included titles such as "Marijuana and Mexicans" and "Marijuana and Jazz." For Anslinger, the jazz of the Roaring Twenties evoked reactions similar to the right-wing reaction to the hip-hop music of our millennium.

A bureaucrat of strong and unbending convictions, Anslinger showed impatience with empirical research and impartial data. In his view, pot prohibition involved not research but patriotism. Tolerance to reefer encouraged the idiosyncratic behavior that disrupted the uniformity he equated with the national fabric. He took personal affront at all forms of civic dissent. When the New York Academy of Medicine issued a report in 1944 concluding, like many other past and present investigations, that marijuana did not cause violent behavior or addiction, Anslinger, true to form in confronting his opposition, castigated its researchers as "dangerous and strange" because their conclusions threatened his personal convictions about the country's need for behavioral uniformity.[8]

Early in his career with the bureau, Anslinger sought to make marijuana illegal under uniform state laws. Mainstream Americans after the First World War had heard little about cannabis. Its use then mostly occurred in small "foreign" or non-establishment segments of the population. He took resolute steps to remedy the publicity deficit about what he termed "this killer weed." In a book entitled *The Murderers*, co-authored with Fulton Oursler, he described his valiant efforts to arouse the apathetic public:

> As the marijuana situation grew worse, I knew action had to be taken to get proper legislation passed. . . . Much of the irrational juvenile violence

and killing that has written a new chapter of shame and tragedy is traceable directly to hemp intoxication.[9]

Anslinger's speeches often featured a rendition of the ancient story of the "Assassins," a vicious hashish-using sect that once terrorized Persia. Pot extinguished their fear of death, claimed Anslinger, inciting them to destructive rampages. The Assassins became a staple in his campaign against America's born-again Assassin potheads.[10]

Some of Anslinger's self-descriptions bordered on the biblical, with echoes of the Apostle Paul spreading the drug prohibition gospel:

> On radio and at major forums . . . I told the story of this evil weed of the fields and rivers and roadsides. I wrote articles for magazines; our agents gave hundreds of lectures to parents, educators, social and civic leaders. In network broadcasts I reported on the growing list of crimes including murder and rape. . . . I believe we did a thorough job, for the public was alerted, and the laws to protect them were passed, both nationally and at the state level.[11]

Part of Anslinger's civics education appeared in a pamphlet titled "Marihuana or Indian Hemp and Its Preparations" issued by the International Narcotic Education Association. Written under the auspices of the federal Narcotics Bureau, it propounded sensational claims about reefer use:

> Prolonged use of marihuana frequently develops a delirious rage which sometimes leads to high crimes such as assault and murder. Hence marihuana has been called the "killer drug." The habitual use of this narcotic poison always causes a very marked mental deterioration and sometimes produces insanity. Hence marihuana is frequently called "loco weed."[12]

Anslinger's prose regularly dispensed with any pretense of medical restraint. While the marijuana habit led to "physical wreckage and mental decay," its effects upon character and morality were "even more devastating." The victim undergoes "such degeneracy that he will lie and steal without scruple" and, despite the best efforts, he "commits high crimes and misdemeanors." Marijuana often generates "the lust to kill." Many cases of assault, rape, robbery, and murder, claimed Anslinger, could be traced directly "to the use of marihuana."[13]

In articles on "Marihuana: Assassin of Youth" and "Marihuana as a Developer of Criminals; Exposing the Marihuana Drug Evil in Swing Bands," Anslinger argued that pot users, notably jazz musicians, eventually became homicidal, suicidal, and insane. He claimed that Mexicans' and blacks' pot-incited promiscuity threatened the nation's stability. This foreign influence—"reefer," in his frequent term—threatened to change healthy Americans into sex-crazed foreign maniacs. He hoped to make reefer so terrifying that young people would fear trying it, perhaps even learning to fear non-Caucasians as well.

Before long, law enforcement attributed astounding exploits to marijuana. Taking its cue from Anslinger, a 1932 law enforcement article on reefer's effects made it into print:

> A Kansas hasheesh eater thinks he is a white elephant. Six months ago they found him strolling along a road, a few miles out of Topeka. He was naked, his clothing strewn along the highway for a mile. He was not violently insane, but crazy—said he was an elephant and acted as much like one as his limited physique would let him. Marijuana did it.[14]

Anslinger's appeal to racism was unabashed. Under the guise of scientific fact, his Bureau of Narcotics reported fictional stories about "colored" students at the University of Minnesota partying with white female students, smoking pot, and eliciting coeds' sympathy with stories of racism. His bureau reported that two "Negroes" took a white fourteen-year-old girl and kept her for two days in a hut under the influence of marijuana. Upon recovery, she was found to be "suffering from syphilis."[15]

Because some twenty-four states had prohibited marijuana use to some degree prior to the bureau's creation in 1930, the narcotics bureau cannot be the sole cause of the nation's early marijuana concerns. However, under Anslinger's impetus, the bureau soon became the primary shaper of public attitudes toward reefer. In 1936, with the bureau's help, he inspired corny but imaginative propaganda films about pot. *Reefer Madness, Devil's Harvest,* and *Marijuana: Weed with Roots in Hell* displayed the extensive horrors of the weed as well as the antiestablishment attitudes of its users. Later in his life, to his dismay, these propaganda films became objects of trendy derision in a counterculture directly opposite his intention.[16]

Anslinger's reefer campaign also fostered cultural and racial symbolism. In the early Depression, fearing immigrants' pot-crazed behaviors, Southwestern politicians, aided by sensationalist newspaper campaigns, petitioned the Treasury Department to outlaw the weed. With Anslinger's inspiration, the Bureau of Narcotics disseminated fictional atrocities committed by marijuana users. Especially prominent was a story about the murder of the Licata family in Florida by an enraged son high on pot who, Anslinger conveniently ignored, suffered from serious mental illness, the true factor in the murders.[17]

Newspapers that printed this and similar fables gave birth to the media's dope-fiend icon for the pothead. Anslinger won strong support for his antipot campaign in the some fifty Hearst papers and magazines that regularly gave headline attention to marijuana-related incidents under such labels as "marijuana-crazed madmen." William Randolph Hearst may have had his own motives as well. If he could eliminate hemp production, his extensive forest holdings would be the prime source of the pulp needed for West Coast paper production. His papers published repeated sensational and not unusual headlines about the evil effects of marijuana: "MARIJUANA MAKES FIENDS OF BOYS IN 30 DAYS; HASHISH GOADS USERS TO BLOOD LUST." Across the country even the staid *New York Times* caught the pot fever: Its Depression-era dispatches included "STATE FINDS MANY CHILDREN ARE ADDICTED TO WEED," and "POISONOUS WEED SOLD FREELY IN POOL HALLS AND BEER GARDENS."[18]

Organizations such as the International Narcotic Education Association printed Anslinger's diatribes as scientific information. "The habitual use of this narcotic poison," one of their publications intoned, "leads to physical wreckage and mental decay. . . . Marijuana sometimes gives man the lust to kill unreasonably and without motive." The lust for pot and crime predominated in foreign stock. Indeed, 50 percent of all violent crimes committed in areas occupied by "Mexicans, Turks, Filipinos, Greek, Spaniards, Latin-American and Negroes," he claimed, "could be traced to the abuse of marijuana." Many cases of assault, rape, robbery, and murder, asserted his propaganda, "are traced to the use of marijuana."[19]

Endorsing this warning in 1940, the *New York Daily Worker*'s health advice column announced that smoking reefer made the face "bloated, the eyes bloodshot, the limbs weak and trembling and the mind [to sink] into insanity. Robberies, thrill murders, sex crimes and other offenses result." The article warned that the habit could be cured only "by the most severe methods. The addict must be put into an institution."[20]

Both echoing and originating these claims, Anslinger traveled around the country with missionary zeal, speaking to Elks, Lions, parents, teachers, judges, and politicians with a message both constant and categorical. "Take all the good of Dr. Jekyll and the worst in Mr. Hyde, the result is opium," he liked to say, concluding that "Marijuana may be considered even more harmful—it is Mr. Hyde alone."[21] He favored such literary allusions for their supposed erudition. "If the hideous monster Frankenstein came face to face with the monster Marijuana," he also often stated, "he would drop dead of fright."[22]

"Marijuana is the most violence-causing drug in the history of mankind," Anslinger once proclaimed, taking his cue from the Assassins story. He added that its use could reduce thousands of boys to "criminal insanity" and "sexual savages." Foreshadowing the gateway argument, he told Congress that over 50 percent of hard drug users started on marijuana: "They took the needle when the thrill of marijuana was gone."[23] His narcotics bureau created this gateway theory as a further basis for pot prohibition after scientific evidence and popular ridicule weakened his original "reefer madness" argument.[24]

Anslinger's arguments regularly linked marijuana to unwelcome minorities. He wrote of "ginger-colored niggers" using pot, an ethnic evil he viewed "as hellish as heroin."[25] He told Congress that half the country's crime stemmed from "Mexicans, Latin Americans, Filipinos, Negroes and Greeks" whose civic aberrations flowed directly from marijuana use.[26]

Personal consistency did not fall under Anslinger's umbrella of concerns. While making these fictional crime claims about pot-using minorities, he was supplying morphine illegally to his good friend Senator Joseph McCarthy, so that "communists would not be able to blackmail this great American senator for his drug-dependency weakness."[27]

By the 1930s, as the West and South associated unwelcome immigrants with pot, Western politicians began to pressure the federal government to control its use. Rank racial motives flourished among some of them. The Colorado legislature learned that pot was especially used "by the Mexican population employed in the beet fields."[28] At times, the racism was barely disguised. In 1929, the Montana legislature began to amend its narcotics laws to include marijuana. On January 27, the Butte *Montana Standard* gave a progress report on lawmakers' "fun" during their deliberations:

> "When some beet field peon takes a few raves of this stuff," explained Dr. Fred Fulsher of Mineral County, "he thinks he has just been elected president of Mexico so he starts out to execute all his political enemies." Everybody laughed and the bill was recommended for passage.[29]

On September 4, 1936, Anslinger's bureau received a letter from the city editor of the Alamosa County *Daily Courier* describing an attack by a supposedly pot-crazed Mexican male on a young girl. The writer indulged in liberal editorializing:

> I wish I could show you what a small marihuana cigaret can do to one of our degenerate Spanish-speaking residents. That's why our problem is so great; the greatest percentage of our population is composed of Spanish-speaking persons, most of whom are low mentally, because of social and racial conditions.[30]

In 1931, as Texas banned marijuana, the *San Antonio Light* editorialized that its legislature deserved thanks for banning a "dangerous and insanity-producing narcotic" that often makes the user "a dangerous or ho-micidal maniac."[31]

THE LEGISLATIVE CAMPAIGN

In 1936, as part of a broad legislative campaign to penalize all pot use, Anslinger issued a nationwide public statement encouraging adoption of uniform state laws against marijuana:

> There is no federal law against the production and use of marijuana in this country. The legal fight against its abuse is largely a problem of state and municipal legislation and law enforcement. All public-spirited citizens should enlist in the campaign to demand and to get adequate state laws and effi-cient state enforcement on marijuana.[32]

By 1936, some twenty-seven states had adopted narcotics laws with partial but haphazard criminalization of cannabis. Nationwide uniformity was still needed. In 1937, the Supreme Court provided a model in up-holding the National Firearms Act prohibiting transfer of machine guns without a tax stamp, which the government, of course, would not issue. To the bureau, taxation appeared as a useful model for the pot war as well.

Anslinger's legislative campaign laid the foundation for the Marijuana Tax Act of 1937. Prior to its enactment, no reliable scientific research had shown any statistical connection between marijuana and criminal behav-ior. The only indictments against marijuana had been conclusory asser-tions, mostly from law enforcement and newspaper sources, that ethnic minorities' use of reefer threatened the stability of the nation's main-stream. Anslinger nonetheless pushed for federal prohibition.

TAX ACT HEARINGS

The 1937 Tax Act hearings conflated more so with anecdotes than with objective research. Here is a sample of Anslinger's testimony:

> Most marijuana smokers are Negroes, Hispanics, Filipinos and entertain-ers. Their satanic music, jazz and swing result from marijuana usage. This marijuana causes white women to seek sexual relations with Negroes.[33]

A physician from the American Medical Association pled for contin-ued permission for medical use of marijuana, then in use only in some medical circles. Speaking against Anslinger's position, Dr. William Wood-ward observed that, in these medical circles, marijuana was considered harmless medicine. In fact, some leading drug companies were distributing small packets of marijuana commercially, and some pharmacies were selling it legally.

This information arrived as unwelcome news in Congress. Its members greeted this information with hostility directed at Woodward personally. "If you want to advise us on legislation," he was told, "you ought to come here with some constructive proposals . . . rather than trying to throw obstacles in the way of something that the federal government is trying to do."[34]

The hearings on the Tax Act offer an insight into Congress's willingness to succumb to forcefully presented fictions. Here is part of the lawmakers' cutting-edge questioning:

> CONG. JOHN DINGELL: I want to be certain what this is. Is this the same weed that grows wild in some of our western states which is sometimes called the loco weed?
>
> ANSLINGER: No, sir, that is another family.
>
> DINGELL: That is also a harmful drug-producing weed, is it not?
>
> ANSLINGER: Not to my knowledge, it is not used by humans.
>
> CHAIRMAN: In what particular section does the weed grow wild?
>
> ANSLINGER: In almost every state of the union today.
>
> CONG. REED: What you are describing has a very large flower?
>
> ANSLINGER: No, sir, a very small flower.[35]

The depth of legislative acumen about the pending bill hardly exceeded this exchange. On the date of the vote in the House of Representatives, the following colloquy occurred:

> MR. SNELL: What is the bill?
>
> MR. RAYBURN: It has something to do with something that is called marijuana. I believe it is a narcotic of some kind.
>
> MR. VINSON: Marijuana is some kind of hashish.
>
> MR. SNELL: Mr. Speaker, I am going to object because I think it is wrong to consider legislation of this character at this time of night.[36]

More insightful than these legislative insights were those from Anslinger himself. As the principal witness before the House Committee, he presented his bulging bundle of newspaper clippings as primary evidence of reefer's evils. He read from his drug-crime file and repeated the fictional story about pot-crazed "colored" college men getting white co-eds pregnant. He told the congressmen about two boys in Chicago who murdered a police officer under the influence of marijuana. He related the story about the fifteen-year-old who went insane from pot, and he told how pot users easily graduate to heroin. Habitual use of marijuana, he claimed, caused a "delirious rage." In the end, he provided Congress with an alarming list of anecdotes portraying marijuana as a menace of crisis proportions spelling the doom of mainstream American society.[37]

When lawmakers asked Anslinger why antipot legislation had not been proposed sooner, he explained the delay as follows: "Ten years ago we only heard about it throughout the Southwest. It is only in the last few years that it has become a national menace."[38] No representatives of pot users testified at the hearings. No attempt was made to check the validity of Anslinger's sensational stories, some culled from Hearst newspaper stories that he and his bureau had planted.

Some of Anslinger's language reappeared in the House Ways and Means Committee recommendation for passage:

> Under the influence of this drug the will is destroyed and all power of directing and controlling thought is lost. Inhibitions are released.[39]

The committee totally succumbed to Anslinger's dire warnings. Its report asserted:

> Not only is marijuana used by hardened criminals to steel them to commit violent crimes, but it is also being placed in the hands of high-school children in the form of marihuana cigarettes by unscrupulous peddlers. Cases were cited at the hearings of school children who have been driven to crime and insanity through the use of this drug. Its continued use results many times in impotency and insanity.[40]

THE TAX ACT

The resulting Marijuana Transfer Tax, which became the Marijuana Tax Act, controlled the weed via a stamp and license transfer tax for which the government refused to issue either stamps or licenses. Users of hemp for defined industrial or medical purposes had to register and pay a tax of $100 per ounce. Those failing to comply faced fines or prison terms, not for drug use but for tax evasion.

The Tax Act did not really target strict medical use of marijuana; its original purpose was to discourage recreational reefer smoking. By forcing some marijuana transactions to be registered and others to be taxed, the government hoped to make it prohibitively expensive to obtain the drug legally. Congress expected that users would be prosecuted for tax evasion, a crime thought easier to prove. The law also rendered medical use of cannabis difficult because of the extensive paperwork required.

Not all doctors were supporters. The Tax Act arbitrarily made criminals of users of a drug that Colonel J. M. Pholen, editor of the *Military Surgeon*, described as "no more harmful than the smoking of tobacco or mullein or sumac leaves." Pholen concluded that the legislation was "ill-advised" because it branded "as a menace and a crime a matter of trivial importance."[41]

The 1937 Tax Act introduced a recurring feature of our nation's reefer war: legislation against the private behavior of minorities, most with recent foreign roots, branded as criminal largely because of their ethnic and musical differences, which differed from the nation's white European establishment. The act's notable achievements included putting some jazz musicians in jail. Not long after pot was outlawed in 1937, Anslinger and his Federal Bureau of Narcotics crafted a plan to accomplish more than an occasional jailing of a jazz musician. The new plan called for a nationwide roundup of all black jazz musicians who smoked marijuana. In his work as head of the bureau, Anslinger had come to believe that jazz and pot use were not only linked together but combined to cause the criminal tendencies of minorities. His plan to arrest and confine all black pot-smoking musicians never got off the ground, not for failure to try but because of his white agents' inability to infiltrate the jazz underworld.

After passage of the Tax Act, Anslinger gradually came to the dawning realization, to his great disappointment, that his bureau could not begin to achieve his personal goal of eradicating reefer nationwide. Contrary to his predictions, no organized interstate traffic in pot appeared nor was organized crime involved in its growth or distribution. From cultivation to consumption, marijuana appeared as a small entrepreneurial interest of mostly law-abiding lower-class private citizens. The Tax Act soon became a pugilist shadowboxing around an empty ring. Law enforcement mostly used the act not as it was intended but against highly visible user groups, including minorities and jazz musicians like Gene Krupa and the occasional reefer-using actor like Robert Mitchum. Their cultural dissonance offended the bureau for lifestyle reasons going well beyond marijuana use. The Tax Act mainly became a law enforcement weapon directed against America's youth, the foreign-born, and nonconforming minorities.

THE NEW YORK ACADEMY STUDY

Not everyone applauded Anslinger's reefer policies or his tax act. The then-mayor of New York, Fiorello La Guardia, himself of "foreign" stock, suspected that the narcotics commissioner did not know what he was talking about in listing pot's parade of horrors. In 1939, two years after the

Tax Act became law, he assembled a research panel of the New York Academy of Medicine—physicians, pharmacologists, chemists, and public health officials. Working with the support of the New York City Police Department and the medical staff of Rikers Island prison hospital, he sampled marijuana provided by Anslinger, who thought he could thereby influence its findings.

The academy decided to conduct a dual study, one part sociological, the other clinical, aimed at finding answers to the following questions: (1) To what extent was marijuana used in New York City? (2) What was its method of retail distribution? (3) What was the attitude of its users toward society? (4) What was its relationship to sex? (5) What was its impact on crime?, and (6) What was its relationship to juvenile delinquency? The clinical study sought to discover by controlled experiments the physiological and psychological effects of marijuana on different users.

This report appeared in 1944 after six years of research and after strong objection to publication by the Narcotics Bureau.[42] The academy's findings echoed an earlier study of cannabis in 1894 by a British team in India, the so-called Indian Hemp Commission. To the consternation of the bureau's menace peddlers, the academy found marijuana only a mild nonaddictive euphoriant. It caused negligible physiological effects; played no role in crime; did not induce physical, mental, or moral degeneration; and caused no permanent negative social effects.

The academy also found that its use was not widespread, being concentrated in black and Mexican ghettos and a small bohemian fringe of musicians, writers, and artists. No evidence existed for its reported epidemic spread. Further, smoking reefer did not lead to medical addiction nor did it serve as a gateway to harder drugs. No evidence showed that its use was rampant in schoolyards or that it was the most popular juvenile euphoriant. New York police themselves debunked the rumor that reefer inspired crime. The report concluded that the publicity concerning its putative horrors was "unfounded."[43]

When he saw that he could not suppress the academy's report, Anslinger resorted to his frequent pattern of personally castigating the researchers involved—the academy and its scholars, he said, were "dangerous" and "strange." Though he lacked medical and psychiatric training, Anslinger retaliated in print with a purported medical refutation of the academy's findings in no less an honored place than the *Journal of the American Medical Association*. There he somehow found the hubris as a nonmedically-trained layman to criticize the academy's psychological experts for overlooking pot's extensive "psychiatric effects," which he described in great detail.[44]

POT CEASES TO BE MEDICINE

Without any effort to evaluate the report's implications for rethinking pot policy, Anslinger next directed his undiminished energy to eliminating marijuana entirely from medical pharmacology. He persuaded Dr. Ernest Cook, chairman of the Committee on Revision of the *United States Pharmacopoeia,* to remove marijuana from its catalogue of recognized medicines, where it had been listed since 1850. Although some AMA doctors believed that marijuana offered medical benefits, he convinced the AMA to reverse its position by appealing to its opposition to remedies containing more than two active ingredients. Soon after the passage of the Tax Act, cannabis disappeared as a therapeutic substance from the *Pharmacopoeia.*

SCHEDULE I LEGISLATION

Once pot lost its protected medical status, the government needed to put it in a defining legal category. Much later, under the federal Controlled Substances Act of 1970, Congress created a series of five schedules establishing varying degrees of control over addictive substances.[45] Marijuana became a Schedule I drug, meaning that (1) it has a high potential for abuse;[46] (2) it has no currently accepted medical use in treatment in the United States;[47] and (3) there is a lack of accepted safety for its use under medical supervision.[48] Though authorized to alter the schedule for each prohibited drug, the Drug Enforcement Administration repeatedly declined to move marijuana into a less restrictive schedule without a prior determination of its safety and efficacy by the Food and Drug Administration.[49]

Anslinger sent his agents throughout the American military to investigate 3,000 suspected pot-using soldiers in World War II. By midcentury, thanks in good part to such displays of undaunted fervor, marijuana had acquired a disreputable image in upper-class establishment circles. It ceased to be a legitimate drug for any medical purpose and fell from legal grace to the point where, instead of being seen as occasionally therapeutic or recreational, it became criminal under all circumstances. Its prohibition illustrated how Congress could succumb to emotional rhetoric rather than dispassionate science and how its demonization thrived more on cultural and racial rather than medical or criminal considerations.

ANSLINGER'S LEGACY

One of Anslinger's lasting legacies remains the use of the penal law to condemn "The Other," people whose skin, ethnicity, work, music, and smoking habits differed from mainstream white Americans of European stock. His habit of supplying morphine to his addicted friend Senator Joseph McCarthy yields a revealing insight into his latent motivation: his animus was less against drugs than against ethnic differences. Anslinger's dislike of these "foreign" elements in American society was intense. His condemnation of these differing peoples and cultures that he saw upsetting national homogeneity could be more powerful if they were labeled "sick" or "insane," transforming their cultural differences into pathologies. To Anslinger, marijuana users not only differed from mainstream America, but worse still, their work, their behaviors, and their music showed them to be suffering from a form of dementia that if unchecked could infect the nation's mainstream.

WORLD WAR II INTERLUDE

Though pot use remained illegal from 1937 onward, the nation's attention gradually shifted after the Second World War to more important matters. The shift appears to be one of cyclic opinion patterns about drugs. National attention about the drug "menace" tended to oscillate between tolerance with less rhetoric to intolerance coupled with severe enforcement and stern rhetoric, all at the behest of politicians capitalizing on differing degrees of public responsiveness to drug fears.[50]

Due to international concerns elsewhere, the Cold War, and the internal threat from McCarthyism, once the Marijuana Tax Act became history, the nation witnessed a gradual decline in official hand wringing about pot. Some enforcers assumed that legislation had totally solved the problem. Others focused on more important international matters like the Korean War and the threat from the "Red Scare." Perhaps most significantly, politicians of the 1950s and 1960s had not yet discovered how to further their political careers by making a link between drugs and crime to posture as the people's saviors. When they occasionally did invoke the threat of crime for political gain, voters responded less to crime issues than to more cosmic matters. The connection between the drug war and electoral success had yet to be forged.

These attitudes would change markedly with Vietnam war protests and the presidency of Richard Nixon, when crime evolved into a code word for national stability and racial differences as pot became identified with antiwar protest. In the period immediately after the Korean War, as a relative truce prevailed among drug warriors and users, the country's concern over marijuana moved toward a quiet consensus that, if there were any pot problem, it was not terribly serious. With the Nixon presidency, however, burgeoning pot use by antiwar college students would redefine the pot and crime relationship into a new paradigm.

2

PRESIDENTIAL POT POLICIES

Over the past four decades, our government's policies toward pot have largely reflected the opinions of the occupant of the White House, who in turn has usually mirrored the strongest voices within his constituency, particularly his drug advisors. Presidential administrations hostile to marijuana share several convictions: First, they believe that pot users eventually become addicts en route to harder drugs like heroin and cocaine, the so-called "gateway" theory. Militant presidential campaigns also emphasize that marijuana use primarily occurs among cultural deviants who undermine the nation's ballast of "establishment values." Hostile administrations have also reflected a self-righteous religious conviction about the sinfulness of using pot, a modern replay of biblical Sodom and Gomorrah.

The opposing picture, though less dramatic, is more charged with frustrated plans. Moderate presidents seeking to lessen penalties have almost invariably fallen well short of their convictions. Usually their failures have resulted not from a changed personal conviction but because policy change on drugs engenders opposition from conservative politicians, entrenched law enforcement, and occasional militant parents groups. These exogenous opponents reflect not only the difficulty of relaxing reefer laws but also the fact that many such groups stand to lose power and financing with any change in the status quo policy.

At a philosophical level, some presidents have opposed pot on consequentialist grounds, finding its evil not in its moral but in its social and cultural effects. Others have taken a more deontological turn, finding reefer morally wrong in itself independent of its social consequences. This clash can be seen as degrees on a Nietzschean scale between the poles of "Apollo" and "Dionysius," uniform rational morality versus the exuberance of individual free expression. These polarities reflect two differing views of how government shapes its ideal citizen. To pot moderates, government should tolerate victimless divergence in order to nurture a wide expression of human spirit. By contrast, those who see the government's relationship to its citizens as parent-to-child conclude that citizens need protection from nonconforming self-expression. In this conflict perspective is everything. While Charles Reich's 1970 *Greening of America* offered a liberal landscape to be sported upon, the political right saw the same scene only as high grass to be mowed down.

KENNEDY-JOHNSON: QUIET BEFORE THE STORM

The political climate regarding pot softened during the early 1960s as Vietnam became a national obsession. Pot enforcement coexisted with a dawning tolerance for citizens' rights to differ on matters of personal privilege, including such unrelated matters as contraception, free love, and support for the war. As college students increasingly adopted pot as an expression of dissent, enforcement of drug laws lessened. Courts tended either to dismiss pot charges or to impose only modest fines.

In academic circles, criminal law ceased to be seen as the primary tool for drug control. A popular sense developed that pot use had been overcriminalized. Marijuana use became seen in some quarters as the prototype victimless crime. That the criminal law was neither the only nor the most potent engine of social control dramatically differed from the paternalism of Anslinger's policymakers, who had crafted the Marijuana Tax Act of 1937 in part to save citizens from their own bad choices.

In 1962, President Kennedy forced Anslinger to resign. Research commissions, notably the 1962 White House Conference on Drug Abuse, again found no direct link between pot and violent crime or hard drugs.[1] The President's advisory commission again challenged a central tenet of reefer prohibition by observing that it was "difficult to believe" that a marijuana user would rationally weigh the penalty awaiting after arrest. It concluded pointedly that the deterrence theory was "weak" regarding criminalization of pot.[2]

By the mid 1960s, widespread use of pot on college campuses generated a broad consensus in student and liberal circles that harsh penalties such as jail time were inappropriate.[3] Local and national groups urged decriminalization. Perhaps the most vocal of the decriminalization groups at that time was the National Organization for Reform of Marijuana Laws (NORML), which helped pot shed its stigma and acquire an image of escapism and protest rather than begin seen as a moral or a health threat.

Momentary echoes of earlier attitudes occasionally surfaced. Henry Giordano, who had replaced Anslinger and shared some of his hard-core convictions, expected the latent evils of pot to eventually appear via improved medical research. "We may soon hope to have the full dangers of marihuana revealed to the public," he declared in 1967, illustrating the recurring dilemma that the credibility of the pot prohibition badly needed support from adverse health findings. None was forthcoming.[4]

The Kennedy-Johnson administrations generally shifted from an exclusively criminal approach to pot to haphazard enforcement coupled with mild punishment. In 1960, only 169 pot felony convictions appeared for the entire nation. Pot had become an accepted symbol of rebellion and independence. A Gallup poll showed most Vietnam War protesters had tried it. Indeed, by the mid-'60s, pot had become the defining symbol of the antiwar movement. Johnson's commission on campus unrest put it this way: "If the rest of society wears short hair, the member of the youth culture wears his hair long. If others are clean, he is dirty. If others drink alcohol . . . he denounces alcohol and smokes pot."[5]

When Robert Kennedy Jr. faced pot possession charges in the late 1960s, newspaper headlines were muted and public outcry subdued. In that day's evening newscast, Walter Cronkite observed that "this case is not unusual; more and more parents across the nation find themselves going to court with their children on drug charges; it's becoming an incident of modern living."[6] *Time* magazine found collegiate pot use an acceptable form of free speech. College pot users ceased to be outcasts to be jailed; instead they became seen as deserving at least toleration if not attention for their political message.[7] After all, their ranks included not only the Kennedys but also upwardly mobile students of middle and upper classes whose promising careers obviously coexisted with pot use. On September 7, 1970, *Newsweek* ran a cover story entitled "Marihuana: Time to Change the Law?"

Echoes of older policy did surface. From retirement, Harry Anslinger in 1968 excoriated marijuana as a deadly, addictive drug. "To legalize marijuana," he said, would be "to legalize slaughter on the highways."[8] To him, pot remained "an assault on the foundation of western civilization," because, in his words, "the only persons who frighten me are the hippies."[9]

Some law enforcement in the late 1960s marched to a different cadence. Though popular sentiment favored softening pot laws, some hardline agencies continued the criminal crusade. Pot arrests rose from a mere 18,000 in 1965 to 188,000 by 1970, in good part due to FBI Director Hoover's aggressive policy to use pot arrests to harass antiwar "leftists."

In a 1968 memo to national FBI offices, Hoover urged that, because pot use characterized "New Left" views, authorities should "be alert" to arresting them on drug charges.[10]

As the Johnson administration ended, the 1970 Comprehensive Drug Abuse Prevention and Control Act, first proposed by his administration, separated marijuana from hard narcotics and reduced federal penalties for possession of small amounts. The act integrated all drugs, hard and soft, into a uniform system, abolished mandatory minimum sentences, and reduced simple possession of all drugs to a misdemeanor. Future president George H.W. Bush, then a representative from Texas, personally spoke on the floor of the House in 1970 against adopting mandatory sentences against drug offenders.[11] His tolerance and that of the act itself were to be short lived.

NIXON-FORD: WAR IS DECLARED

By 1970, crime generally and drugs in particular were becoming code words in some conservative groups for racial hostility, cultural stereotypes, and suburban isolationism. Right-wing religious voters also expressed alarm at cultural turmoil, social disarray, and ethical relativism. The civil rights movement, the Vietnam War, equal rights for women, changing sexual roles, increased racial diversity, and economic restructuring contributed to increasing anxieties in status quo mind-sets. As control and structure began to appear as social values, pot became seen as one of the primary catalysts for national disorder.

At the start of his presidential campaign, Nixon adopted a neoclassical approach to crime, finding its true cause not in poverty—seen by some liberals as the prime crime cause—but in insufficient government restraint on hedonist urges. His solution would not involve fighting poverty but "increasing the numbers of convictions." If cultural "permissiveness" caused social disarray, crime could be reduced if government suppressed the attitude of "anything goes." Narcotics and marijuana in particular become symbols of the permissiveness undermining crime control. Nixon's resulting war against hard drugs and pot became his attempt to reduce crime by eliminating its precursor, illicit drug usage of all kinds.

Both a product and a devotee of Anslinger, Nixon harbored deep disgust for illegal drugs and their users. Contrary to his immediate predecessors' indifference, he saw drugs as the showcase in the fight against crime, shaping the campaign squarely for the first time on the assumed effects of drug use on national cohesion. With the nation reeling from assassinations, campus unrest, antiwar protests, and Nixon's asserted rise in street crime, repression of cultural disarray would occur via a new punitive paradigm: "Doubling the conviction rate in this country," he repeated on the campaign trail, "would do more to cure crime in America than quadrupling the funds for (Hubert) Humphrey's war on poverty."[12]

Nixon saw hard and soft drugs as a massive cultural problem transforming America's youth into longhaired, unruly, anti-authoritarian peace freaks. In a 1968 campaign speech in California, he called drugs "the modern curse of youth" capable of "decimating a generation of Americans," adding later that pot users were like "foreign troops on our shores."[13] Conservative writer S. K. Oberdeck, a Nixon devotee, echoed the essence of the president's concern in a 1971 *National Review* article: "The weed is an . . . instrument of initiation for a lifestyle that generally rejects or seeks to bring down 'ordered life as we know it.'"[14]

Assuming that the Religious Right's "Silent Majority" favored coercive restoration of national order, Nixon briefly contemplated creating a new and more militant political party embracing conservative Republicans (excluding Nelson Rockefeller and the Ripon Society) and emphasizing right-wing religious groups like Southern Baptists (excluding Catholics, Episcopalians, and Jews, who were all too liberal). In Nixon's mind, religious right-of-center groups constituted the ignored "Silent Majority" able, if aroused from slumber, to counteract Democrats' permissive constituencies of the young, the poor, racial minorities, and students.[15] These right-wing groups, he believed, would support coercive steps to restore national cohesion.

Nixon heard mainstream America singing in the voice of the "Okie from Muskogee," the hero of Merle Haggard's 1966 country and western hit. Okies "don't smoke marijuana in Muskogee" because Okies "like livin' right and bein' free." So impressed was Nixon with the song's equation of political freedom with freedom from pot that he invited Haggard to perform the song at a formal White House dinner.

With Haggard's help, Nixon moved pot from a medical to a cultural issue afflicting the national body politic more than the individual human body. A kindred believer, Attorney General John Mitchell observed about pot: "Why should we use it when it has no redeeming value? The desire of someone to get high and out of this world by puffing on marijuana has no redeeming value."[16] Indeed, pot's evil far surpassed alcohol's, explained Nixon, because while people drink alcohol "to have fun," they smoke pot to "get high." These two flights from reality were somehow different, the former acceptable, the latter not.

Pot liberalization remained out of the question; proponents of relaxing drug laws became suspect. Legalizers appeared especially troublesome for reasons echoing Anslinger's views. To chief of staff Bob Haldeman Nixon once shared the off-the-cuff observation that "it's a funny thing—

everyone of the bastards that are out for legalizing marijuana is Jewish. What the Christ is the matter with the Jews, Bob?"[17]

As it began to produce unintended consequences, the campaign against antiwar protesters and cultural deviants soon fashioned a coveted badge of honor for these very groups. Student protesters found a symbol for their movement in the pot leaf itself. Pot use became a form of anti-government protest. The Presidential Commission on Campus Unrest discovered about student protests that "If others drink alcohol, [the pot user] declares himself an alien in a larger society with which he is fundamentally at odds."[18]

Antiwar and antiestablishment protesters sometimes admitted exactly that. In a speech at the University of Virginia in May 1970, antiwar protester Jerry Rubin, a member of the "Chicago Seven" disrupting the Democratic convention in that city, asserted that "Smoking pot makes you a criminal and a revolutionary," traits that in his circles had become accolades. "As soon as you take your first puff," he boasted, "you are an enemy of society." Being an enemy of the government had become an honor. The comedians Cheech and Chong became the embodiment of a new culture honoring the "stoned" anti-war, anti-government protester. The same year as Rubin's speech, Attorney General Mitchell, in remarks to a smaller, more conservative audience, apologized for the administration's legal difficulties in curbing nonconforming collegians' reefer use by observing that conservative Americans like himself "don't like the Constitution."[19]

Early in the Nixon administration, CBS presented a program on drug use by Vietnam service members showing a GI smoking pot from his rifle barrel, prompting the Senate to convene immediate hearings on military drug use. Observing Congress's penchant for scientific explanations for pot use, Nixon saw an opportunity to combat pot under the pretense of scientific objectivity. Only eight years after President Kennedy's 1962 White House Commission's tolerant report on drugs, he decided to create yet another ad hoc presidential body to study pot, which he termed the National Commission on Marijuana and Drug Abuse. His expectation, of course, was for different results.

Similar drug commissions sprang up almost simultaneously in other countries facing related drug concerns. In Holland, the Dutch convened the Baan Working Party to conduct similar research about drugs. The United Kingdom formed a prestigious committee under leading criminologist Baroness Barbara Wootton. In Toronto, law school Dean Gerald Le Dain headed the Canadian government's Commission of Inquiry on Marijuana. Pot had assumed the stature of an international cultural concern.

Nixon's idea of another presidential commission enjoyed a considerable pedigree. Recommendations from preceding presidential commissions had uniformly but calmly attacked penal overreach on drugs. Three earlier commissions had recommended that sentencing discretion return to judges: The President's 1963 Advisory Commission on Narcotics and Drug Abuse (Prettyman Commission), the 1967 President's Commission on Law Enforcement and the Administration of Justice (the Katzenbach Commission), and the 1969 National Commission on the Causes and Prevention of Violence (the Eisenhower Commission) echoed these moderating themes. Ensuing reports by other presidential commissions on Civil Disorders (Kerner, 1968), Campus Unrest (Scranton, 1970) and Pornography (Lockhart, 1970) suggested government should recognize a limited but legitimate sphere of private expression.

No fan of these permissive conclusions, Nixon relished the prospect of yet another seemingly independent presidential commission, properly constituted, of course, that would reach different conclusions. Fellow conservatives shared his views. By 1970, congressional Republicans viewing marijuana as an issue of renewed national import also thought that another carefully constituted presidential commission would enjoy the unique authority to resolve, on a scientific basis, the vexing questions about pot once and for all.

Nixon wanted to use the commission's objective research to anchor a condemnation of pot that, in his words, would be "really strong," one that would "tear the ass out of them." Among other goals, he wanted to know, again, "why all the Jews seem to be for legalizing pot," a question he answered this time with his own conviction that "those bastards" were all "psychiatrists."[20]

THE 1972 MARIJUANA COMMISSION

The ensuing "Presidential Commission on Marihuana and Drug Abuse," front-loaded with approved conservatives, was headed by Raymond Shafer, the former Republican governor of Pennsylvania. Nixon expected its conservative members, some of whom he appointed, to inveigh against marijuana on scientific grounds, providing him quotable data showing pot's dire unraveling of the nation's social fabric.

The contemporaneous foreign commissions studying pot presented an obstacle. In almost simultaneous published findings, these three commissions found marijuana about as dangerous as alcohol but, like alcohol, undeserving of criminal penalties. The English report went a step further: The evidence of a link with violent crime, it found, was far stronger with alcohol than with reefer. Without exception, these three disparate research committees, featuring some of world's leading legal, medical, and scientific specialists, recommended relaxing sanctions against marijuana.

In the United States, however, the story would turn out differently. As his marijuana commission was drafting—and leaking—its recommendations, Nixon publicized his personal views. A questioner at a press conference observed that his earlier White House Conference on Youth had recommended legalizing marijuana. Asked his view, Nixon replied with an eye on cultural disarray: "I am against legalizing marihuana. Even if the commission does recommend that it be legalized, I will not follow that recommendation."[21] He elaborated:

> I can see no social or moral justification whatever for legalizing marihuana. I think it would be exactly the wrong step. It would simply encourage more and more of our young people to start down the long, dismal road that leads to hard drugs and eventually self-destruction.[22]

He would have to do just as he predicted. His Commission on Marijuana and Drug Abuse concluded in its March 1972 report that marijuana—a "rather unexciting compound"—should be decriminalized and demythologized. The "experimental or intermittent use" of pot, said the report, results in "little proven danger of physical or psychological harm." The commission declined to endorse outright legalization or even limited regulation because either "would institutionalize availability of a drug which has uncertain long-term effects." This innocent language resurrected a central unstated dilemma in the pot war: having criminalized pot without first knowing whether it produced harmful effects, the government now, after its prohibition, badly needed to identify some objective ill effects via medical research to support the prohibition. None appeared.

The commission did recommend that marijuana be decriminalized but not fully legalized. A violator would face a fine like that for a speeding violation. Policy makers, it admonished, had erred in their assumption about the consequences of pot. "In our considered judgment," wrote commission members, pot ranked "very low" as a social threat. Finding no causal support for the claim that it contributed to "amotivational syndrome," the commission observed that policymakers knew very little about the effects or social impact of marijuana because many of their hypotheses were speculative and, in large measure, incorrect.[23]

REACTIONS TO THE COMMISSION REPORT

Betrayed by his commission and its modest recommendations, and especially by fellow Republican Shafer, Nixon, like Anslinger before him, denounced the commission's findings on personal grounds. His hope for scientific support against reefer succumbed to research by conservative researchers no less. His anger extended to the commission's medical professionals sympathetic to marijuana's health claims. "Soft-headed psychiatrists" he called them, "who are all on the stuff themselves." "I oppose the legalization of marihuana and that includes sale, possession, and use," he repeated, adding that American culture and its criminal justice policy could not rest on "a philosophy that something is half-legal and half-illegal."[24]

Nixon's moral reaction to the commission's research echoed among other conservatives in his camp. Vice President Agnew, a tireless opponent of youthful permissiveness, said that it was "wrong" to encourage any use of pot; the commission's recommendations, which he misread, "frightened" him that the nation was to suffer like "Asian countries" where pot use, from his highbrow view, had "really debilitated those societies."[25] Mayor Frank Rizzo of Philadelphia, a former police commissioner, opined that the members of the commission, including his state's former governor, needed their heads cleared of "cobwebs."[26] Former drug czar Anslinger again emerged from retirement to offer similar horrors if pot were legalized: "I think in a couple of years we'll have about a million lunatics filling up the mental hospitals and a couple of hundred thousand more deaths on the highways—just plain slaughter on the highways."[27] Conservative Nixon mouthpiece Jeffrey Hart, writing in *The National Review*, insisted that pot prohibitions should aim "to lean on, to penalize, the counterculture," because that culture was "bad"; weed would cease to be a political issue when the counterculture died, a consummation likely to occur "about six months from now."[28] Perhaps the enemy was not really reefer but the counterculture.

Nixon remained convinced that marijuana use was a cultural escape, or, in his bohemian words, a "way out want." His radio address reminded his audience that

> In recent days there have been proposals to legalize the possession and use of marijuana. I oppose the legalization of the sale, possession or use of marijuana. The line against the use of dangerous drugs is now drawn on this side of marijuana. If we move the line to the other side and accept the use of this drug, how can we draw the line against other illegal drugs? Or will we slide into an acceptance of their use? There must continue to be criminal sanctions against the possession, sale or use of marijuana.[29]

Perhaps due to the intensity of his reaction, no states then adopted the commission's recommendations except for Oregon, which decriminalized pot in 1973.

Nixon reacted similarly to the nonpartisan conclusion of the Le Dain Canadian Commission, whose later 1972 recommendation also called for decriminalization of marijuana. He ignored Baroness Wootton's similar English findings. A decade later, when the National Academy of Sciences Substance Abuse Commission again called for marijuana decriminalization, President Reagan would adopt the model of Nixon's calumny to denounce these researchers for also contradicting his personal views.[30]

Though Nixon dealt with unwelcome pot research by denouncing its researchers, Holland, where social science research evokes less polemics, simply followed the Baan researchers' recommendations without personal invective. Like the other national commissions, the Baan Working Group found a significant difference between marijuana and harder drugs and concluded that continued pot prohibition wasted government resources without any commensurate public benefit. The Dutch simply followed the Baan recommendations, built a legal wall between hard and soft drugs, and permitted a limited, controlled use of pot without political posturing or ad hominem attacks on their researchers.

With Nixon at the helm, however, the United States declined to adopt impartial research or to follow the example of other countries. Pot had to be condemned for endorsing offensive countercultural traits. If the countercultural pot smoker was passive, rude, and escapist, then, by this logic, pot itself caused these traits. Pot became a way to define the "amotivational" counterculture without confronting greater contributors to social unraveling. In this sense, pot became the gateway to Communism; it softened the nation's moral and patriotic backbone by lowering resistance to seductive ideologies of all sorts. Nixon's final word on the drug menace, especially marijuana, was the creation of the Drug Enforcement Administration (DEA) to prosecute, as he told Congress in 1973, an "all-out global war on the drug menace" threatening the country from within, just as Communism did from without.

NIXON IN RETROSPECT

Nixon's rejection of the Shafer commission recommendations exposed two rifts, one scientific, the other diplomatic: on the scientific front, a refusal to accept independent research findings about pot on moral-religious rather than scientific grounds, and, on the international scene, scorn directed at Dutch pot policy, a 1970s flashpoint igniting right-wing ire as a wanton aberration from morality.

Though Nixon's reefer policy seemed harsh by contrast with preceding administrations, it pales by comparison with later administrations. His attitude toward pot coexisted with a concerted effort to offer treatment for users wanting help. His mix of strict enforcement with a realistic treatment alternative created a marriage that would not last.[31]

GERALD FORD

When Gerald Ford suddenly became president in 1974, the country was occupied with the trauma of Watergate and Nixon's resignation. Ford moderated his predecessor's pot rhetoric in degree rather than in kind. His Domestic Council issued a white paper advocating tolerance of the nation's drug problems, including reefer, and acknowledging their permanency: "We should stop raising unrealistic expectations of total elimination of drug abuse from our society," recommended the council.[32] However, Nixon's extermination goal remained with Ford, though with less rhetoric. While suggesting further study of decriminalization, Ford's official position on reefer confirmed "the basic strategy of balancing mutually supportive supply reduction and demand reduction activities."[33]

CARTER: TOLERANCE UNDERMINED

Shortly after taking office in 1977, President Carter addressed Congress on the harm done by marijuana prohibition. Penalties, he argued, should not damage the user more than pot itself. His goal was not merely to relax enforcement but also to repeal parts of earlier pot prohibitions while discouraging alcohol and tobacco excess. Noting the impotency of four decades of pot prohibition, he sought to replace criminal penalties with a modest civil fine and elimination of federal penalties for less than one ounce of pot.[34]

Carter's initial efforts at relaxing reefer laws enlisted drug advisors left over from the prior administration, including one of Nixon's chief advisors, Robert Du Pont. While serving under Nixon, Du Pont wisely kept to himself his personal view that marijuana deserved no severe penalties. To him, at least at that time, pot appeared no worse than tobacco. In November 1974, in a talk to the NORML, he admitted candidly that he could not endorse marijuana because of possible but "unknown" health consequences, but pot prohibitions, he added, should not be allowed to produce harmful social effects on the public's well-being. True to the Shafer commission's recommendation, he hoped, like Carter, to erase penal sanctions for simple marijuana possession. By 1975, five states followed this recommendation and decriminalized pot possession: Alaska, California, Colorado, Maine, and Ohio.

Carter had chosen as his main drug advisor Peter Bourne, a genteel Englishman with a trusting naivete regarding drug politics and the traps in its political minefields. He failed to grasp that many conservative politicians like Nixon saw pot less as a medical or criminal justice issue and more as a quasi-religious issue of cultural deviance discernible in long hair, war protests, free love, and unusual lifestyles. Bourne also failed to grasp that independent pot research remained secondary to preserving political image. He also failed to see that the medical issues lay decidedly subordinate to religious and cultural considerations.

In 1977, Carter sent Bourne a note requesting that, with Du Pont's help, he prepare a congressional proposal for an enlightened drug policy. Borrowing Du Pont's ideas, Bourne's draft called for broad marijuana decriminalization. Carter's ensuing recommendation to Congress advocated that "We can and should continue to discourage the use of marijuana, but this can be done without defining the smoker as a criminal." The message noted that the six states that had already decriminalized pot had not suffered any increase in marijuana smoking. Pot sanctions would yield to a civil fine to express disapproval short of a criminal conviction. His message concluded by urging Congress to "eliminate all federal criminal penalties for the possession of up to one ounce of marijuana."[35]

In 1978, a variation of Carter's proposal was appended to the revision of the federal criminal code that, if enacted, would have treated possession of small amounts of pot as a minor infraction. One of the most liberal parts of the proposed criminal code revision, it went down to defeat in the House of Representatives along with the entire bill.

Carter's proposals were never implemented primarily because of opposition from two quarters. Law enforcement pressed Carter and Congress to receive its expected increased financial resources for an expanding drug war. It prevailed both in finances and in policy. Its drug budget escalated from $382 million under Ford in 1977 to $855 million by 1981. Carter's reforms failed to loosen the propriety grip of the enforcement bureaucracy on the pot turf. Law enforcement's tenacity reflected institutional empire-related goals wholly separate from pot's evils. Thus arose not the first but one of the clearest instances of enforcement agencies thwarting efforts to relax the pot war for reasons less related to drugs than to maintaining their enforcement empires. Funding remained a big part of law enforcement opposition. Indeed, law enforcement's very inability to win the drug war became a reason for providing still more funding to continue that effort.[36] If all the king's horses and king's men could not prevail, the solution would be simply to add more horses and men.

PARENTS' GROUPS

Carter's second obstacle came from a more unexpected source. The same pot policy that appeared humane for users seemed inhumane to their parents. In the second half of the 1970s, several right-wing parent groups combating marijuana use among their children blamed their parenting problems on a spreading culture of government indifference. Among the early leaders in this movement were Ron and Marsha "Keith" Schuchard of Carter's hometown of Atlanta, whose discovery of marijuana joints at a daughter's party in August 1976 generated anger not so much at their daughter and her friends but at the federal government's shoulder shrugging. Strengthening her Democratic but conservative convictions, Ms. Schuchard—"Keith" to her friends—rallied neighboring parents to her message that the federal government needed to aggressively combat the reefer "menace" undermining parents' discipline of their kids.

In reading a magazine interview of Robert Du Pont, Schuchard noted his opposition to sending young potheads to jail and his concern over pot as a social problem. She sent him a letter expressing her group's concern with teens' pot use. Du Pont used a 1977 business trip to Atlanta to meet with her and a group of students, who confirmed widespread peer pot use. He came away from the meetings convinced that he had been misguided in seeing heroin as the nation's major drug menace. Instead, these "real people" had convinced him that the mainstream public cared less about hard drugs' proven liabilities and more about pot's antiestablishment assault.

Du Pont fervidly converted to the cause of the Atlanta parent groups. Never again did he say a word in public in favor of pot decriminalization. "No issue," he confessed later, "has been more frustrating to me in five years as director of National Institute on Drug Abuse (NIDA)" than the difficulty of communicating "the risks of marijuana use," now looming as the "single biggest new health threat in the nation," one that "harmed health, social activities, family living, and work."[37] Pot had become omnipotent.

Schuchard and an across-the-street chain smoker, Sue Rusche, soon formed "Families in Action" to lobby lawmakers in the fight against youthful pot use. Rusche, Schuchard, and their allies pressured youth-oriented shops to stop promoting pot-oriented paraphernalia and music. Schuchard fired off a letter to Du Pont and to Carter attacking Bourne as "sitting on a political powder keg" by treading lightly on the pot problem plaguing the nation's youth.[38]

Schuchard, Rusche, and their conservative followers eventually founded another parents' group called "Parents' Resource Institute for Drug Education," or PRIDE, to whom Bourne's leniency toward pot became anathema. Sending repeated complaints to the White House, these groups joined other drug conservatives to urge his removal, which eventually occurred with his resignation in July 1978, via a letter to Carter concluding, "I fear for the future of the nation far more than I do for the future of your friend."[39]

Bourne's resignation undermined Carter's tolerant attitude toward pot while energizing the grassroots parents' war against the administration's moderate goals. Jubilation swelled in some conservative religious quarters. Utah Senator Orrin Hatch peppered the media with his view that Bourne had done "more harm than any public official in the history of government."[40]

With liberal Bourne off center stage, the new chief of the Drug Enforcement Administration, Peter Bensinger, announced to the media that marijuana penalties would increase rather than relax. That pot could offer some therapeutic or coping benefits now was bunk. As proof, "The American Cancer Society," he volunteered, had found that the weed "represents a more serious cancer threat than cigarettes." Surprised at hearing this news for the first time, the society responded that it had neither conducted such research nor been consulted on any or on Bensinger's personal views but that it remained very interested in marijuana "for treatment of pain for cancer victims."[41]

Bourne's successor, Lee Dogoloff, had served as an assistant to Bourne and had also worked as a disciple of Nixon's first drug czar, Dr. Jerome Jaffe, who had also quietly believed in a health rather than a penal model for reefer abuse. When the Schuchards, Sue Rusche, and other conservative and religious parents' groups visited Dogoloff in his White House office in 1978, their insistence on official resistance against their kids' pot use and antiauthority attitudes undermined Dogoloff's belief in a distinction between hard and soft drugs and the relative harmlessness of the latter. Their advocacy formed his new belief akin to that of the similarly converted Du Pont: Youthful pot use constituted the number one national threat to family stability.[42]

Like Du Pont, Dogoloff now saw the militant parents' groups echoing forgotten mainstream values. These "real" people—the long-suffering parents on the front lines—confronted practical traumas about child rearing that Dogoloff never read about in his scientific journals. These parents, as unsung heroes, combated "changing permissive social attitudes" while hungering for government help needed for "strengthening the family."

The parents' issues put official pot policy in a new light. Dogoloff could no longer see marijuana simply as an impersonal public health concern; it had become a moral and religious value choice affecting human lives and the upbringing of children, a primordial issue of right versus wrong, like sin or murder, without middle ground, tolerance, or compromise. The only approach to drugs and to pot in particular had to be "zero tolerance," a rallying slogan for Dogoloff and for subsequent presidential administrations.[43]

PARENTS AND POT PUBLICATIONS

Du Pont and Dogoloff found a way to channel Keith Schuchard's antipot energies into writing a parents' handbook on ways to combat teenage pot use. The National Institute of Drug Abuse gave its imprimatur and minimal edits to her manuscript, written under her maiden name Marsha Manatt.

The book laid out, definitively, the evils of pot. Published in 1979 by the National Institute on Drug Abuse, *Parents, Peers and Pot* excoriated both government indifference and the teen culture for undermining parental authorities trying to "nurture a young person's ability to reject drug use."[44]

The heart of the booklet throbbed with an exposé of reefer's medical side effects. An English literature Ph.D. specializing in William Blake's romantic poetry and lacking any medical training, Schuchard somehow found the confidence to assert in print, without suffering NIDA's editorial knife, that pot caused cancer, sterility, heart disease, severe lung damage, panic attacks, and a weakened immune system. It also transposed right and left sides of the brain, decreased production of sex hormones, and endowed teenage boys with "enlarged breasts."

Exactly contrary to the findings seven years earlier by Nixon's National Commission on Marijuana and Drug Abuse, Schuchard declared that marijuana definitely served as the "gateway" to hard drug use. Her booklet made no detailed mention of more serious drugs. Nor did she mention that, as of the 1978 University of Michigan annual "Monitoring the Future" student survey, nearly half of all high school students had never smoked pot and two-thirds did not use it on even a monthly basis, while 30 percent smoked cigarettes daily and 40 percent became drunk every two weeks.[45]

To the surprise of the nation's drug czar, *Parents, Peers and Pot* became a best seller with a million copies sold to anxious parents troubled over their kids' reefer use. The parent groups now not only had an ally in the office of the drug czar, they also had co-opted his printing press and used it to recast, even contradict, prior government views, especially Carter's, about the petty effects of pot. The parent groups also triumphed over the Carter policy of discouraging tobacco use while lightening up on pot. The gateway theory became vindicated. Cigarette smoker Sue Rusche took to calling pot users "pre-addicted."

CARTER UNDERMINED

Presidential priorities quickly shifted without the president's consent. While Carter personally considered tobacco worse than marijuana, all references to tobacco disappeared from his speeches and collected papers. His original congressional message had criticized "excessive use of to-bacco" as more serious than pot use, regretting that the 55 million Americans smoking cigarettes daily cost the nation some $25 billion annually in health costs while illegal drug abuse then cost only 40 percent of that amount. Notwithstanding these convictions—subsequently vindicated by major tobacco settlements—tobacco's evils disappeared not only from Carter's speeches but also from much of the nation's consciousness for another seventeen years.[46]

Carter became the first but not the last president to see his pot policies undermined by law enforcement and grassroots parents' groups. Federal and state law enforcement agencies demanded expanding finances and empire building in their respective turfs. Unable to separate marijuana use from their teens' general rebelliousness, parent groups sought government help to bolster their parenting efforts. A devoted officer and family man himself, with both law enforcement and parental experiences, Carter could deny neither of these constituencies. Despite his early reformist intentions, the pot war continued to thrive throughout his administration almost by default.

REAGAN: MOBILIZING MORALS AND MILITARY

After Carter's exit, the pot war greatly expanded in the Reagan administration. Anslinger's depression-era policy of pot extermination became reborn not as a medical or cultural clash but as a moral clash supported by military might and the salvific fervor of the Religious Right.

Sociologists and criminologists have long recognized a political phenomenon called "moral panic" that occurs when political or religious hysteria fuels excessive policies that later come to be regretted. The Salem witch trials and alcohol prohibition offer examples.[47] The Reagan approach to drugs and to pot in particular fits this description of a beginning moral panic.

Reagan's pot policy germinated at a gut level not refutable by social science research because, unlike Nixon, he did not engage the issue as a subject for transient social science research. To the extent that a public increasingly upset over cultural dissent and youthful rebellion demanded toughness on drug crime, Reagan enjoyed the rhetorical advantage of replacing social science data with nonempirical and supposedly universal moral arguments beyond statistical refutation.

To conservative parents like the Schuchards, who supported moral militancy against cultural deviancy, marijuana epitomized the permissive attitudes of liberal and disdainful youth. In her view, the government needed finally to get tough. For Reagan, who shared these views, marijuana's negative features became newly expanded into a modern version of a medieval morality struggle. Reefer's evils lay not primarily in its medical harm or social disarray but in moral degeneracy, a religious "fall" like that in the Garden of Eden, a beguiling image for the Religious Right.

To the Reagan mind-set, pot-bred hippies rewarded lethargy and generated moral relativism deeper than mere cultural dissonance. An expanded drug war, including the reefer war, could generate support among the moral conservatives crucial to the right-wing base of his constituency. His attack and his wife Nancy's "Just Say No" campaign not only validated the parent groups but served as a subtle symbolic attack on the left, the antiwar counterculture, and permissive liberal humanism. Right-wing parents and religious devotees sharing these beliefs applauded. They prompted him to expand the pot war nationwide, in concert with the subtle racial and cultural attitudes of the Anslinger era. Shortly into his administration, staffer Peggy Mann published *Marijuana Alert* describing how pot was turning America's kids into lazy, moody, insolent, bored, slovenly, disheveled monsters—traits she conceded could also be explained by adolescence alone. First Lady Nancy Reagan's foreword termed the book "a true story about a drug that is taking America captive."

Reagan emphasized his get-tough attitude toward drugs by institutionalizing the "zero tolerance" approach. Despite his general sunniness about America, he harbored an especially dark view of reefer. No social solutions to pot existed, he maintained, because pot use, like hard drug use, raised not a social but a moral issue, "a problem of the human heart"; it was not an economic or cultural problem but a defining ethical issue facing each individual. The country had fatally indulged the dual liberal fallacy regarding social engineering: the conviction that reducing poverty would diminish drug abuse, coupled with the companion fallacy that "there is nothing permanent or absolute about human nature."[48]

The war against drugs and against pot in particular tied into Reagan's larger war on crime. The roots of drug abuse, like crime itself, he saw spreading from a permissive Nietzschean moral vacuum where the user, like Dostoyevsky's Raskolnikov in *Crime and Punishment*, became a law unto self alone. In place of this Übermensch philosophy, Reagan offered an undeveloped natural law theory reflecting a drug user's voluntary choice for evil over virtue. The pothead was thus neither sick nor dependent; instead, he was unnatural, evil, and a born-again Satan whose taking of forbidden pot reenacted taking forbidden fruit in the Garden of Eden. Both kinds of violators deserved punishment, if not banishment.

Drug users and "welfare cheats" became targeted staples in Reagan political discourse. A gross connection existed among crime policy, drug policy, and economics. Free-market and "trickle-down" economics depended on the drug user and welfare cheat appearing as folk devils sapping the nation's moral and economic energy. These groups needed salvation—if not exile—via coerced repentance. No longer victims of circumstance as Carter viewed them, the poor appeared as an undeserving, dangerous class of grasping takers whose moral depravity threatened upper-class industry and righteousness.

Like Nixon, Reagan paid much attention to the problem of street crime that, once he took office, morphed into drug crime, the latter the cause of the former. As he fanned public fear around pot use, he presented his penal policies as a messianic salvation against these immoralities battering the nation's walls. Rather than poverty, illness, or bad environment, drug use, particularly pot use, throbbed at the heart of street crime. A newly fearful, angry segment of the public, weary of drug tolerance and moral relativism, supported the administration's strong measures of condemnation and punishment.[49]

Reagan's compliant policy makers accordingly decried the "tumultuous change in values" among the young—their deviant lifestyles and lack of responsibility—and located the leading edge of their moral poverty in marijuana use.[50] If pot symbolized both culture clash and moral disarray, war had to be declared against these barbarians bringing moral degradation to the city gates. If the administration wanted a "strong federal law enforcement capacity in a highly popular manner," recommended Reagan's Attorney General William French Smith, a new federal war on drugs would loosen the criminal's "upper hand" from America's neck.[51]

As governor of California in the tumultuous sixties, Reagan had vetoed a popular bill approved by the assembly that would have reduced pot possession to a simple misdemeanor. During the 1980 presidential campaign, he had taken a hard line against reefer, claiming that medical research showed it to be "probably the most dangerous drug in America today."[52] He brought these views in full bloom to the White House. Youthful drug use lay at the core of the nation's problems, and marijuana lay at the core of drug use. By this logic, pot lay at the center of all the nation's problems. Parent groups, like PRIDE, exulted. After so much foot dragging by Carter's tolerant experts, new hope arose in religious and conservative quarters that government severity would combat the reefer scourge undermining America's youth and parents' efforts to control them.

In 1981, in the Rose Garden, Reagan redeclared the war on drugs with a broadside: "We're taking down the surrender flag that has flown over so many drug efforts. We're running up a battle flag." One drug received special mention: reefer. The federal government, warned the president, needed to "let kids know the truth, to erase the fake glamour that surrounds drugs, and to brand drugs such as marijuana exactly for what they are—dangerous, particularly to school-age youth."[53]

In his 1983 state of the union address, moral panic became Reagan's leitmotif. "An all out war" had to be declared against "big time organized crime and the drug racketeers who are poisoning our young people."[54] Coddling of drug offenders would end first. The federally funded drug treatment network, begun under Nixon and nourished by Carter, became the first to get the ax. The same law enforcement agencies that thwarted Carter's efforts at moderation supported Reagan's drug war escalation, which, of course, expanded their power, turf, and funding.

By the end of his first year, Reagan had drafted the CIA and the military into the pot war by amending the posse comitatus act outlawing military involvement in civilian law enforcement. He enlisted the Navy, the Coast Guard, the Customs Service, the IRS, and the U.S. Marshals Service as well as the DEA in the pot campaign. He propelled the budget for this military expansion from $4.9 million in 1982 to over $1 billion by the end of his term.[55]

NATIONAL ACADEMY OF SCIENCES REPORT

Reagan's declaration of war against marijuana faced an early but timid challenge. In 1982, as he was gearing up the military for the revived pot campaign, the National Academy of Sciences released its own nonpartisan study—with only 300 printed copies—of the medical effects of hard and soft drugs, including marijuana.

Acknowledging its untimeliness, the Academy's Committee on Substance Abuse concluded its detailed scientific study by saying that reefer did not deserve a severe criminal approach, that it caused no damage to the brain or nervous system or to fertility, and that its prohibition should be "seriously reconsidered." The academy added that "alienation from the rule of law," remained the "most serious cost of the current marijuana laws." There was more: "Cannabis and its derivatives," added the prescient report, "have shown promise in the treatment of a variety of disorders, (including) glaucoma, . . . asthma, . . . and the nausea and vomiting of chemotherapy."[56]

With his associates lobbying the National Academy's president to disavow the report, Reagan himself indulged none of its scientific balm. Like those of Nixon's National Commission on Marijuana and Drug Abuse, he excoriated the National Academy's apolitical conclusions as deviant, even dangerous. "The mood toward drugs is changing in this country," he responded, because "the momentum is with us. We're making no excuses for drugs—hard, soft, or otherwise. Drugs are bad and we're going after them."[57] He derived much satisfaction from law enforcement reports of massive pot seizures, tempered, however, by his surprise that the considerable amount of pot being seized exceeded by one-third his administration's estimates of the nation's entire crop.

Recalling the financial consequences of Reagan's expanded drug war is a sober exercise in trickle-down economics. Because so many military resources became enlisted in this war, spending on drug eradication significantly increased the federal deficit. As of 1991, by the end of the Reagan-Bush administrations, the pot war had generated more than $30 million in annual public expenditures (while the annual federal drug budget that year was only about $10.5 million),[58] expanding by the year 2000 to an annual budget of $1.2 billion.[59] In the first five years of the Reagan administration, Pentagon funding for the military portion of the drug war grew from $1 million to $196 million. By the end of his "fiscally conservative" administration, while national spending on education rose 70 percent, spending for police and prisons rose 600 percent during years when all the nation's crimes declined except murder.[60]

TURNER'S TENURE

Shortly after taking office, Reagan created a new White House Drug Policy Office. He appointed as its head a thirty-seven-year-old chemist, Carlton Turner, director of the Marijuana Research Project at the University of Mississippi where, on its enclosed pastoral farms, he had been legally growing well-protected crops of government marijuana for researchers trying to find something wrong with it. With a graduate specialization in plant chemistry and well versed on the perils of marijuana, Turner had been traveling around the country exposing pot's evils to parent groups like PRIDE who received his doomsday pot predictions with enthusiasm.

Turner took special pride in his expertise regarding the evil effects of his collegiate pot crop. In 1980, testifying before the Senate on pot's harms, he stated that its active ingredient, THC, was really not its only powerful agent; in fact, pot possessed as many as sixty-one additional cannabinoids, all harmful to body and mind.[61] These ingredients stayed in the user's body "for days" and remained "in every organ of the body," and "particularly the brain." There was "more cancer in a joint," he liked to say, "than in a Camel." Marijuana exceeded the harm caused by all other drugs because "no other drug used or abused by man has the staying power and broad cellular actions on the body as do the cannabinoids."[62]

Neither medical doctor nor physiologist nor pharmacist, Turner was unqualified by training to work even as a pill dispenser at Walgreen's. His studies had made him an expert on the chemical composition of organic plants like cannabis, but his professional qualifications extended only to observations of plant potency levels. His knowledge of pot's human effects remained secondhand at best. Nonetheless, his talks to antidrug groups carried an air of scientific authority, if not outright dogmatism. Parent groups like PRIDE and National Federation of Parents (NFP) lauded his categorical assertions about pot's parade of medical horrors.

Reagan's hard-line attorney general Edwin Meese, also advising the president on drug policy, took a liking to Turner in his first interview. Sensing evangelical militarism as the right approach, Turner told Meese that "most of all" the big issue was to "clean up society," which meant, "stop talking about whether marijuana is good or bad for you; I'm here to tell you it's bad."[63] After a third pep rally interview in this messianic mode, Meese offered Turner the job of drug czar, only to discover to his dismay that Turner was, of all things, a Democrat. The political affiliation problem handily disappeared with Turner's hasty assurance that his political registration served only as an academic front to mollify his liberal colleagues, for in reality he was a closet Republican. Turner then came aboard the administration with a militant agenda matching the aggressive invasion of the Carter administration by parent groups.[64]

From prior work with other administrations, Turner knew Jerome Jaffe, Robert Du Pont, and Lee Dogoloff and their policies. He now announced that these experts really knew nothing at all about an effective national marijuana policy. Their convictions about real distinctions between hard and soft drugs and between addicts and recreational users were simply wrong. All drugs of whatever kind, even soft drinks—but not tobacco— were dangerous. All required a policy of zero tolerance. "I was hired by the President of the United States," Turner began boasting, "to clean up America." Shortly after taking office, in an interview in *Government Executive*, he attributed enormous ideological power to pot: use of marijuana alone caused "anti-military, anti-nuclear power, anti-big business, anti-authority attitudes."[65]

Turner's pot strategy adopted the criminal rather than the medical model. Users would be better motivated to change their habits by the threat of punishment than by the benefit of treatment. "Our philosophy is to get rid of the psychiatrists," he announced, because "they're trained to treat and treatment isn't what we do."[66] The treatment budget accordingly was cut by 43 percent of what it had been under Carter.

Under Turner, law enforcement emphasis shifted from hard drugs to the real danger to national well-being, the deliberate moral choice of the evil weed. The president acted in tandem. After the November elections, working behind the scenes, Reagan cut a billion dollars from the $4 billion drug bill announced during the campaign, including most of the treatment budget plus all drug treatment grants to state and local police.[67]

With Reagan's blessing, Turner suspended the venerable doctrine of posse comitatus preventing American armed forces from policing internally within U.S. territory. Urged to focus on pot rather than hard drugs, the DEA soon was actively eradicating pot plants in seven states, a figure ballooning to forty by 1983. To eradicate pot in the national forests—a popular and safe growing area—Turner enlisted the Forest Service and the Bureau of Land Management. To combat maritime pot from the Caribbean, he deployed a new federal pot task force taken from the ranks of the FBI, the DEA, Customs, the Coast Guard, and other traditional law enforcement agencies. He enlisted Vice President George Bush to head the South Florida Task Force to interdict reefer seeping into the country's porous Caribbean coast.

With Turner's encouragement, the Reagan administration gave its blessing to the DARE drug education program ("Drug Abuse Resistance Education") to enlist police officers to teach fifth and six graders about the perils of marijuana. DARE was the brainchild of Reagan's friend Daryl Gates, police chief of Los Angeles, who had first proposed the program in the early 1980s. Testifying before Congress, Gates had recommended with a straight face that "the casual drug user ought to be taken out and shot."[68]

With Reagan guarding the White House, Bush monitoring South Florida and the Caribbean coasts, and Turner keeping lookout over military patrols, marijuana officially became a more dreaded immigrant than heroin, cocaine, or any other hard drug. Tobacco—then the subject of only modest government interest—remained so innocuous as to deserve no official negative thoughts at all.[69]

In hindsight, these conflicting priorities about pot and tobacco were unsurprising. In his prior life as an actor, Reagan had repeatedly endorsed

Chesterfield cigarettes. His image had graced numerous holiday ads show-ing him smoking them while boasting that he planned to give them as holiday gifts to his best friends. Turner urged ceasing any further research on tobacco as a matter of little toxic importance.[70]

Under Robert Du Pont, the DEA had seriously contemplated pot de-criminalization before the Reagan administration took office. Now, un-der conservative political pressure from Turner and right-wing religious and parent groups, it backtracked into proclaiming marijuana the nation's "most urgent" drug problem. The administration's twin goals of zero tolerance and user accountability became political slogans. Pot offenders became national security threats deserving severe punishment. Enthusi-astically spreading that gospel, Turner regularly joined up with Schuchard and Ross Perot on a traveling road show—the "Texans War on Drugs"—preaching to Lions, Elks, PTAs, law enforcement, and especially the Re-ligious Right about pot's fraying of the nation's social fabric and the universal moral law, while offering audiences homespun parental strate-gies to combat its horrors.[71]

NEW LAWS

This militant ideology spread to Congress as well, which was itself reel-ing from the contagious moral panic over drug excess. The drug death of basketball star Len Bias and the swelling crack cocaine epidemic even-tually led, at Reagan's urging, to passage of the 1984 Sentencing Reform Act establishing the federal sentencing commission to mandate federal sentences in drug cases.

Contradicting many of the penal policies of the 1970 Comprehensive Sentencing Act, the commission's "reforms" compelled adherence to rigid sentencing guidelines, effective in 1987, placing a heavy presumption of mandatory imprisonment on most drug offenders with little regard for mitigating circumstances. "If we have mandatories for a first offense," explained Turner, "we won't have people back on the streets committing crime."[72] The sentencing guidelines quickly provoked widespread criti-cism as being rigid and excessive, leading America's top sentencing scholar Michael Tonry to describe them as "the most controversial and disliked sentencing reform in U.S. history."[73]

Reagan's legislative assaults on drugs flourished with a Congress as quiescent as in the era of Anslinger's comparatively tepid 1937 Tax Act. The Anti-Drug Abuse Act of 1986 and the Anti-Drug Abuse Amendment of 1988 raised federal penalties for possession, cultivation, and traffick-ing in pot, reflecting its assumed medical and cultural harms, though no evidence supported those conclusions.

The 1986 Anti-Drug Abuse Act greatly increased the penalties for federal drug offenses, established mandatory minimum sentences, and effectively transferred sentencing power from judges to prosecutors. Hatred of drugs swelled into hatred of the drug user, particularly the long-haired pothead stereotype. Marijuana use brought draconian sentences and specious suggestions of links to marginalized racial groups. The country was in thrall to an almost unending panic over crime problems supposedly related to drugs, with pot at their core, culminating in mandatory minimum sentences of unprecedented length for drug crimes, including simple possession of reefer.

Passed without serious congressional cost-benefit or deterrence analyses, these new sentencing laws reflected not the degree of participation in a drug transaction but simply the indiscriminate quantity of drugs. Prosecutors rather than judges decided whether a mandatory minimum sentence would apply. The public health approach of the 1960s thus yielded to severe criminal repression. All use of pot became as serious as hard-drug crime, the contagion a personal moral failing as well as a threat to national stability.

Comforting and self-fulfilling successes in this pot crusade appeared with trumpet flourishes. In August 1985, in one of a series of similar triumphs, Attorney General Meese boasted to the press the daring achievements of daunting drug agents eradicating pot. "This week alone we have confiscated and eradicated over 200,000 marijuana plants . . . confiscated numerous weapons, taken over greenhouses where marijuana was being grown," he exclaimed, adding with pride that "approximately 2,200 federal, state and local law enforcement officers joined in a coordinated campaign to uproot the plants."[74] He made no mention of the serious crimes this considerable manpower diversion had overlooked.

Eventually Turner's fortunes took a turn for the worse, due in good part to his own unfounded beliefs. Late in 1986, while being interviewed by a *Newsweek* reporter on drug policy, he asserted a causal connection between marijuana and homosexuality. While visiting drug treatment centers, he explained, he had been told that 40 percent of the treated addicts had engaged in a homosexual act. Homosexuality "seems to be something that follows along from their marijuana use," he concluded. *Newsweek* ran the interview under the heading: "REAGAN AIDE: POT CAN MAKE YOU GAY."[75]

Much controversy followed, culminating in a sense that it was time for Turner to move on to plants in other gardens. In December, some six weeks after the article appeared, he resigned as Reagan's drug advisor to join a Princeton, New Jersey, drug-testing firm expanding rapidly under the administration's mandate on workplace drug testing.

SCHUSTER TAKES OVER

Reagan's choice for Turner's successor, Charles Schuster, a Ph.D. in psychology, enjoyed close ties to the drug treatment community. He had been associate director of the Illinois Drug Abuse Program and had taught and conducted drug research at the University of Chicago. His son had suffered a lengthy marijuana problem, a trauma endearing him to the parent groups, many sharing similar frustrations. In March 1986, Schuster took over NIDA's directorship.

Almost immediately, Schuster faced the renewed dilemma of needing medical evidence to support the prior reefer criminalization. Shortly after taking office, he received a call from a prominent Republican senator demanding to know why the millions of dollars given his agency had not yet revealed "something wrong with marijuana." The call was not isolated. During his tenure in the Reagan administration, as Schuster later acknowledged, "the pressure became, 'Find something wrong with marijuana.'" Reacting to the same urgency, NIDA spent a good portion of its million-dollar budget in desperately seeking to uncover toxic effects of any kind from reefer use. "For many years," Schuster later admitted, "we tried to determine whether marijuana produced brain damage. We didn't."[76]

Schuster's fruitless search for pot's ill effects reflected a continuing policy dilemma for Reagan and other presidents: pot had been criminalized without any verifiable assessment of its harm—in fact, in the face of denials of such harm. To maintain the criminal sanctions, it became urgent, after the fact, to find some medical justification to make the criminalization credible. None was forthcoming during Reagan's tenure.

REAGAN'S LEGACY

Reagan's marijuana legacy remains militantly clear: a stiffening of the punitive approach to pot via a confiscatory policy that his Associate Attorney General Stephen Trott described as not only sending pot users to jail but also "forfeiting everything they own—their land, their cars, their boats, everything." As Michael Pollan notes of Reagan's pot forfeiture policy, pot use "not only could get you temporally expelled from your garden but can get your garden taken away forever."[77] Any property obtained through an illegal marijuana transaction became subject to forfeiture. Some people who never faced actual marijuana charges but had only been investigated saw their properties forfeited to law enforcement agencies.

Reagan's confiscatory forfeiture policy served as a materialistic incentive for greedy law enforcement agencies to swell their possessions. As of

1998, according to Pollan, most law enforcement asset forfeitures derived directly from pot arrests.[78] In the analogy of the war on drugs, Reagan's forfeiture policy gave his troops authority to loot, with the spoils going to the troops.

Criminalization and forfeitures during the Reagan administration may have generated an unexpected reaction among drug users. Just before Reagan's presidency, about a third of America's high school seniors admitted to smoking pot in the prior month. By 1988, as the Reagan administration was winding down, that percent had been cut in half, so only about one in six admitted to using it. The parents' movement took credit for the downturn. Sue Rusche boasted that, thanks to their efforts, "We stopped decriminalization. We stopped the head shops. We reversed the nation's attitudes about marijuana."[79]

A closer inspection of these drug numbers, however, reveals another interpretation lurking beneath the plaudits. While youngsters' reefer use was drifting downward, hard core drug use during Reagan's watch dramatically moved upward. The logic of the gateway theory—that pot initiated its users to hard drugs—suggested the very opposite: if the gateway theory were accurate, as pot use declined, so also would hard drug use. Drug statistics for the waning Reagan years showed the exact contrary. Pot and hard drug usage moved independently of each other, with pot declining while hard drug usage, especially crack, increased. Reagan's militancy on reefer had pushed young Americans away from marijuana and toward truly dangerous hard drugs like crack cocaine—a reverse gateway.[80]

GEORGE H.W. BUSH: MORAL PANIC REDUX

When George H.W. Bush took office, the war on pot declared by his predecessor raged in full force. True, some loyalists had voiced occasional dissent. Before he became Bush's vice president, then Representative Dan Quayle had declared, in March 1977, that "Congress should definitely consider decriminalizing possession of marijuana. . . . We should concentrate on prosecuting the rapists and burglars who are a menace to society."[81] That conviction, of course, evaporated when Quayle became Bush's running mate.

Surrounded by a chorus of voices from the left claiming that the marijuana war had failed and many more from the right demanding more punitive measures, Bush opted for yet another new war against drugs, including reefer. Unlike the Democrats' platform, the 1989 Republican platform located the pot problem squarely in degenerate American youth. "Drug use directly threatens the fabric of our society," it announced, adding that pot was "part of a world-wide narcotics empire" that the Reagan-Bush administrations had "set out to destroy."[82] "We support stronger penalties," proclaimed the Republican platform, "including the death penalty for drug traffickers." Echoing Reagan's moral philosophy about the voluntary choice of evil, the platform underscored the need to "assert absolutes of right and wrong concerning drug abuse."[83]

"This scourge will stop," the newly inaugurated president proclaimed about drug usage. A compliant media generated feature stories, investigative reports, and news stories about the "drug menace" requiring Bush's renewed war. No longer the "wimp" caricatured during the campaign, a resolute Bush sought to exterminate once and for all time the common enemy debilitating a cohesive America: drugs, with pot, again, at their core.

Presidential endorsements of fear easily spread to the citizenry via the media. Within a month of his call to arms, thanks to the renewed equation of the drug war with patriotism, news polls reported that two-thirds of the citizenry agreed that all drugs, pot in particular, had become the major issue facing the country. After a year of only modest success against drugs, however, public opinion polls then revealed that only 10 percent of the electorate still continued to support this militaristic approach, showing, not for the first time, how public support offered a fickle reed for an aggressive pot policy.

Bush needed a dramatic scene to illustrate the renewed drug war. On September 1 of his inauguration year, undercover drug agents arranged a drug sale in Lafayette Park directly across from the White House. Shortly thereafter, according to plan, the president appeared in a special televised news conference where he displayed the seized cache as he announced with alarm that drug activity was now occurring "just across from the White House."[84] The barbarians—at least the scripted ones—were at the very door of civilization.

WILLIAM BENNETT COMES ABOARD

Bush offered the job of crafting drug strategy to William Bennett, a bright and brash thirty-seven-year-old political enthusiast who had been Secretary of Education under Reagan. Bennett lobbied Bush for the job by phone. "If you're really serious about it [the drug war] and want someone to go after it for you, I'll volunteer." In a later call, he told Bush of the need for a strong and aggressive federal role in the drug war. Bennett was one of the very few academics who had supported Ronald Reagan, a distinction making him politically unique in academic circles. The president happily crowned him as drug czar—or, in his ascendant persona, as the nation's virtue entrepreneur.

Bennett's forte was not drugs but liberal arts. He knew nothing of drugs or crime apart from reading newspapers. His training had been in educational philosophy, for which his Ph.D. earned him several teaching positions before he moved on to the National Endowment for the Humanities and the Department of Education. Like Reagan, Bennett saw the nation torn asunder by liberal ideology—tolerance, permissiveness, and especially pot experimentation, all eroding the nation's moral stability and, in his appropriated word, its collective virtue.

In his view, the evil of pot was not primarily medical or cultural but moral. As a chosen vice, the weed caused antiauthoritarian, nihilist, and anticonformist behaviors reflecting the user's choice of self-destruction. Drug use, especially pot use, "destroys character," he thundered, because it "destroys dignity and autonomy." "It subverts productivity, it makes a mockery of virtue," he proclaimed in a talk to the Kennedy School of Government at Harvard in 1989. As he became more upset about drugs, he found himself increasingly dependent upon his two-pack-a-day cigarette habit.[85]

Bennett harbored strong convictions about the moral impact of drugs but not about other addictions like tobacco, his own chosen addiction. Like Anslinger and Reagan before him, he saw pot, not tobacco, as *the* symbol of cultural deviance and as *the* threat to civic virtue. He was among the first drug czars to announce that the children of his administration faced a more powerful blend of pot than their parents had used in the heady 1960s. Some reports did indicate that the THC in the new varieties was forty times greater than just two decades earlier. This discovery lent alarm to his deontological pronouncements about the evils of the weed. "The simple fact," he asserted, is that "drug abuse is wrong. And the moral argument, in the end, is the most compelling argument."[86]

Data about pot potency were ambiguous at best. The administration's long-term studies of pot potency at Turner's marijuana farm in Mississippi partly undermined Bennett's alarm. Its research showed that the average THC seized by law enforcement agencies after 1981 had fluctuated between 2.3 and 3.8 percent. Other researchers found that the average THC in the 1970s ranged from 2 to 5 percent, with some samples reaching 14 percent. Depending on one's view, Bennett could argue either that pot potency had dramatically increased or that it had decreased since the 1970s. What seems beyond doubt, however, is that the Bush administration's militant crusade began to drive pot growers indoors, where they could safely bathe their plants in uninterrupted floodlights generating higher potencies than in outside-grown plants.[87]

Whatever the data, Bennett spoke plainly to his staff and public audiences about his favorite subjects of virtue and coercion, two concepts he viewed as blood relatives. Believing wholeheartedly in moral reform by compulsion if not by consent, he tirelessly repeated that pot use ultimately constituted moral evil. To stamp out this evil, "a massive wave of arrests" became his "top priority."[88]

VIRTUE BY COERCION

Trained as an educator, Bennett as drug czar promoted a unique educational philosophy for the country: the best way to learn virtue was through coercion. Just as literalist Christians viewed hell as a prime motivator of moral observance, Bennett called for the "reconstitution of legal and social authority through the imposition of appropriate consequences for drug dealing," especially regarding pot.[89] Punishment played for the drug war what hell provided for the Religious Right. "I'm not a person who says that the first purpose of punishment is rehabilitation," he lectured Congress; instead, "the first purpose is moral, to exact a price for transgressing the rights of others."[90] An eye for an eye, the joint for a joint.

Bennett announced that the administration "had little choice but to pursue get-tough law enforcement strategies" against pot. What about a parallel approach to alcohol? Alcohol, he admitted, constituted the nation's primary medical and criminogenic problem, greater than all other drugs, including pot. How then handle alcohol abuse? The most effective strategy, he proposed, would not be enacting new punitive sanctions against drinkers but instead crafting new zoning laws around liquor stores.[91]

Sterner strategies, however, were needed for the serious but lesser pot problem. Bennett gave no quarter to students' drug use. Drugs reflected "bad choices of immoral school kids." If caught using pot a second time, students should be kicked out of school and put in jails. Counseling or treatment? No, that smacked of "moral relativism." "No ifs, ands, or buts," he insisted; what was needed was a "clear message to all kids that if you're using drugs, you're out of school" and back on the streets or in jail.[92] Action even more dramatic might be needed. On *Larry King Live*, he announced that "beheading" drug dealers was a suitable albeit "legally difficult" strategy. Asked for clarification, this author of books on virtue responded with "Morally, I don't have any problem with it."[93]

The womb of many of these strategies, Bennett's office became a popular staff-gathering place for debating the great issues of political philosophy, topics about which he did know something. Each week his 130 staff associates, chosen as much for their ability to debate weighty affairs of governance as for their drug expertise, spent hours debating how to restrain an unruly populace, confine youthful instincts, and use force to shape drug immorality into the one-dimensional national conformity the office equated with virtue. Given that reefer's evil was moral rather than medical, the logical remedy was not treatment programs but individual will power or, failing that, coercion. The pot problem was moral, not medical.

The very year that Bennett became drug czar, tobacco killed 395,000 citizens and alcohol another 46,000. Alcohol abuse, he admitted, certainly needed some creative strategy. His prime remedy for it was "strengthened will power." He acknowledged that alcohol was a "multiplier" of crime, far worse than hard drugs. But for alcohol abuse his practical solutions, beyond self-control, became, in order, (1) more zoning around liquor stores, (2) more research, and (3) limiting liquor advertising.[94] For drugs, however, though they caused far fewer deaths, injuries, crime, or health problems, the death penalty, beheading, or lengthy incarceration became the most effective strategies. Though alcohol caused more than ten times the deaths caused by hard drugs, its abuse would be best addressed through the three nonpunitive techniques of self-control, limited advertising, and urban zoning.

The same year Bennett took office, cocaine killed 3,618 people, fewer than the 5,500 who acquired cancer from legal pesticide spraying. Heroin killed another 2,743. Pot killed no one. On the crime front, more than half the nation's killers in 1989 were using alcohol at the time of their killings; only 6 percent were using drugs alone. In 1990, while 17 percent of twelfth graders had tried pot, 60 percent were drinking alcohol almost weekly, and 20 percent of the nation's high school seniors were regularly smoking carcinogenic cigarettes, like Bennett himself, to the tune of more than a pack a day.[95]

These alarming statistics, however, did not disrupt the lofty debates in Bennett's office. His staff's favorite afternoon discussion topics of political philosophy, morality, and virtue eventually helped convince Bennett that both for health and consistency reasons he needed to strengthen his own will power regarding his personal tobacco addiction. He put himself into a $700 a week tobacco treatment program—the kind denied drug users—and successfully graduated. To keep his mouth and hands off tobacco, he took to gulping bags of sunflower seeds, popping, crunching, and ejecting them with gusto while presiding over the afternoon office deliberations. Shelled sunflower seed debris littered the office, desk, and floor much like a birdcage after feeding. His staff philosophers took to calling his office "the aviary."

Bennett quickly tired of a job for which he had little expertise. He tired, too, from the embarrassment caused by the nation's burgeoning use of drugs during his reign, an eighteen-month tenure relieved by spending the pleasant summer months of 1990 campaigning in Alaska for a Yes vote to recriminalize marijuana. He also wanted to devote more time to writing books about moral perfection.

In November 1990, he announced with triumph his resignation, declaring victory over the drug scourge—"Victory," he exalted, "beyond my wildest dreams." With victory now officially decreed, Bennett returned to private life, where he could earn upwards of $25,000 for each speech he gave on the relationship among drugs, civic virtue, and coercion.

Not everyone applauded Bennett's claim of victory in the drug war. Representative Charles Rangel, chair of the House Committee on Narcotics, termed Bennett's tenure "a colossal failure," with no progress in the drug war at all, least of all a victory. "He must be smoking cigarettes," said Rangel, "if he thinks he can . . . find anybody who will say, 'Thank you, Bill Bennett, there's light at the end of the tunnel.'"[96]

Retirement gave Bennett a chance to indulge some long-lasting hobbies. His hastily published anthologies on civic virtue reflected a different persona from that of drug czar. In his books, compassion appeared near the top of the virtue hierarchy. "Compassion seeks to retain our hold on this very early awareness that we are all in the same boat, that there but for the grace of God go I."[97] Later, he wrote that, of all the virtues, "compassion may bring the greatest degree of fulfillment. It enriches our lives with a sense of nobleness and purpose, makes us morally awake."[98]

Bennett also had more time in retirement to indulge some favorite but secret hobbies. In May 2003, major newspapers acquired casino documents in Atlantic City and Las Vegas revealing that Bennett, a compulsive high stakes gambler and "preferred customer," had lost over $8 million of his family assets because of his addiction to late-night gambling, a topic overlooked in his virtue books. According to a gambling expert consulted by the *New York Daily News*, Bennett needed to devote 800 to 1,600 hours to gaming to hemorrhage the $8 million he lost. The author of *The Death of Outrage*, lamenting President Clinton's sexual misbehavior, eventually issued a Clintonesque apology to the nation, saying that he had done nothing wrong at all and promising never to do it again.

Ultimately, the Bush-Bennett coercive criminal justice approach made little difference in drug statistics. By the end of Bush's third year in office, the nation's drug problem continued to be, in Bush's words, a "scourge."[99] While 17 percent of high school seniors were smoking pot once a month, 60 percent of them were drinking alcohol to excess at least once a month. Whatever zoning existed around liquor stores failed to diminish alcohol's predominant contribution to the nation's drug problem.

THE COMPASSIONATE USER PROGRAM

President Bush Sr. did accomplish something both lasting and ironic in his war against marijuana. In 1978, in the wake of a lengthy lawsuit filed by glaucoma patient Robert Randall, the federal government had implemented a "compassionate user" program to provide marijuana directly to sick people for whom it was expected to provide relief, glaucoma and epilepsy patients in particular.

The rationale for this unusual "Investigational New Drug Program" was medical necessity. Eligible patients could get relief from no medicine other than marijuana. Compassionate while at the same time conservative, before those terms became politicized, the DEA thought it could arrange distribution of small amounts of marijuana to carefully screened patients whose ailments were thought responsive to pot.

During the height of the Bush campaign against the weed, after more than a decade of this program's quiet service to sick patients, someone saw the contradiction between this program and the policy of unqualified drug prohibition. In 1991, fearing a public relations fallout from an appearance of compassion toward the weed—a "wrong message"—the Bush administration closed the program to new entrants after only eight patients had been certified. The decision slammed the program's doors in the face of thousands of sick persons who had applied. Thus Jacki Rickert, denied entry into the compassionate user program, became a target for arrest and conviction for using once-approved but now-unapproved pot to alleviate her serious illnesses.[100]

By the end of the Bush administration, the marijuana tolerance of the 1970s had retreated along with conceptual distinctions between hard and soft drugs and between law-abiding behavior and pot use. The campaign against all undifferentiated drugs reached new heights of coercion and punishment under the Bush-Bennett contention that fear, not compassion, offered the best way to stem pot use.[101]

Under the Bush-Bennett regime, policymakers' fear of drugs morphed into fear of the drug user, generated draconian sentences, and forged specious links between drugs and marginalized groups, exactly as had happened with alcohol during Prohibition. Forfeitures, fast becoming an institutional motivator for law enforcement agencies, increased dramatically. Toward the end of the Bush presidency, a 1990 Justice Department memo to U.S. Attorneys urged prosecutors to "increase our forfeiture production" as the best means to "increase our forfeiture income."[102]

CLINTON: POLITICS TRUMPS CONVICTION

Bill Clinton's election in 1992 initially suggested a more tolerant approach to pot. For one thing, as he unabashedly acknowledged, he had smoked the weed himself. A decade earlier, his brother had been addicted to cocaine to the point of receiving intensive treatment. While Clinton promoted his brother as a poster child against drug legalization, including legalization of marijuana, the president nonetheless urged more compassion and less punishment for users—at least initially.

Intimations of a more lenient policy appeared in his campaign's scathing critiques of his predecessor's confrontational drug policies. "Bush confuses being tough with being smart," he said in 1992. "Bush thinks locking up addicts instead of treating them before they commit crimes— or failing to treat them once they're in prison, which is basically the case now—is clever politics. That may be, but it certainly isn't sound policy, and the consequences of his cravenness could ruin us."[103]

As happened with Carter, Clinton's troubles with pot moderation began almost immediately after the election. Early in his first term, the University of Michigan released its annual "Monitoring the Future" survey of substance use among high school seniors. Of twelfth graders, more than one-fourth admitted to smoking pot in the prior year, an increase of about 5 percent since the last report, the first increase in student pot-use numbers in fourteen years. Similar reports showed heavy pot usage even among eighth graders, in some instances doubling. The student increase in pot usage spelled trouble for the president's preferred policy of penal relaxation.[104]

Of course, the president had himself largely to blame for his own contribution to the burgeoning marijuana problem. For one thing, there was his highly publicized admission to smoking it but not inhaling. Moreover, shortly after taking office, in an MTV interview, he was asked if he could turn back the clock, would he use pot and even inhale? Viewers could interpret his grinning, unqualified yes as a presidential green light to smoke pot, exactly what the Michigan "Monitoring the Future" study showed teens doing in greater numbers. After the MTV interview, a dramatic increase in marijuana use appeared for eighth, ninth, and twelfth graders, virtually doubling between 1993 and 1997.[105]

By 1995, Clinton's tolerant pot policy was in trouble, castigated especially by Representative William Clinger (R-PA), the leader of the House Committee on Government Reform and Oversight. Justice subcommittee chair Bill Zeliff (R-NH) also condemned the president's "shocking disinterest" in the war on pot.[106] Representative Charles Rangel (D-MI) expressed similar sentiments: "I've never seen, never never, found any administration that's been so silent on this great challenge [drug use]."[107]

In the wake of the Michigan report, the press spread the bad news: "STUDY FINDS MARIJUANA USE IS UP IN HIGH SCHOOLS" proclaimed the *New York Times*'s front page on February 1, 1994, noting that Clinton had rarely mentioned the drug war while campaigning except to criticize his predecessor's severity. At ensuing White House strategy sessions, Clinton's advisors insisted that the reefer increase would be read to mean that his administration played soft on drugs. His political survival beyond a first term depended on crusading vigorously against all drugs, pot included.

The administration's drug office convened a group of prevention experts to worry over the rise in student marijuana. Their concern may have been misdirected. While the Ann Arbor report found that the nation's increased pot use was a "wake-up call" about a "general rise in deviance," its other messages about substance abuse went unheard. While pot use was growing, its increase was less than one-fourth what it had been during peak years. The most dramatic but ignored data involved not hard or soft drugs but alcohol. More than one-fourth of the nation's high school seniors admitted to five or more drinks in one sitting during the previous two weeks. One-fourth of the nation's twelfth graders were regularly drunk.[108]

For Clinton to make an issue of this excessive use of alcohol by comparison with marijuana would have been indelicate if not ungrateful. Given that his Democratic party was the major recipient of financial contributions from the alcohol industry, silence appeared the better part of any new alcohol crusade. Clinton's missed opportunity reflects yet another theme interwoven into the country's twisted pot saga: presidential administrations' repeated ignoring of the far greater social and health consequences from tobacco and alcohol compared to marijuana, simply because of political ties to the alcohol and tobacco lobbies.

As with Carter, Clinton found resistance to drug liberalization coming from law enforcement agencies. Early in his first year, he learned that it would be no easy task to dismantle the many bloated governmental agencies fighting against drugs. Tentative efforts in that direction generated resistance from lawmakers and agency heads, notably the DEA and the Federal Law Enforcement Officers Association representing the fifty federal agencies involved in the drug war. All feared loss of workers, funding, and turf.

Law enforcement resistance reflects another ironic logic of the pot campaign. Given their impossible task of total pot eradication, law enforcement would never have sufficient resources to eliminate pot completely, thus generating their continuously expanding resources for their endless, fruitless efforts. The very futility of their campaign ensured its continuing funding.[109]

A NEW POT CAMPAIGN

Fearing the image of softness on pot, the Clinton administration launched a new antimarijuana campaign in late 1995, contemporaneous with the president's reelection campaign. The crusade began with the claimed discovery of a new link between marijuana and violent behavior, a claim inviting but escaping scholarly scrutiny. Despite friendly suggestions to research this link in more depth, the White House did not want to put marijuana policy before another truly independent advisory commission, given the consistency with which such commissions had reached politically unacceptable conclusions favoring tolerance.

Needing decidedly strong messages, the same Clinton, who famously voiced "feel your pain" messages, refused to reopen the government's compassionate user marijuana program to new patients wanting pot to relieve their illnesses. In a 1999 legal brief, Clinton's Justice Department adopted the denounced Bush administration policy in asserting that medical use of marijuana was "bad public policy," meaning, of course, not medically but politically problematic.

In December 1993, as the concern over increased pot usage was building, Surgeon General Joycelyn Elders gave a speech suggesting that the crime rate might diminish if drugs were legalized, including marijuana. While cautioning that more research needed to be done before any such change, she cracked open the policy door ever so slightly to suggest official discussion of a more moderate attitude toward drugs, marijuana in particular.

The president's reaction was immediate. His press secretary quickly responded by saying that Clinton remained personally opposed to legalization of any drugs and, further, remained "not interested" in any more scientific studies about their true effects. The president put pressure on Elders to correct her discordant views about marijuana. She was fired a year later in December 1994.[110]

Given this crack in the official armor, antipot efforts would have to be redoubled. At Clinton's urging, his first drug czar, Lee Brown, marched into a Kentucky marijuana field and vigorously chopped down cannabis plants as TV cameras purred. "My message is simple and clear," Brown proclaimed from between cannabis stalks. "Marijuana is not benign, it is not harmless and should not be legalized. It's a very dangerous drug that can cause you to fight for your health and life in a hospital emergency room."[111] Just what pot-induced illness could send a user to the emergency room was not mentioned.

In focusing on pot, Brown, like his predecessors, ignored the nation's continuing increase of heroin and alcohol, drugs with a true claim on emergency treatment. The new policy also contradicted Clinton's campaign statements during the 1992 election. "A President should speak straight," he then had said, "even if what he advocates isn't popular. If he sticks to his guns, the results will prove the wisdom of his policy."[112]

Not long after his second inauguration, Clinton signed a bill earmarking $195 million for an antidrug ad campaign, the first installment of a $1 billion public relations campaign against all drugs, including pot. The ad campaign became the nation's third largest ad campaign ever.[113] The ads ended with the words "Partnership for a Drug-Free America" sponsored by the "Office of National Drug Control Policy." The Partnership had modestly emerged in 1986, the year basketball star Len Bias died with cocaine in his system, when President Reagan had signed the bill creating mandatory federal prison terms for possessing any illegal drug. Now, under Clinton, the slogan "Drug-Free America" became shorthand for declaring the "policy of the United States Government to create a Drug-Free America by 1995," with pot slated to be the first drug to expire.[114]

Clinton's public relations concerns over pot arose not only from the University of Michigan's "Monitoring the Future" reports but also, of all places, from evening sitcoms on television. In 1997, following successful medical marijuana initiatives in California and Arizona, the CBS comedy show *Murphy Brown* presented a prime-time segment featuring leading lady Candice Bergen suffering serious aftereffects of chemotherapy from cancer treatment, with a friend providing her marijuana to relieve her pain and stimulate her appetite.

Drug enforcement administration chief Thomas Constantine immediately attacked CBS for "doing a great disservice," by "trivializing drug abuse," and by "pandering to the libertarian supporters of an 'open society' and to the myths of legalization." The nation could not tolerate such televised views. "I am extremely troubled," he lamented, "that at a time when teenage drug abuse is doubling . . . a television show of the caliber of *Murphy Brown* would portray marijuana as medicine." He asserted that pot was definitely "not medicine" and promised to research whether CBS had broken any laws by airing the program.[115] This clamor against medical marijuana on TV, which of course increased the show's ratings, arose near the time when Vice President Gore disclosed his sister's real-life treatment of her cancer with government-provided medical marijuana.

GENERAL McCAFFREY: WARRIOR OF HOAX

After Brown's tenure, Clinton passed the role of drug czar to General Barry McCaffrey, a decorated Vietnam veteran who had lost partial use of his left arm in the course of three woundings in action, earning two Distinguished Service Crosses, two Silver Stars, and three Purple Hearts. The drug war needed such valor, and a general seemed the ideal figurehead for waging it anew. A four-star general was also the ideal figure to garner patriotic votes for Clinton's second term.

With McCaffrey in charge, the war on drugs continued at its highest level ever in terms of tax dollars, arrests, numbers incarcerated, and lengths of prison sentences.[116] However, this war continued to fail to achieve the promised victory of a drug-free America by 1995. While antidrug efforts reduced some use and trafficking, increases in arrests and incarceration did little to curb widespread drug use, violence connected with drugs, or the deterioration of American families. The renewed pot war revealed a desperate effort by the Clinton administration to prove to the public, for political gain, that the president was tough on crime by responding punitively to the pot problems of the nation's youth, the same population then using alcohol twice as frequently as pot.

McCaffrey particularly fumed at the specter of the Netherlands, where the drug policy permitted limited legal access to pot in coffee shops. Before traveling to Holland for an official—and denunciatory—look-see in 1998, he announced that the murder rate in that degenerate country amounted to "double that of the United States—that's drugs."[117]

His indiscreet exaggerations about Holland's "unmitigated disaster" were grossly incorrect, echoing those of Anslinger a half century earlier. In fact, the per capita Dutch murder rate then was barely one-fourth the murder rate in the United States. The percentage of Americans who used marijuana during their lifetimes, or even in the last month, then doubly exceeded the percentage of Dutch citizens using pot, and Americans were then three times more likely to have used cocaine as Dutch citizens. Twenty-eight percent of Dutch tenth graders had then used marijuana, while 41 percent of American tenth graders had tried it.[118] McCaffrey's misstatements impugned both his credibility and Dutch integrity.

The Dutch ambassador to the United States, Joris Vos, responded to McCaffrey's unfounded accusations about Holland with a plaintive letter sent to the White House, saying in part:

> I am confounded and dismayed by your description of Dutch drug policy as an unmitigated disaster and by your suggestion that the purpose of that policy is to make it easier for young people. . . . Your remarks have no basis

in the facts and figures which your office has at its disposal and which certainly do not originate only from Dutch sources. . . . I find the timing of your remarks—six days before your planned visit to the Netherlands with a view to gaining first-hand knowledge about Dutch drug policy and its results—rather astonishing.[119]

While championing the first amendment, the Clinton administration strained to suppress potentially embarrassing pot research. In 1997, the World Health Organization completed a major comparative study of pot's effects. Its final report compared the adverse effects of the weed against alcohol and tobacco. The results showed marijuana far less harmful than either was. When the Clinton administration learned of its imminent release so near the elections, it urged NIDA officials to lobby to suppress that part of the report for fear of encouraging pot legalizers. However, suppression only raised the specter of forbidden fruit. A British magazine, *The New Scientist,* acquired and released an early copy of the deleted section showing alcohol far more harmful than pot in seven of nine categories, including injuries and deaths. *The New Scientist* then editorialized against the "anti-dope propaganda that circulates in the U.S."[120]

ELEVENTH-HOUR DECRIMINALIZATION

Far from the least of the lasting ironies of the Clinton war on pot occurred toward the very end of his second term in an interview in *Rolling Stone* magazine in December 2000, less than a month before leaving office. No longer politically motivated to send stern antipot messages or to confront parent groups, law enforcement, or irate lawmakers or to seek re-election, Clinton allowed his true convictions to surface by asserting, for the first time as president, that the time had come for the nation to decriminalize marijuana. His recommendation appeared far more categorical than the timid hints that had prompted him to silence his Surgeon General Joycelyn Elders's earlier and more modest hint in that direction. Clinton's decriminalization suggestion, politically safe for a lame-duck president, appeared especially untimely for the 4,175,537 Americans arrested for pot during his terms in office—88 percent for simple possession—and even more untimely for the 21,424 sentenced to federal prisons for marijuana convictions during his presidency, all untimely sacrifices on his reelection altar.[121]

After having severely criticized his predecessor's harsh drug policies and reprimanded his surgeon general merely for suggesting studying drug moderation, the same Clinton administration that favored pot decriminalization imprisoned more Americans for marijuana crimes than any other administration in our history. Twice as many people were arrested for using the weed during the Clinton presidency than during the entire presidency of the seemingly draconian Richard Nixon.[122] While Washington had its back turned, real people were suffering from severe penal consequences. Aristophanes's play "The Frogs" tells the story of boys playing near a stream who find a frog and kill it in jest. Aristophanes recounts that, although the boys killed the frog in jest, the frog itself died "in earnest." Incarceration of drug users was a reality rather than an abstraction.

Clinton's reefer crackdown also expanded workplace drug testing, funded research on new forms of biological warfare against marijuana plants, and terminated the student loans of convicted pot smokers—but not of violent criminals or even alcoholics. Within days of Clinton's *Rolling Stone* reefer decriminalization interview, full-page antipot ads appeared in the *New York Times* and other papers composed by Clinton's "Partnership for a Drug-Free America," his administration's $2 million advertising attack on the same marijuana the president now favored decriminalizing.[123]

Retiring General McCaffrey's final report to the president resembled that of William Bennett. "Substantial progress" he now claimed in the administration's fight against drugs, pot included. Though much of the report addressed treatment, only 31 percent of the Clinton drug budget addressed treatment, with the remaining 69 percent dedicated to enforcement and interdiction, including pot enforcement. Despite Clinton's 1992 anti-Bush campaign statements about the priority of treatment over enforcement, his administration had waged a more intensive war on pot than any other presidency in history. There were more arrests for pot use in 1998 than for murder, rape, robbery, or aggravated assault combined, costing in 1996 alone some $13 billion just for pot arrests, approximately $21,400 for each one.[124]

In retrospect, Clinton's resolve for a more temperate approach to drugs suffered from weak backbone and hypocrisy. Sensing opposition from legislators and law enforcement and anticipating reelection obstacles, he abandoned his announced policy of pot tolerance for fear of being labeled soft on drugs. His convictions about moderating marijuana enforcement thus surrendered to political expediency.

Surrendering principle for political gain has become a hallmark of American drug politics. Clinton's self-serving pot policy in this respect pervades the justice system. Commenting on the passage of a congressional resolution rejecting more moderate federal drug sentencing, the *New York Times* reported in 1995 that, while no one in Congress supported the administration's severe drug sentencing policies, Attorney General Janet Reno and President Clinton both chose to continue the disliked policy because "they simply were afraid to appear even remotely soft on drugs."[125] Aristophanes's modern "frogs" were dying not only "in earnest" but also in vain.

GEORGE W. BUSH

In May 2001, newly designated President George W. Bush, who had refused to answer all electoral questions about his own prior drug usage,[126] chose John P. Walters to replace General McCaffrey as head of the Office of National Drug Control Policy. Walters had been executive director of the conservative Council on Crime in America and president of the New Citizenship Project. He also had served as deputy director for Supply Reduction in the Office of National Drug Control Policy, acting as chief deputy to drug-and-virtue czar William Bennett in President Bush Sr.'s administration. One of Bennett's "moon howlers," he had been a frequent participant in the philosophical debates in Bennett's "aviary."

Along with John DeJulio and Bennett, Walters had coauthored *Body Count: Moral Poverty and How to Win America's War against Crime and Drugs*, a hard-line 1996 handbook addressing the moral bankruptcy caused by declining use of capital punishment and drug use, including pot use. He shared Bennett's emphasis on publicly stigmatizing drugs and using American military might against drug runners. He also favored severe prison sentences for marijuana smugglers and repeat offenders. *Body Count* announced that ultraviolent, morally vacuous young druggies called "superpredators" were victimizing America's beleaguered cities.

No enemy of imaginative ideas, Walters in 1996 had urged Congress to increase support for a South American drug policy of shooting down planes suspected of transporting drugs, including marijuana. He rejected concerns that such a policy would endanger innocent passengers on the planes. As Bush's drug czar he withdrew his support for this idea in April 2002 when Peruvian military authorities shot down a plane carrying an American missionary and her daughter—but without any drugs.

Before Walters became Bush's drug czar, General McCaffrey, a self-described hardliner, had expressed dismay at Walters's unbending punitive views. McCaffrey particularly disagreed with Walters's attitude that treatment failed to offer a realistic policy option because, in Walters's view, "too much treatment capacity in the United States" already existed. In testimony before the Senate Judiciary Committee in 1996 and thereafter, Walters criticized "this ineffectual policy" of government-sponsored drug treatment as a waste of effort compared to incarceration.

Co-authored with like-minded Bennett, the same who favored "beheading" drug users, Walters's *Body Count* book branded young criminals "superpredators" attacking mainstream American values "without remorse." Drug-using criminals, he maintained, suffer from an extreme form of "moral poverty," for which the only remedy remains "stiff and certain punishment." Pot poses a moral issue because it "enslaves the mind and destroys the soul." "Smoking marijuana is clearly detrimental both physically and mentally," he wrote in *Body Count.* "It impairs judgment and short-term memory, reduces the ability to concentrate, and diminishes motor-control functions." In a word, marijuana acts like a glass of alcohol.

Walters also saw marijuana as the gateway to hard drugs because teen potheads were eighty-five times more likely to use hard drugs than non-users. Lax pot laws vastly increased numbers of potheads admitted to emergency rooms for marijuana use.[127] In fact, however, the consistent main contributor to this nation's emergency rooms has long been the commonplace practice of mixing legal prescription drugs with legal alcohol, a practice exceeding emergency room admissions for cocaine, heroin, marijuana, and LSD combined.[128]

Walters's drug policies mirrored classical penology, especially the idea that incarceration motivates virtue. In an interview in the conservative *Weekly Standard,* he urged abandoning "the three great urban myths": that the nation was locking up too many people for drug possession, including pot; that their sentences were too long; and third, that the justice system was "unjustly punishing young Black men."[129]

These sentiments signaled little change from prior Republican administrations except for a significant dissonance in aggression from his boss, President Bush, who had said more than once while campaigning that "long minimum sentences for first time offenders may not be the best way to occupy jail space and/or heal people from their disease."[130]

Walters's supporting data about his three myths were also suspect. Data from the Bureau of Justice statistics in 2000 showed that teenage crime had steadily decreased in the prior decade—the "superpredators" were dying out. Every year since 1989, the number of people imprisoned for nonviolent drug offenses had exceeded the number of violent offenders. In 1980 about 10,000 people went to state prisons for drug offenses; by 2000, the majority of inmates in all the nation's prisons and jails were nonviolent offenders, of whom the greatest portion were drug users.[131]

Like Bennett, Walters asserted that marijuana use leads to other kinds of more serious crime. But in 2003 researchers at Harvard's Kennedy School of Government, in conjunction with the Rand Corporation, tested that theory by looking at statistics on marijuana use among persons arrested for various kinds of crime. They found that the arrestees for property and financial crime were disproportionately likely to have used pot at some time, but when they looked at crime rates rather than arrest rates, the connection completely disappeared. Their conclusion was that pot use may not make its users more likely to break the law but it does make them much more likely to get caught.[132]

Walters also shared the Religious Right's view of the criminal law as an instrument of virtue via coercion. This segment of conservative voters, predominant in the Bible Belt, traditionally has linked drug use to sin, moral depravity, and the decline of the family. For them the prospect of secular jails and prisons for drug users borrows on divine authority for a parallel secular hell on earth as punishment for sin and as a disincentive to immorality. To such groups Walters, like Bennett, appeared as an ideologue of virtue whose drug office should define for young people what virtuous human life was really about and the hellish sanctions available if they missed the message.

In November 2002, Walters called a press conference to announce a major new interagency campaign against "drugged driving," which focused on driving while smoking marijuana. Under this initiative, pot smokers should not drive during the two weeks needed for pot's metabolites to wear off. Violators would be arrested and cited for "drugged driving," just like alcohol-impaired drivers. Walters did not take the additional step of urging that alcohol be made illegal.

During the same period that Walters announced his new campaign against stoned driving, major research appeared both in Australia and in the United States showing that potheads actually drive more safely while "drugged" than the general drug-free driver population. Curiously, many studies of marijuana and traffic safety found that the odds of causing death or injury while driving were slightly lower in cannabis users than in people who had not consumed drugs. The study of Australian motorists showed that consumers of cannabis were 30 percent less likely to cause accidents than drivers who had not used the drug. Another investigation of more than 1,800 crashes in the United States found that drivers who used only cannabis were only 70 percent as likely to have caused an accident as the drug-free group.[133]

Walters also continued the campaign by the Office of National Drug Policy Control to publish anti-marijuana messages in major publications. Some of the ads resorted to emotion and hysteria if not rank exaggeration. One ad in 2003 showed televised images of a teen being molested and another girl becoming pregnant during times they were using marijuana. Another showed a teenage male accidentally shooting his best friend after the gun-user had taken marijuana. A causal connection between pot and pregnancy and pot and shooting does not appear in any serious marijuana research, though the connection between homicide and failed gun control does.

With President George W. Bush and his drug czar, it becomes indisputable that his "compassionate conservativism" in the war on drugs involves a move decidedly toward the latter rather than the former term. Under Walters's view, the federal government has the duty to impose and subsidize certain morals over others, including the immorality of drugs, though not of drugs like tobacco and alcohol. Citizen free choice or self-definition is out of the question. Unlike alcohol and tobacco, drug use and marijuana in particular become moral evils defined by the White House, leaving no room for competing definitions. For Bush and Walters, the government's job is to save its citizens from hell.[134]

CONCLUSION

Apart from the hyprocrisy and occasional humor, the vagaries of the past six presidential administrations reveal nuances both contrary and ironic. Hard-liners like Nixon focused on social consequences assumed to be causally linked to pot. Deontological hard-liners like Reagan and Bush Sr., while agreeing on the social ills of pot, emphasized the moral poverty of pot users, while overlooking the greater poverties and social harms of tobacco and alcohol. More tolerant presidents like Carter and Clinton, who initially sought to relax reefer laws, succumbed to pressures from parents (Carter), law enforcement (Carter and Clinton), and to re-election priorities (Clinton), in the end augmenting the very policies they wished to relax.

The interplay between morality and utilitarianism in these administrations shows a consistent but rarely acknowledged pattern. William Bennett used moral explanations to castigate marijuana, finding "the moral argument, in the end, the most compelling."[135] General McCaffrey, Clinton's most vocal czar, argued that marijuana's evil lay in the fact that it is "destructive of a person's physical, emotional and moral strength."[136] Walters follows Bennett's view regarding the immorality of marijuana.

Reliable data showing the claimed moral destruction, however, remains hard to find. Such moral assertions usually reflect only highly idiosyncratic and disproportionately stern ethical views linked to coerced virtue, but the moral argument has the advantage of being beyond the reach of research or statistics. In the end, despite the deontological claims, many recent presidents' and drug czars' moral condemnations of pot drift into utilitarian rationales focusing on cultural disarray and social protest, behaviors more readily measurable but difficult to attribute to marijuana alone.

Each administration since Nixon finds a locus on the Apollo-Dionysius continuum. To Carter and Clinton, the nation's ideal citizen ought to be trusted to choose a mode of victimless personal self-expression with minimal government coercion, even if the by-products of self-expression become socially or culturally unusual. To Nixon, Reagan, and both Bushes, on the other hand, the citizenry cannot be trusted to choose its pleasures or vices without government direction. Instead, the government must selectively dictate those choices for its citizens in order to promote their compliance and virtue, using when necessary legal and military coercion from on high.

3

ENFORCEMENT PRACTICES

ENFORCEMENT PRACTICES: GEOGRAPHY, GATEWAYS, GAUNTLETS, AND GUMPTION

The vagaries of pot policies across different administrations appear dramatically on the nation's streets where law enforcement officers implement—or ignore—lawmakers' statutory prohibitions. One of the most striking aspects of the nation's pot war is its capriciousness. Law enforcement directed at pot resembles pot growing and use: It is haphazard, discretionary, and geographically uneven. This chapter addresses the vagaries of the different approaches of enforcement agencies to the spectrum of legal enforcement, including enforcement efforts on cultivation, location, and production.

UNEVEN LAWS

Not the least of the enforcement inconsistency appears in the wide disparity in state and federal reefer laws. As of the new millennium, state marijuana laws varied in an arbitrary checkerboard fashion in scope and severity from coast to coast.

In the six years after the 1972 Shafer report, beginning with Oregon in 1973, eleven states reclassified marijuana possession as a misdemeanor, petty offense, or civil violation punishable only by a negligible fine. Reefer use in those tolerant states and in states with stricter sanctions remained indistinguishable, suggesting the futility of the penal sanctions in the strict states.[1]

A 1988 scholarly evaluation of the Moscone Act, California's 1976 decriminalization law, estimated that the state had saved $958 million in arrest costs through 1985 because the new laws encouraged more tolerance and less involvement of police and courts.[2] California's message did not reach many policymakers. Under conservative pressure, national public opinion began to take a more punitive shift in the late 1970s. No other states decriminalized marijuana, and some like Alaska, which had decriminalized it in 1978, recriminalized it, thanks in part to high-season campaigning there by drug czar and states' rights advocate Bill Bennett. Some states increased penalties for using pot under specified circumstances, such as driving, using pot near a school or housing project, or receiving a student loan.[3]

Enforcement of pot laws has also varied dramatically because of different legal standards across different jurisdictions. Some states classify marijuana with drugs like mescaline and heroin; others put it in a separate category by itself. The mélange of disparate state laws yields widely different penalties for the same conduct. In Connecticut, cultivating as little as a kilo merits a mandatory five-year jail sentence. In New York, possessing slightly less than an ounce brings a $100 fine, rarely collected, but if pot is found in an automobile in New York City, the entire car can be forfeited. In Nevada, possessing any amount of marijuana is a felony. In Rhode Island, possession of over 5 kilograms (11 pounds) can lead to a fine of $1 million. Montana penalizes selling a pound of marijuana as a first offense as eligibility for a life sentence. In 2000 in New Mexico, where Governor Gary Johnson opposed the war on drugs, selling 10,000 pounds of marijuana as a first offense can result in a prison term up to three years. In Idaho, selling water pipes could earn nine years in prison. Growing any amount of pot in Oklahoma can bring a life sentence.

In Kentucky, a major pot-growing state, products made of hemp, such as paper and clothing, carry the same penalties as an equivalent weight of marijuana. Until the 1960s, Texas had laws on its books ranging from two years to life imprisonment for marijuana possession. In Arizona, as of 2004, if a death occurred for any reason (e.g., heart attack) during any kind of marijuana transaction, the offender qualified for the death penalty.[4]

Ohio sports one of the most liberal marijuana laws; possession of up to three ounces is a misdemeanor punishable by a $100 fine.[5] In 1996, Ohio decriminalized the cultivation of small amounts of marijuana for personal use.[6] Otherwise, pot remains illegal to some extent in all other states. The federal crime bills passed in 1996 by a conservative Congress now specify the death penalty for any marijuana offender caught with 60,000 plants or more. These instances of geographical and penal disparity reflect Marvin Frankel's 1972 complaint in his influential *Criminal Sentences: Law Without Order*[7] that the nation's drug enforcement, prosecution, and sentencing are haphazard and capricious to the point of lawlessness.

Caprice extends squarely to pot enforcement. Like patternless street enforcement, pot prosecutions often reflect geography more than ideology. In Milwaukee, possession of marijuana for many years was classified as a state misdemeanor while the same behavior in the suburbs involved a violation of a municipal ordinance. The city's mostly nonwhite prosecutions resulted in jail time and a criminal record while most white offenders cited in the suburbs suffered only a ticket and an erasable fine.[8] Nationally, as Milwaukee's experience epitomizes, the choice of who gets busted depends on place more than conduct. Geographical disparity typically reflects the arbitrary decisions of police and sheriffs deciding locally, at their whim, whether to enforce pot prohibitions on their turf.

As of 2004, small-quantity pot sales and smoking occurring privately generally merited little official fanfare. Place and its notoriety play a continuing role in arrests. Pot transactions tend to cluster on corners on or near high school and college campuses and on inner city streets and parks. Although the total number of pot sellers likely exceeds the total number of hard drug sellers, pot-selling arrests as of 2003 averaged much fewer than the annual total of 220,000 heroin and cocaine arrests. Black and Hispanic Americans continue to be overrepresented among outdoor pot sellers because of their concentration in inner cities and their relative scarcity on college campuses. These factors help explain why white high school and college-age students compose the highest number of pot users, but inner-city blacks and Hispanics compose the most numerous arrestees.[9]

Arrest data released in 2000 showed more than a third of all marijuana arrests occurred in only ten counties in the nation. Alaska, New York, Nebraska, Mississippi, and South Carolina achieved the country's highest marijuana arrest rates, even though the first four of these states decriminalized light pot possession decades ago. In those states, as well as in Oregon, California, Maine, Colorado, Minnesota, Ohio, and North Carolina, first possession of less than an ounce typically brings punishment by fines ranging from $200 to $400. The National Organization for the Reform of Marijuana Laws (NORML) study reviewed more than 1.4 million arrest reports from 1995 through 1997 and found highly selective enforcement and inconsistent punishment for violations even within counties in the same state.[10]

Effects of these varied levels of enforcement on extent of pot usage appear minimal or even inversely related. States that decriminalized possession of small amounts of marijuana for personal consumption in the 1970s showed no increase in marijuana use.[11] Marijuana consumption declined in those states just as it did in states retaining stronger sanctions.

When California saved $958,305,499 between 1976 and 1985 by reducing pot possession to a finable violation, the percent increase in pot use in that state during that same period was zero.[12] The Netherlands saw the identical pattern when it decriminalized marijuana consumption in 1976 as a result of implementing the Baan recommendations.[13]

As Presidents Carter and Clinton unwittingly discovered, much to their frustration, more permissive pot policies largely depend on political support from law enforcement. However, enforcement agencies typically fear that government relaxation will endanger their jobs and funding. Thus, both law enforcement and drug traffickers oppose legalization for common reasons of empire building. In 2000, in addition to Governor Gray Davis, the main opponents of California's Proposition 36 to replace drug incarceration with treatment were elected district attorneys and prison guards, groups fearing job loss from diminished convictions, along with enforcement officers fearing loss of authority on the streets.

Former Kansas City and San Jose police chief Joseph McNamara explains why most police chiefs balk at pot legalization efforts:

> It's asking an awful lot for them to come out and say, "Look, this drug prohibition is a stupid thing we shouldn't have started in 1914 and it gets worse and worse every year." That's a big step for a police chief. That's asking them to commit career suicide.[14]

Checkerboard legislative and enforcement policies about reefer reveal much about inequality, inconsistency, and caprice. Reefer prosecution reflects location and status more so than conduct or degree or quantity of pot. Behavior condoned in one state could be severely punished just across the state line or in an adjoining county or ignored just across the street.

Campus marijuana enforcement offers a dramatic illustration. Under the loan policies of Presidents Clinton and George H.W. Bush, pot-using college students automatically lose their eligibility for college loans pursuant to the Higher Education Act of 1999. To avoid this result, some college administrators, siding with students rather than the government, have instructed their campus police to ignore student marijuana violations. At Florida State University in Tallahassee, for example, marijuana arrests by campus police dropped from over 1,200 in the 1999–2000 school year to a grand total of 11 the following year. For institutional and student reasons, Florida regents had instructed campus police to de-emphasize pot violations to avoid jeopardizing students' government loans.[15]

The disparity goes beyond administrative edicts. Pot sales occur in great numbers in college dorms and campus watering holes. While arrests occur relatively rarely in those places, they predominate on urban streets and parks. Thus, whites who predominate on college campuses are under-represented in marijuana arrests while inner city minorities such as blacks and Hispanics are overrepresented.[16]

POT AND POLS

Courthouse observers, judges included, have regularly found that children of the upper and middle classes are rarely charged and even more rarely sent to prison for reefer use. When they are caught, they often enter private treatment programs before trial to avoid prosecution and conviction. Sentencing decisions thus reflect not only geography and race but also political favoritism.

Examples abound. In 1994, the son of Indiana Congressman Dan Burton, an outspoken proponent of life sentences for some marijuana crimes, was arrested for transporting nearly eight pounds of pot to Indiana in the trunk of his car, for which he received probation. Months later, he was rearrested at his apartment with thirty marijuana plants and a shotgun. Under federal mandatory minimum sentencing, these behaviors would have merited a minimum of five years in a federal penitentiary, plus another year or more for violating probation. The Indiana prosecutor gained dismissal of the original charges, reduced the remaining one to a state misdemeanor, and a state judge sentenced him to community service, probation, and house arrest rather than the incarceration his father demanded for offenders other than his son.[17]

Other politicians have seen family potheads receive similar lenient treatment from police, prosecutors, and courts. In June 1993, Richard Riley Jr., son of President Clinton's education secretary of the same name, was indicted by a federal grand jury in South Carolina for distributing cocaine and marijuana, crimes carrying a penalty of ten years to life in prison. His sentence: probation and six months' house arrest. Riley was one of the many pardoned by President Clinton in his final days in office.[18]

Early in the Clinton administration, when Vice President Al Gore's son, Albert Gore III, was found smoking pot at the exclusive St Alban's school, his sentence was a mere suspension. His father managed to suppress the story, thereby avoiding having his son fingerprinted and suffer a permanent pot offense on his record.[19]

Marijuana remains popular with professional athletes, academics, scholars, and upper-class society, groups that, as a whole, rarely if ever appear in court or in police dossiers. In ten years serving on a major urban trial court and twelve years on an appellate court, I saw no member of these groups convicted of any marijuana sale or use. Instead, those prosecuted for pot are overwhelmingly isolated lower-class inner-city blacks, whites, and Hispanics who foolishly use pot in public places less protected than college dorms, private clubs, and the seemingly immunized locker rooms of professional sports or the entourages of media stars.

In January 1999, police stopped singer Whitney Houston at a Hawaii airport, searched her and found 15.2 grams of marijuana, earning a potential Hawaii penalty of six months in prison and a $500 fine. Told to wait for more police to arrive, Ms. Houston simply boarded her plane and flew away from the problem to San Francisco. After considering at length whether to prosecute such a famous diva, Hawaii prosecutors conceded in April 2000 that they had decided not to file any charges.

In 1982, the same year that President Reagan launched his war on weed, the son of his chief of staff, John C. Baker, sold less than an ounce to an undercover cop at the Baker family ranch in Texas. Under Texas law, such conduct constituted a felony carrying a prison term of between two and twenty years. Instead, charged with a misdemeanor, he pled guilty and was fined $2,000.[20]

In 1996, Representative "Duke" Cunningham, a Republican from California, given to advocating harsh drug penalties, attacked President Clinton for being too "cavalier" about illegal drugs and for appointing federal judges who were soft on drug crime. "We must get tough on drug dealers," he then proclaimed, asserting that all peddlers must pay "dearly." Four months after this ringing call to arms, the DEA arrested his son Todd for transporting 400 pounds of pot from California to the east coast as part of a marijuana smuggling ring peddling tons of pot across the nation, a crime with a potential life sentence in some states.

Offered a plea bargain, Todd pled guilty to distribution of a mere 400 pounds, and the prosecutor recommended only fourteen months at a boot camp and halfway house. Forgetting his complaints about President Clinton's lenient pot policies, Representative Cunningham appeared before the sentencing judge begging for a deviation from his own penal policy because, as he put it, "my son has a good heart."[21] What is the public message? Good-hearted scions of politicians escape the penalties reserved for less fortunate pot peddlers. Put differently, the marijuana laws and their penalties apply only to The Other.

Inconsistencies are not limited to cases involving family potheads; ideology and politics also rise to the surface. Before he became George Bush Sr.'s running mate, Dan Quayle had called for the decriminalization of small quantities of pot.[22] In 1981, as a new representative from the state of Georgia, Newt Gingrich had introduced a bill in Congress that, if enacted, would have legalized the medicinal use of marijuana. Some fifteen years later, as Speaker of the House during the Bush-Quayle "Contract for America" era, Gingrich, himself a former youthful pothead, took a more militant stance by sponsoring a bill requiring a life sentence or the death penalty for anyone caught importing anything more than two ounces of marijuana into the country.[23]

POT AND JOCKS

Pot is equally alive and well in sports circles where a parallel kind of arbitrariness reigns. Contrary to the wholesome image marketed by the NBA, 60 to 70 percent of its 350-plus players smoke marijuana. If they tested for pot, there "would be no league," once asserted Richard Dumas, the former Phoenix Suns guard. "Weed is something guys grow up doing, and there's no reason for them to stop. Because almost everyone does it, no wants to test for it. They're afraid to." The NBA's drug policy protects its players despite their illegal behavior. The NBA has co-opted reefer enforcement. The policy is "ridiculous," said Karl Malone, Utah's 1997 and 1998 All Star. "Marijuana is not tested for."[24]

In 1997, after a series of off-court incidents involving NBA players possessing marijuana, the *New York Times* reported that the majority of NBA players smoked marijuana.[25] As of 1999, the league began testing for marijuana. Twelve of 430 active players tested positive during training camp in the fall of 1999. That only 2.7 percent of players tested positive at first seemed to quell concern over marijuana use among NBA players. But the results reflected the fact that players were told *in advance* when they would be tested, a privilege given no ordinary nonathletic pot users.

Before the league and the players reached the collective bargaining pact in January 1999, the NBA tested only rookies and then only for cocaine and heroin. Though the old agreement seemed a model for professional sports when it took effect in 1983, only seven players were suspended in sixteen years. Their numbers included the former Knicks and Nets player Michael Ray Richardson, who was suspended for cocaine use and reinstated after two and a half years, and Roy Tarpley, who was disqualified for cocaine use in 1991, reinstated in 1994, and disqualified again in 1995 for failing his after-care agreement.

Dumas was the last player suspended for pot use in the United States under the rookie testing provision of the old program. By warning the players that the pot test would occur sometime during training camp, the NBA was saying, in effect, "Go get ready for it and please don't mess up." Nonathletes in the general population receive no such advance warning. "The players who use marijuana say to themselves, 'All right, I'll chill out, make my money and wait for the summertime,' Dumas has said.

Believe me, it's more of a cover for all the players who got caught with possession."[26] Would more testing work? Once they pass the test, "smart users," according to former NBA player and coach John Lucas, "do whatever they do."

Baseball's attitude toward its pot users shows similar caprice. Three baseball stadiums are named after beer companies—Coors Field, Busch Stadium, and Miller Park. Similar marijuana promotions, of course, would violate the law. Nonetheless, reefer remains popular with baseball players too. The New York Mets ended their lackluster 2002 season amid allegations of widespread unprosecuted pot use by its players. Newsday said marijuana use was widespread on the team and cited Tony Tarasco, Mark Corey, and Grant Roberts as prime weed violators. Roberts, a relief pitcher, appeared in a *Newsday* photo doing a bong hit. Perhaps more bonging would have helped the Mets' batting. *High Times*, a New York-based magazine for pot enthusiasts, has long fielded a local softball team, the "Bonghitters," which between 1996 and 2002 went 50-8-4, with a three-year winning streak.[27]

Reefer is also popular in less popular sports. Bob Burnquist, one of the nation's better-known skateboarders, and his girlfriend Jen O'Brien, a top female boarder, openly advocate pot. They admit that it helps them deal with the pressures of their sport. "A lot of skateboarders use marijuana for relaxation," says O'Brien, who appeared on a 2003 cover of *High Times* magazine with a marijuana bud. "I think it's better than popping Vicodin or Valium or drinking alcohol."[28]

This highly selective pot war directed largely away from important people like politicians, athletes, and students and aimed at young and poor urban minorities announces the exact opposite of what drug warring politicians profess. Three decades into our current war, over $40 billion has been spent annually to date at the state, federal, and local levels to fight marijuana; millions of people stand convicted of marijuana felonies with thousands sent to prison, while the reefer leaf remains the rallying cry for disaffected youth, pop divas, athletes, and frumpy professors. Instead of scorn, reefer has come to symbolize an image of thoughtful liberation from bourgeois government propaganda.

SENTENCES FOR MARIJUANA

In 2000, 734,000 people were arrested for marijuana-related offenses. In that year, one of every six inmates in a federal prison system—roughly 15,000 people—lived behind government bars primarily for a marijuana offense. Other inmates were serving life sentences in state correctional facilities for growing, selling, or possessing marijuana. In 1980, almost twice as many violent offenders resided in federal prisons than drug offenders; twenty years later, more people resided in our nation's prisons for nonviolent marijuana behavior than for manslaughter or rape.

Between 1992 and 1998, some 21,424 Americans were sentenced to federal prison terms for marijuana convictions.[29] In 1997, 38.7 percent of all federal sentencing guideline cases were drug offenses. The largest percentages of those offenses involved marijuana. Of the 27,000 drug offenders sentenced to probation in seventeen states in 1986, 49 percent were rearrested for a felony offense within three years, of which 26.7 percent were drug related.[30] Attempts to reduce dangerous prison overcrowding suffer from these inconsistent penal policies. In 1992, violent offenders, on the average, earned release after serving less than half their sentences. In that year, the average punishment for a violent offender in the United States was forty-three months in prison; the punishment under federal law for a marijuana offender that same year averaged fifty months in prison.[31]

HAS CRIMINAL PROHIBITION WORKED?

Teenage marijuana use grew since 1992 when President Clinton took office; by one measure, it doubled. That increase cannot be attributed to any slackening of marijuana enforcement. The number of Americans arrested each year for marijuana offenses increased by 43 percent after Clinton took office, with more marijuana arrests during his first three years than during any other three-year period in our history.

In 2000, the nation's police arrested more than 734,000 people for marijuana violations, a new record. About nine out of ten of those arrests were for possession, the remainder for personal sale, manufacture, or cultivation. In 2000, more Americans resided in prison for marijuana violations than at any other time in our history.

As incarceration for pot violations continued to grow, teenage marijuana use also grew. School kids of the late 1990s were more likely to smoke pot than teens a decade earlier. In 1998, *Time* reported that urine tests showed 13 percent of teenagers used the weed in 1997 compared to 2 percent in 1989.[32] In 1982, when President Reagan declared war on drugs, 88.5 percent of high school seniors said it was "fairly easy" or "very easy" for them to obtain marijuana. In 1994, well after a decade of the drug war, the proportion of seniors who said they could "easily" obtain it remained at 85.5 percent, marking no improvement in user rates in over a decade of expensive and aggressive police enforcement.

In June 2001, drug analyst Andrew Golub, a researcher at New York–based National Development and Research Institute, reported that marijuana had replaced crack cocaine as the drug of choice among young people in legal trouble. Nearly 60 percent of eighteen- to twenty-year-olds arrested during the late 1990s tested positive for pot, according to the Justice Department's Bureau of Justice Statistics in June 2001.[33]

In the four years before the millennium, the nation's pot arrests doubled from 300,000 to 600,000. In 1996, 641,642 people were arrested for marijuana violations, 85 percent of them for possession, not sale.[34] In 1997, there were 606,519 arrests for marijuana possession and 88,862 arrests for sale or manufacture. Over four million persons were arrested for pot violations, mostly simple possession, during the Clinton presidency before his announcement in December 2000 that pot should be decriminalized. Those imprisoned included an Oklahoma man with severe rheumatoid arthritis who received ninety-three years in prison for growing marijuana plants in his basement. His prosecutor told the jury that, in sentencing, they should "pick a number and add two or three zeros to it."[35]

In 1996, the U.S. Department of Health and Human Services surveyed almost 18,000 Americans and concluded that marijuana use among youths ages twelve to seventeen rose 105 percent from 1992 to 1994 and 37 percent between 1995 and 1998. At the Phoenix House Foundation ten years before, 13 percent of adolescents sought treatment for marijuana; by 2000 that figure had jumped to 40 percent. Mark Kleiman, a UCLA specialist in drug policy, then said:

> It's destructive to focus the country on one small part of drug use. Focusing on marijuana ignores the rising use of methamphetamine and the fact that heroin appears to be coming back, and ignores the No. 1 drug of abuse among high school kids—alcohol.[36]

Marijuana accounts for nearly 90 percent[37] of illegal drug use.[38] Our pot prohibition has given all these young people a lifelong criminal record as well as a potent rallying symbol to counter adult values, including the adult addictions of tobacco and alcohol.

CRACKING DOWN ON THE GATEWAY

Politicians and drug czars regularly assert that reefer enforcement should be harsh because its use inevitably leads to harder drugs such as crack, heroin, and cocaine. This belief became almost a mantra for drug czars McCaffrey, Bennett, and Walters. Proponents of this gateway argument urge strict enforcement of pot laws, particularly against young people, in order to intercept their pot use before the alleged transition to harder drugs. This gateway theory explains the DARE drug education program and the concentration of law enforcement attention on high school campuses and other youthful watering holes such as shopping malls. All this energy reflects the mandate to apprehend young potheads before they pass through the pot gateway to graduate to hard drugs.

The gateway theory originated at least as early as 1937, when the Federal Bureau of Narcotics began to widely publicize this view, though not under the "gateway" label. The gateway assumption became a common slogan for Harry Anslinger and President Nixon despite lack of evidence that pot presaged harder drug use any more so than did alcohol, tobacco, or food in general. In the Anslinger era, the gateway theory regularly appeared in congressional testimony as the "tragically familiar story" of young potheads moving on to hard drugs and violent crime.[39]

Credibility of the gateway theory suffered its earliest critiques in the reports of both the 1944 New York Academy of Medicine and President Nixon's 1972 Marijuana Commission. Nonetheless, drug czar William Bennett asserted that teenage pot use increased the risk that teens would move on to hard drugs "more than 80 fold."[40] The same theory appears in a 1994 report by the National Center on Addiction and Substance Abuse at Columbia University, whose authors asserted that juveniles smoking marijuana are eighty-five times more likely to use cocaine than those who do not smoke it. The survey reported that 17 percent of interviewed potheads admitted to trying cocaine. Only 0.2 percent of those who had not used marijuana admitted to trying cocaine. Put another way, 83 percent of the pot smokers, or nearly five out of six, said they had not tried cocaine, a figure undercutting the threat of marijuana as the "gateway" to hard drugs.

Proponents of the gateway argument often confuse causality with correlation. The Columbia researchers reached the gateway conclusion by first taking the estimated number of cocaine users who had smoked pot and dividing that sum by the estimated number who had not (almost nobody). The same procedure can establish that coffee, alcohol, tobacco, and cherry pie are also gateways to hard drugs.

The actual experience of users does not mesh with the official line. Of the seventy million Americans who smoked pot in 1994, 98 percent did not wind up on anything harder than martinis. Only a tiny fraction went on to become heroin or cocaine addicts, and the cause-effect connection for this group was less evident than the connection to coffee.[41]

The same gateway argument leads to indiscriminate conclusions. "Beer and cigarettes seem to be gateways to marijuana," said the British journal *The Economist* in illustrating the fallacies of this gateway research.[42] The gateway argument takes on a different hue in light of older but representative University of Michigan "Monitoring the Future" surveys in 1978 and again in 1993 and 1994, where more than 70 percent of all high school seniors admitted to an alcoholic drink in the prior month, double the number using weed. Of this group, 40 percent said that over the prior two weeks, they had engaged in binge drinking, consuming five or more drinks in one sitting, a number four times higher than those who had smoked pot daily. Young beer drinkers were far more likely than pot users to get into fights, smash cars, or have sex.

As these statistics suggest about the "precursor" rationale, alcohol, not marijuana, appears as the true gateway. Yet the government has not chosen to ban soft drinks because they precede alcohol or to prohibit alcohol merely because alcohol regularly precedes or even correlates with violent crime.[43] Nor does the government attach severe prison sentences to teenagers' greater use of alcohol, nor has it adopted Bill Bennett's preferred strategy of imposing zoning restrictions around liquor establishments.[44] In 1972, Nixon's Commission on Marijuana and Drug Abuse debunked the gateway theory, finding that only a small portion of pot users became persistent users of other drugs. "The majority [of users] appear to experiment only," wrote the commission.[45]

Even if the overheated argument about the pot-cocaine connection were true, its logic is wanting. Not everything that precedes another is the cause of the latter—this is a classic *post hoc, ergo propter hoc* fallacy. If every antecedent were the cause of a subsequent event, the gateway argument would logically lead to the criminalization of all predrug food. After all, probably well over 90 percent of hard drug users at some time in their early years ate peanut butter and jelly sandwiches with gusto.

Marijuana researcher Mitch Earleywine sums up the scientific status of the gateway theory as of 2003:

> There is no evidence that cannabis creates physiological changes that increase the desire for drugs. The idea that marijuana causes subsequent drug use appears unfounded. . . . Only a minority of marijuana smokers try cocaine, crack, or heroin.[46]

THE ECONOMICS OF GROWING PAINS

Pot enforcement and its economics meet under the law of unintended consequences. Long prison sentences given to marijuana offenders have turned marijuana into a precious commodity whose increased pricing reacts to increased law enforcement efforts. Two decades ago, policy analysts Peter Reuter and Mark Kleiman observed that the price of an illegal drug reflects not only its supply, demand, and production costs but also the risks of selling it. As the risks of strict enforcement increase, so do profit and value.[47]

Marijuana prices rose after the war on drugs began. In 1982, the street price for an ounce, adjusted for inflation, was about $75. By 1998, it had reached about $325; in some places like New York, high-grade marijuana reached over $600 an ounce by 2000.[48] Although cultivating costs rose during that same period, most of the price increases represented sheer profit, the reward for evading law enforcement. Anticultivation crusades encourage more potent strains that in turn bring a higher price and lower sales.

Mexican reefer imports sell in the $100 to $200 range, often under street names like "Chronic" or "Chocolate," usually smoked not in rolling papers but in hallowed-out cigars known as "blunts." In California, better grades such as "Maude's Mighty Moss" ("large and luscious") go for about $18 a gram. Cheaper varieties such as "Adobe" ("fresh and tasty") go for as low as $4 a gram.

Large profit margins have transformed marijuana cultivation from a hippie fringe into a multibillion-dollar industry. Unlike heroin and cocaine that require importation, almost half our nation's marijuana now grows within our own borders, mostly in the vast area between the Appalachians and the Great Plains and in a second, smaller area in Northern California known as the Emerald Triangle. For the value of this annual crop, plausible estimates start at $4 billion and extend to $24 billion. In 1993, the value of our largest legal cash crop, corn, was roughly $16 billion.

The highest-quality weed grows indoors in the Emerald Triangle north of San Francisco. No other area, however, surpasses the Midwest for high volume. There neighborhood greenhouses flourish in pastoral farmlands. With names like "Hydro" and "Bubble Gum," high grade Midwest strains like "hydroponic," grown without soil, and "wet," soaked in formaldehyde, possess increased potency, bringing as much as $6,000 a pound, more than ten times the typical price for average quality marijuana from Mexico.[49]

Harvesting and profits interact with enforcement policy. During the Second World War, our government encouraged farmers to plant thousands of acres of marijuana to replace fiber supplies interdicted by the Japanese. The "Hemp for Victory" program left marijuana growing wild in the countryside as "ditchweed," where it spread over thousands of Midwestern acres. Growing conditions ideal for corn also nurture marijuana. In 1999 dollars, a bushel of corn sold roughly for $2.50; a bushel of manicured marijuana sold for about $70,000. By 1997, marijuana had become the largest cash crop in the United States. In Indiana, its value rivaled that of corn; in Alabama, it rivaled cotton; in California, it has surpassed wine. The threat of long prison sentences has enriched some marijuana growers but hardly affected the burgeoning cultivation.

ERADICATION

During the Reagan administration, because of this widespread pot cultivation in California, various law enforcement groups there tried to exterminate pot plants, end cultivation, and prosecute growers. The effort remains instructive for the rest of the nation.

In 1983, under pressure from drug czar Carleton Turner, then State Attorney General John Van de Kamp, with one eye on the governor's office, vowed that the aggressive military-assisted "Campaign Against Marijuana Planting," or "CAMP" for short, would run reefer growers out of the state. Military helicopters began to swoop low on hillsides in the Emerald Triangle in Northern California, particularly at harvest time. In the Emerald Triangle and the Silicon Valley, locations of high potency cultivation, few growers were arrested. Only a tiny fraction wound up in prison. Sheriff David Renner of Humbolt County, who began as a dedicated advocate of CAMP, arranged for low-flying helicopters to conduct these annual autumn raids. After more than a decade, Humbolt county voters had enough and threw Renner out of office in 1994. Van de Kamp himself soon disappeared from the radar screen of governor contenders.

Though he had led the attack on marijuana, Renner, after removal from office, raised a white flag. "I say go ahead and legalize it," he confessed in 2000. To him, as to retiring President Clinton, pot had become a black hole for law enforcement because of mixed official messages. One message is that marijuana appears to be a dangerous drug that must be harshly suppressed. Another competing message is that pot is a minor matter best ignored. The emerging hempster movement promotes still another message of pot as a useful economic product. California's politicized CAMP efforts reflect the growing militarization of American law enforcement agencies regarding marijuana. Some 90 percent of police departments in cities with populations over 50,000 and 70 percent of those in smaller cities now boast paramilitary units for drug forays. These "special weapons and tactics," or SWAT, teams often possess tanks and grenade launchers and semi-automatic weapons. Initially created to confront hostage crises, SWAT teams increasingly undertake drug raids and pot assaults, including plant uprootings and burnings, adding an aggressive military dimension to the enforcement checkerboard.

CULTIVATION PRACTICES

California tops the list of fertile states for growing marijuana. Hawaii and Kentucky vie for second and third places, each bringing in about half California's 900,000 annual average of discovered cannabis plants. Seemingly, as a result of law enforcement efforts, pot cultivation increasingly appears dominated by large, sophisticated, and clandestine operations producing a plant much more potent than existed in the 1960s and 1970s. The payback for greater potency can be significant. As of 2001, cured marijuana sold for an average of $4,000 a pound, nearly the price of gold. In 1998, the National Organization for the Reform of Marijuana Laws (NORML) analyzed the market value of the California crop and concluded that it exceeded $3.8 million.[50]

Marijuana cultivation in the national parks and forests, especially those in California and the northwest, has increased steadily since the mid-1990s. Since 2001, the number of plants seized in California's national parks has increased by up to eight times. Many of the pot fields are financed by Mexican drug cartels whose planting areas hide in the steep Sierra Nevada foothills in parks like Sequoia or in isolated fields many miles from ranger headquarters. For the first half of 2004, California's Bureau of Narcotics estimated that 84% of the marijuana plants seized on public lands were controlled by Mexican gangs, who find it safer and more profitable to grow their crops in this country rather than trying to smuggle them across the border.

SUCCESS?

Has enforcement worked to reduce the use and growing of marijuana? In 1980, the federal government and the states spent about $4 billion on drug control. As of 2000, that figure reached at least $32 billion. In the two prior decades, the number of people in prison on drug charges multiplied by about eight times, from 50,000 to over 400,000. Pot farms in the Emerald Triangle northeast of San Francisco morphed into large cartel operations growing from 2,000 to 10,000 plants and bringing in some returns averaging over $4,000 a pound. About 74 percent of this area's pot confiscated in 2002 came from aggressive Mexican cartels who find it safer to grow plants here rather than in Mexico. As of 2003, more than half their crops grow on the nation's public land, especially western national forests, particularly those near the Emerald Triangle.

Canada, whose pot policies are far more liberal than those of the United States, presents the different picture of importation rather than internal cultivation. An estimated $2.5 billion yearly in "BC Bud" and "Quebec Gold"—nicknames for powerful Canadian hydroponic hybrids—reaches

American pot smokers by being smuggled across the Canadian border into Washington and Montana. Some 95 percent of the marijuana grown in British Columbia crosses the Washington border into the United States each year. Most of these imports arrive at lightly guarded border crossings or in areas lacking border guards. Outlaw biker gangs also bring some into this country.[51]

California has witnessed a series of bumper crops despite the CAMP campaign. Pot has become even more available than when CAMP first started, suggesting that aggressive enforcement promotes aggressive growing. As to rates of use, the Alaska experience suggests no correlation at all between legalization and degree of use. That state decriminalized marijuana in 1975. As of 1992, daily use of pot in that state by high schoolers was one-third lower than high school usage in the rest of the country—6.3 percent to 4 percent.[52] Alaska data suggest what has happened, or not happened, elsewhere. Ten other states removed criminal penalties for simple possession of pot by 1979—California, Colorado, Maine, Minnesota, Mississippi, Nebraska, New York, North Carolina, Ohio, and Oregon. In these states, decriminalization led to no discernible change in marijuana use either by adults or by high school students.[53]

CONCLUSION

As of 2004, marijuana enforcement efforts in this country resemble an unpredictable and haphazard checkerboard of activity and inactivity. Being busted for reefer possession or use remains as capricious as being struck by lightning—and potentially as injurious.

4

HEALTH EFFECTS

Growing pot for medical use can generate legal and geographic troubles. As this is being written, American prosecutors in California and Canada want to send Emily Boje back to the United States to face charges of conspiring to grow and sell marijuana. Boje's case dates from 1997 in Los Angeles, where she met Todd McCormick, a cancer patient and activist for the use of marijuana to treat cancer and AIDS. McCormick hired her to illustrate a book on growing marijuana for medical use. She started hanging out at his mansion in tony Bel-Air, which police raided on July 29, 1997.

There police found 4,116 high-grade marijuana plants that McCormick claimed to be using to treat his cancer. Boje was among nine people arrested that night. According to police affidavits, the strongest evidence against her was that she was seen watering some of these plants. The punishment she faced was draconian: a mandatory minimum of ten years in prison without parole for watering pot plants for a friend who was using them to fight cancer. Deciding to duck the bullet, she fled to British Columbia in 1998.

HARMFUL?

Is marijuana really harmful? Some think so. The nation's most vocal drug czar, General Barry McCaffrey, regularly insisted that marijuana is both harmful in itself and acts as a gateway to harder drugs. George W. Bush's drug czar, John Walters, has echoed similar convictions. In a vein typical of this medical-based antipot argument, the conservative *Arizona Republic* editorialized in 1997 that pot needs strict criminalization because of its "craving effects." Its argument is a medical prototype for what some crusaders describe as marijuana's unhealthy side effects:

> One study on rats suggests that people who regularly smoke large amounts of pot are changing the chemistry in their brains in exactly the same way as those who regularly abuse cocaine, heroin, amphetamines, nicotine and alcohol.
> By measuring the effect of the sudden withdrawal of marijuana on rats, scientists were able to measure a neurochemical reaction identical to what occurs when a heroin addict goes cold turkey.
> The difference is that the active ingredient in marijuana, THC, lingers in the bloodstream long after the high is over. That lingering effect masks some of the more extreme sensations associated with withdrawal. Addicts don't realize they are addicted. This research suggests that regular smokers of pot continue smoking not so much to get high as to ease the anxiety of withdrawal caused by the drug itself.[1]

At bottom, this argument leads to criminalizing all food and drink because people eat and drink in order to "ease the anxiety" caused by pangs of hunger and thirst.

REEFER CRITICS

Perhaps the leading scientific light of the marijuana prohibition movement has been Dr. Gabriel Nahas, retired from his academic position at Columbia University's College of Physicians and Surgeons. A sworn enemy of cannabis, Nahas over the last quarter century has sought a scientific rationale for continuing the prohibition on pot, notably in his books *Marijuana: Deceptive Weed* and *Keep Off the Grass* that in part argue for the gateway theory by confusing temporal correlation with causality.[2]

Probably no drug-abuse scholar in the past half century since Anslinger has been the subject of such scathing criticism in scientific journals.[3] The *New England Journal of Medicine* called his research "psychopharmacologic McCarthyism" peppered with "half-truths, innuendo and unverifiable assertions." The *Journal of the American Medical Association* found his research littered with "examples of biased selection and [that] omissions of facts abound in every chapter."[4] *Contemporary Drug Problems* called his research "meretricious trash."[5] Nahas's papers, which often heavily quote himself, offer repeated references that have been found misleading or distorted.[6] Nonetheless, his work remains a primary source of pseudoscientific justification for research-hungry warriors, especially gateway theorists, seeking medical justification for the pot prohibition.

Nahas's rationale for pot prohibition is not really medical or scientific. Like that of President Nixon, his opposition is primarily cultural, resting solidly on psychosocial bases, especially the symbolic meaning of marijuana in a drug-induced society:

> Drug taking is symptomatic of the dissatisfaction and the craving for fulfillment of disillusioned youth seeking new values. Such fulfillment cannot be found in any lasting way through any type of intoxication. . . . If the American dream has lost its attraction, it will not be retrieved through the use of stupefying drugs. Their use only delays the youth in their quest to understand the world they now live in and their desire to foster a better world for tomorrow.[7]

Dr. Nahas's point, then, is really more cultural than medical: pot is bad because of what it does to the American dream.

Another classic bias in scientific research on pot appears in a 1975 study of monkeys by Robert Heath of Tulane University, which supposedly proves that marijuana smoke causes human brain damage. The bias involves grossly different and involuntary use of unrealistic quantities of marijuana. Because rhesus monkeys do not normally smoke, Dr. Heath liberally forced reefer smoke on them through a gas mask locked to their faces. When Heath's monkeys involuntarily puffed up to ninety joints a day, he concluded that the apes' brain damage resulted simply from these large amounts. A subsequent study of rhesus monkeys at the National Center for Toxicological Research repudiated Heath's findings.[8]

No agency has disseminated as much falsehood about marijuana as the $195 million government-sponsored Partnership for a Drug Free America. Its TV commercials, beginning in 1998, have included one showing two young men in their twenties smoking marijuana, one watching TV as the other downplayed its warnings about pot. The skeptic says he has been smoking for many years and "nothing has ever happened," at which point his mother's voice asks him if he has looked for a job today. The announcer's voice concludes: "Marijuana can make nothing happen to you too." Another ad features a bleary-eyed teen, seemingly stoned, who says that before using pot he was a straight-A student, liked by neighbors and friends but then, when he began using pot, he found himself "getting thrown out of my house . . . a total loser."

Another Partnership ad portrays potheads suffering from pot-induced IQ deficiencies. One of these shows a comparison between smoking pot and being repeatedly hit over the head by a professional boxer. Another, in the same vein, makes the IQ argument directly. A cartoon shows a flowerpot repeatedly hitting a user's head as the voice-over predicts that such pot banging may not kill the user but "if you keep smoking it, you might just get dumber and dumber and dumber and dumber and dumber."

All these ads about the listless, drowsy pothead reflect the long-standing—and totally discredited—theory that marijuana provokes not Anslinger's mania and hysteria but instead its very opposite: amotivational syndrome, a condition of wakeful sleep.

HARM FROM POT USE

Dispassionate medical data about pot offer the most helpful starting point for assessing pot's true health effects. Viewed only as a health issue, marijuana creates a physical dependence in some but not for all users. THC diffuses widely throughout the body and remains within cells and vital organs just the same as legal drugs, such as valium, thorazine, and quinine. However, studies of lifelong heavy marijuana users in Jamaica, Greece, and Costa Rica reveal little psychological or physiological damage. Short-term memory deficiencies in heavy smokers, though reversible, may endure long after smoking marijuana stops. Laboratory animals injected with marijuana do suffer mild immunosuppression, but no study has conclusively linked THC to lasting immune-system changes. Horror stories from the 1970s, like those of Keith Schuchard's *Parents, Peers and Pot* book—that marijuana kills brain cells, damages chromosomes, and prompts males to grow breasts—endure as imaginative fictions without medical support.

Smoking marijuana can indeed damage the pulmonary system in a way similar to inhaling tobacco smoke. UCLA physician Donald P. Tashkin found that marijuana smoke can cause chronic bronchitis, changes in cells of the central airway, and cellular impairment. A joint of pot delivers somewhat more carcinogenic tar than a tobacco cigarette of the same size. Some heavy marijuana users may eventually suffer cancers of the mouth, throat, and lungs as do some tobacco and alcohol users. At times smoking pot causes respiratory irritation akin to smoker's cough as well as lung illness.[9] Doctors have also found precancerous changes in the lungs of potheads. Massive pot use does suppress sperm counts, but users have the same infertility rate as nonusers.

Contrary to the claims of Keith Schuchard and others, no lasting damage to the brain results even from decades of daily use. If marijuana ever caused a single death, it did not leave any fingerprints. The most comprehensive research—a study of sixty-five thousand users in the Bay area over ten years—found "no association between marijuana and overall mortality."[10]

Admittedly, Dr. Tashkin's pulmonary findings ought to trouble chronic marijuana smokers. For more than a decade, he compared the lungs of pot smokers, cigarette smokers, and nonsmokers, looking for damage leading to lung cancer. Pot smokers who inhaled three or four joints a day suffered from chronic bronchitis as often as cigarette smokers who lit up a pack or more a day. Pot and cigarette smokers showed similar damage to the trachea and bronchial tubes, as cells that sweep soot from the lungs die off to be replaced by proliferating mucus cells. The greatest damage appeared in the lungs of people smoking both marijuana and tobacco because their common effects intensified each other.[11]

While long-term marijuana use does not produce memory, attention, and thought debilitation typical of chronic alcohol use, it can nonetheless impair short-term mental functioning, including memory and perception, to a transitory degree. A minority of users may suffer impairments to the lungs, throat, or mind roughly comparable to what long-term cigarette smokers experience. But lung problems from pot are less serious than those related to tobacco because, unlike alcohol and tobacco, THC is not toxic at high levels and also because it delivers its high almost immediately, thus eliminating the need for repeated doses. By comparison with tobacco, less pot is needed to generate the desired effect.

A 1991 Department of Health and Human Services report to Congress found that medical problems with reefer were "infrequent" and "tolerance and dependence are not major issues at present." No one knows what serious marijuana treatment would look like. MacCoun and Reuter write that "severity of addiction is modest enough that there is scarcely any research on treatment of marijuana dependency."[12]

A major breakthrough in understanding marijuana's negative medical effects came in 1988 when Allyn Howlett of St. Louis University discovered the chemical receptors that react to THC, the ingredient causing a high. The receptors differentiate pot from other substances including heavily addictive drugs such as heroin and morphine. Marijuana is "completely different from all other drugs," according to Miles Herkenham, a brain researcher at the National Institute of Health in Bethesda, Maryland, who helped map the receptors in the early 1990s. Pot's influence on the immune system seems relatively subtle. "The paucity of receptors in the brain stem is crucial for explaining why it's a safe drug," says Herkenham. "It's impossible to take a lethal overdose."[13] Smoked marijuana has yet to be linked with any death.[14]

POT'S HEALTH BENEFITS

Drug sociologist Lynn Zimmer and narcotics researcher John P. Morgan have found significant health benefits from pot. For glaucoma, marijuana reduces the fluid pressure in the eyes that causes irreversible damage to vision. For AIDS patients, marijuana addresses their immunosuppression and the danger posed by lung irritants and fungal illnesses such as aspergillosis. Many AIDS patients with treatment-induced nausea, appetite loss, and wasting syndrome claim that marijuana saved their lives by motivating them to eat.[15]

Almost half the oncologists in a 1990 study recommended pot to their patients.[16] By then, pot's core ingredient was already legal: Dronabinol, marketed as Marinol, a synthetic THC compound using the active ingredient in pot, continues as a legal drug in pill form prescribed for nausea, depression, and spasticity. The federal taboo on pot thus acquires an Orwellian irony: prohibition of the same substance the government has previously approved under a different name.

Marinol, a 1985 creation by Unimed Pharmaceutical and selling for about $15 per 10-mg pill, acts as a poor substitute for marijuana because doses cannot be titrated as precisely. Marinol can cost upward of $500 per dosage or between $600 and $1,000 per month, considerably more than even high-quality marijuana. Opponents of medical marijuana claim that all medicines need approval by the FDA, but drug companies have little incentive to overcome the regulatory and financial obstacles for a plant that cannot be patented.

As of 2001, the capsule form of Marinol was more cumbersome than smoked marijuana in delivering pain relief. Here are the major differences between the two:

- The onset of relief from the capsule takes an hour or more: smoking takes effect within minutes.
- The one-hour lag time means that oral dosage by capsules is difficult to adjust and monitor; a patient can cease or continue smoking in response to minute-to-minute results.
- Oral THC is metabolized through the liver, neutralizing more than 90 percent of the chemical; smoking pot delivers the THC directly to the bloodstream.
- An oral dose lasts six unpredictable hours, with variable effects; in the same patient, smoking pot lasts a more manageable and predicable hour or two.
- Some patients whose livers metabolize the synthetic delta-9 THC into a more psychoactive 11-hydroxy-THC get more stoned on a metabolite.
- According to 2003 figures, a moderate Marinol regimen can cost about $1,000 a month while the cost of smoking quality marijuana for a month is much less and would be negligible if medical cultivation became legal.
- Compared with most painkillers and sedatives based on opiates, medical marijuana reduces pain without causing physical addiction, nor does it carry the risk to patients of developing tolerance to the extent of requiring increasing doses.

Many approved non-THC alternatives to pot present serious side effects. The antimetics Compazine and Decadron pose a great risk of liver damage. Marijuana is safer than many over-the-counter drugs. Asked to evaluate the medical benefits of marijuana, the DEA's own administrative judge Francis L. Young declared in a ninety-page decision in 1988— impoliticly, from the DEA's point of view—that marijuana was "one of the safest therapeutically active substances known to man."[17]

The DEA's politicians concluded otherwise. In 1992, brushing aside the ruling while ridiculing medical marijuana as a dangerous and "cruel hoax," DEA officials slammed the door on Judge Young's findings by reversing his decision on unstated political grounds.[18] Thus arose a continuing anomaly: the more costly, more cumbersome, less effective drug Marinol remained legal while the more efficient, less costly same drug under the suspect name of marijuana remained criminal.

PAIN-KILLING ABILITIES

Ironically, this excoriated drug also has pain-killing powers. Animal studies by research groups at the University of California–San Francisco, the University of Michigan, and Brown University have shown that a group of potent cannabinoids, including the active ingredient in marijuana, relieves several kinds of pain, including the inflammation of arthritis as well as severe forms of chronic pain.[19] In 1997, a panel of experts convened by the National Institute of Health's Society for Neuroscience reported at its annual meeting that the active chemicals in marijuana cause a direct beneficial effect on pain signals in the central nervous system. Unlike opiate-based painkillers, pot's painkillers are not addictive; continued use does not develop tolerance.[20]

Although the government continues to claim that the vast majority of American physicians remain opposed to the medical use of marijuana,[21] a 1990 survey of oncologists by researchers at the Kennedy School of Government at Harvard revealed that nearly half of those who responded said that they would prescribe pot to cancer patients if it were legal to do so.[22]

Despite some medical folklore about the negative therapeutic effects of smoked marijuana, studies indicate that the active chemicals in marijuana directly mitigate pain signals[23] and that marijuana, unlike prescribable opiate-based drugs, carries no risk of patients developing a tolerance requiring increasing doses.[24] For the government to prosecute physicians for recommending medical marijuana denies viable medical treatment, perhaps the best existing treatment, for patients suffering from debilitating illnesses. Indeed, such prosecutions contradict the government's original rationale for setting up its Compassionate User Program.[25]

SAFETY COMPARISONS

Though it remains criminal, pot offers a vastly superior safety record in comparison to legal drugs. Although the misuse of over-the-counter medications such as aspirin, acetaminophen, ephedra, and antihistamines each year kills thousands of Americans, pot is one of the few drugs that has yet to cause a fatality. Nor is there any known fatal dosage. It is that rare drug without risk of overdose—except to force-fed monkeys.[26]

Harvard's Lester Grinspoon has shown that marijuana can relieve nausea associated with chemotherapy, prevent blindness induced by glaucoma, serve as an appetite stimulant for AIDS patients, act an antiepileptic, ward off asthma attacks and migraine headaches, alleviate chronic pain, and reduce the muscle spasticity that accompanies multiple sclerosis, cerebral palsy, and paraplegia.[27] As of 2002, the federal government remains deaf and blind to Grinspoon's research as well as to the statistical differences in mortality between pot and legal drugs. For the past quarter century, and particularly in the Reagan, Bush Sr., and Clinton administrations, drug policy wonks focused more on seeking marijuana's professed but illusive ill effects than in trying to lessen the country's dependence on far more detrimental drugs such as alcohol and tobacco.

Pot's medical benefits have eminent references. The well-known Harvard geologist Stephen Jay Gould developed abdominal cancer in the 1980s, suffering such intense nausea from intravenous chemotherapy that he came to dread chemotherapy with an "almost perverse intensity." The treatment, he remembered, acted "worse than the disease itself." Initially reluctant to smoke marijuana, Gould eventually found it "the greatest boost I received in all my years of treatment." "It is beyond my comprehension," he concluded, "and I fancy myself able to comprehend a lot, including such nonsense that any humane person would withhold such a beneficial substance from people in such great need simply because others use it for different purposes."[28]

RECENT POT RESEARCH

The 1990s saw increased medical studies on the effects of medical marijuana. A 1997 study performed on experimental animals at the University of California found that THC effectively relieved pain without the adverse side effects associated with opiates.[29] In 1995, the British medical journal *Lancet* reported research showing that pot is safer than alcohol or tobacco; it editorialized that smoking pot, "even long term, is not harmful to health," and added that more recent research showed it to "reduce the pain and muscle stiffness of multiple sclerosis."[30] In 1999, the *American Journal of Psychiatry* reported German research showing that THC in pot successfully treated Tourette's syndrome. The National Academy of Sciences reported in its 1998 *Proceedings* that marijuana protects brain cells during a stroke.[31] In early 2000, researchers in England reported pot effective in controlling the muscle spasms of multiple sclerosis.[32]

Given these medical benefits, some doctors have become willing to recommend marijuana for a variety of ailments. In response to a DEA inference that only fringe doctors would recommend marijuana as an antiemetic agent, a random sample of members of the American Society of Clinical Oncology interviewed by Harvard scientists in 1990 revealed that of the more than 1,000 oncologists responding, about 44 percent admitted that they had already recommended marijuana to at least one patient. Further, those responding indicated that they believed pot to be more effective than oral dronabinol.[33]

MEMORY BENEFITS

Not the least of marijuana's benefits is a modern version of the Lotus Eaters' visit to Lethe in Homer's *Odyssey*: selective forgetfulness. Allyn Howlett, the St. Louis University medical researcher who discovered a specific receptor for THC in the brain, has shown that cannabis models the work of natural neurotransmitters such as serotonin, dopamine, and the endorphins. Like these other transmitters, pot's THC contributes to anxiety relief by softening painful memories. "It's a palliative that enables us to get up and back to work on Monday mornings," writes drug researcher Michael Pollan.[34]

Almost identical results have come from German research in 2002 at the Max Planck Institute of Psychiatry in Munich. There neurological researchers found that pot's cannabinoids can wipe out bad memories by dampening nerve cell action contributing to the anxiety stemming from remembered bad experiences. Cannabinoids bind to the brain's chemical receptors to create a feeling of euphoria as they mask painful memories, a result comparable to that achieved by Xanax, Wellbutrin, Prozac, Valium, and a host of similar legally permitted drugs.[35]

POT, TOBACCO, AND ALCOHOL

A 1991 U.S. Department of Health and Human Services report to Congress stated: "Given the large population of marijuana users and the infrequent reports of medical problems from stopping use, tolerance and dependence are not major issues at present." Indeed, no one can be very certain what "marijuana treatment" would look like.[36] Long-term heavy marijuana use does not produce the severe or grossly debilitating impairment of memory, attention, and cognitive function found with chronic heavy alcohol use," says the British medical journal *Lancet*.[37] Only a small minority of users eventually smoke enough of it for a long period to suffer impairments matching those of prolonged tobacco use. Jailing such users clashes with the government's approach to the more harmful effects of tobacco and alcohol, whose abuses do not generate alerts, arrests, forfeitures, or convictions.

In 2001, two of the weed's strongest political critics, Republicans Mitch McConnell of Kentucky and Bob Barr of Georgia, tried without success to ban all medical use of marijuana and to increase penalties for its use. "All civilized countries in the world," according to Barr, "are under assault by drug proponents seeking to enslave citizens."[38] Both lawmakers come from tobacco-producing states. Despite the fact that over 400,000 citizens of this country die each year from tobacco, these two anti-addiction crusaders focused their legislative energies on demonizing marijuana, a drug that, unlike their homegrown tobacco, has never caused a single death.

In its March 19, 2002, issue, the British medical journal *New Scientist* reported that a single glass of wine impairs driving more than smoking one marijuana joint. The report refutes a common misconception that weed smoking poses as great a threat to safe driving as does alcohol. Conducted by the Transport Research Laboratory in Crowthorne, Berkshire, the study showed that marijuana affected just one test category, the ability of drivers to follow the middle of the road while driving a figure eight loop. Drivers who drank the equivalent of a glass of wine fared much worse on the task than did those who had smoked an entire joint.[39] A similar California study of over 300 drivers in fatal accidents in that state focused on drivers who tested positive for pot but no other drug. Surprisingly, they were found to be half as likely to be responsible for accidents as those free of all substances.[40]

NATIONAL INSTITUTE OF MEDICINE REPORT

The most exacting—and politically unwelcome—research findings on pot's medical effects appeared in a nonpartisan March 1999 report from our government's Institute of Medicine. Entitled *Marijuana and Medicine: Assessing the Science Base*, the 250-page report, commissioned by none other than drug czar General McCaffrey, found that smoking marijuana effectively treated nausea and severe weight loss associated with AIDS and cancer treatment.[41] To improve its medical effects, the Institute urged development of new delivery mechanisms, such as bronchial inhalers used by asthma patients. The report recommended that pot be provided, under close supervision for a limited time, to patients not responding to other medical therapies.

The institute's conclusion causing the biggest stir, however, impacted policy more than medicine. The eleven medical researchers found no evidence that ill persons' marijuana use increased illicit drug use in other populations. Contrary to Ms. Schuchard, Bill Bennett, John Walters, and other imaginative medicine men and women, these independent medical researchers found marijuana does not act as a gateway to more dangerous narcotics like cocaine and heroin. The institute's $896,000 study concluded that the future of pot's medicinal use lay not in lighting up joints, since smoking pot can lead to lung damage and low-birth-weight babies, but in the development of safer delivery systems, like a vaporizer or patch to more effectively deliver pot's active ingredients to sick users.[42]

The Institute of Medicine report suggested interim solutions for some sick and dying patients unable to benefit from approved painkillers and antinausea drugs. "There are limited circumstances in which we see recommending smoked marijuana for medical uses," wrote Dr. John Benson Jr., former dean of Oregon Health Sciences University, one of the two principal medical investigators. According to the report, thousands of patients with nausea and vomiting from chemotherapy could benefit from marijuana in carefully controlled trials.[43]

Not surprisingly, the Institute's report touched a sensitive nerve within the Clinton administration, especially with its suggestion that the federal government commit to doing medical marijuana research to deliver pot's benefits for certain classes of sick patients. In the meantime, the researchers recommended, the government ought to reopen the "compassionate user" medical marijuana program suspended by the Bush administration in 1992 (because of "the wrong message") to provide legal access to medical marijuana to seriously ill persons.

In a muted response to this government research, McCaffrey quoted only the report's conclusion that the future of cannabinoid drugs "lies not in smoked marijuana, but in chemically defined drugs that act on . . . human physiology." He then called for still more pot research, thus continuing the government's longstanding search for some ill effect to justify pot's prior prohibition, a task made more difficult by this latest government report denying, again, the very ills drug warriors sought.[44]

In May 1999, shortly after the Institute of Medicine report, and in response to it, the Department of Health and Human Services released new guidelines on "Procedures for the Provision of Marijuana for Medical Research," to allow the National Institute on Drug Abuse to sell government pot plants from its Mississippi pot farm to privately funded scientists for "scientifically valid investigations" preapproved by NIDA. The new guidelines contained numerous impediments to medical marijuana research and continued to deny lawful access to medical marijuana by seriously ill patients. The guidelines explicitly rejected the Institute's recommendation that the government expand its compassionate user program.[45]

In December 2001, the Drug Enforcement Administration announced limited research, to begin in 2002, on the medical uses of marijuana for neuropathy and muscle rigidity. The new research did not make it legal for doctors to provide pot as medicine to their patients but allowed pot for limited use only in scientific experiments. Approval for this research ended a two-decade-long federal de facto prohibition on medical research on marijuana. One of the principal researchers, Dr. Donald Abrams of the University of California, noted that the important factors in getting the new research approved were successful medical marijuana referenda in Arizona and California in 1996.[46]

RAND INSTITUTE STUDY

In December 2002, the Rand Drug Policy Research Center in California published a lengthy study casting further doubt on claims that marijuana acts as a medical gateway to harder drugs.[47] According to Rand, an alternative, simpler, and more compelling explanation accounts for the pattern of transitioning to hard-drug use. Associations between marijuana and hard drugs result from known differences in the ages at which youth have opportunities to use marijuana and hard drugs and known variations in their willingness to try any drugs. Rand researchers tested the gateway theory by creating a mathematical model simulating drug use. The model's rates of pot use and hard-drug use matched youthful drug-use data.

Without use of a gateway effect, the model produced patterns of drug use remarkably similar to the real-world data, showing the marijuana gateway theory to be an unnecessary construct for explaining hard-drug use. Rand's chief researcher Andrew Morral concluded that the study "suggests that policies aimed at reducing or eliminating marijuana availability are unlikely to make any dent in the hard drug problem." He added that "Enforcement resources used against heroin and cocaine if used against marijuana could have the unintended effect of worsening heroin and cocaine use," as seems to have occurred toward the end of the Reagan presidency.

The National Institute of Medicine and Rand studies helped to convert some former drug warriors. President Reagan's former drug czar Charles Schuster responded to the Rand study by saying he could "only hope that this report will be read with objectivity and evaluated on its scientific merits, not reflexively rejected because it violates most policy makers' belief."[48]

CONCLUSION

While marijuana is not harmless, its harms pale compared to over-the-counter drugs and euphoriants like alcohol and tobacco, and common pacifiers like Valium and Xanax. In the view of the British medical journal *Lancet*, an objective person can reliably judge pot "less of a threat than alcohol or tobacco." Merely on the medical evidence alone, according to *Lancet*, "moderate indulgence in cannabis presents little ill-effect on health."[49] Drug czar McCaffrey's sponsored Institute of Medicine report in March 1999 reached similar conclusions about the medical benefits of marijuana and the absence of any evidence that it "primes" its users to move on to harder drugs.

University researcher Mitch Earleywine, the author of America's definitive compendium of pot medical research, has reached parallel conclusions in reviewing all the current medical data. Medical research, he finds, shows that marijuana's medical harms approximate those of tobacco when it is used with equal frequency, which it rarely is because its effects are more immediate and less toxic.[50] Pot's medical benefits extend to nausea, appetite stimulation, convulsion control, relief from glaucoma pressure and pain, and memory softening. It is neither as toxic nor as fatal as our legal drugs alcohol and tobacco, nor is it a gateway to harder drugs.[51]

5

SEEDS OF THE MEDICAL MARIJUANA MOVEMENT

Undoubtedly, one of several major motivators for the medical marijuana movement has been our government's own encouragement of medical marijuana through its Compassionate Investigational New Drug Program. Though mentioned previously, the program—and its several ironies— deserves greater attention.

THE COMPASSIONATE INVESTIGATIONAL DRUG PROGRAM

Under this federal program, first operational in 1978, seriously ill patients for whom marijuana offered promising medical relief could petition the government for permission to use marijuana legally in order to relieve their suffering. Shortly after its inception, however, the program generated so much red tape that only about three dozen patients received marijuana through it.[1] As of 2003, the government's compassionate user program continued with eight surviving, previously approved patients receiving 300 low-potency government-issued marijuana cigarettes per month, the equivalent of 10.75 ounces, or 300 grams. The dried marijuana was shipped from the government's pot farm at the University of Mississippi to a post office in Raleigh-Durham, rolled into cigarettes, shipped back to Mississippi, and from there sent to the patients' pharmacies for pickup.

The first patient to benefit from this proclaimed "compassionate" user program was Robert Randall, who succeeded in 1978 after lengthy litigation in receiving government pot to relieve his glaucoma pressure. His regular use of marijuana through the compassionate user program helped keep the glaucoma pressure from causing total blindness. He was nonetheless arrested for possession and cultivation, leading to protracted legal battles before he became one of the few long-term authorized users of government-provided marijuana. Twelve other patients received conditional acceptance into the program shortly after his initial approval.

By 1990, the FDA's compassionate user program overflowed with applications, particularly from AIDS patients seeking marijuana to relieve their nausea. In 1992, twenty-eight very sick patients headed the program's waiting list. The increase in patients posed a dilemma for the first Bush administration. Later that year, opting for political security over compassion, Bush closed the program because, in his words, it was sending "a wrong signal" by contradicting the administration's official position that pot lacked any health benefits whatsoever. Already suffering pot image problems of its own, the Clinton administration refused to reopen the compassionate user program to new patients despite the 1999 urging of the National Institute of Medicine. In a court brief that year, Clinton's Justice Department acknowledged that the program's use of medical marijuana "was bad public policy."[2] As of 2003, the program remained closed to new patients beyond those like Randall who had been previously approved. Nonetheless, its continuation even with a small number of approved patients suggested the government was indeed sending different, even contradictory, messages about medicinal pot.

STATE PROGRAMS

The early federal compassionate pot program of the mid-'70s sprouted some contemporary state analogues. By the early 1980s, following the federal government's lead, thirteen states approved laws permitting medical marijuana distribution by their public health departments. By 2000, none of these state programs was operating, largely due to the legal difficulty in obtaining marijuana from the federal government's pot farm in Mississippi.

New York offers one of several examples of legislated medical pot permission. In 1980, the New York legislature and Governor Hugh Carey, with little fanfare, enacted a medical marijuana law as one of the first state programs of its kind. The mechanisms to obtain and distribute the marijuana in New York, however, never materialized because of federal red tape. As similar experiences occurred in other compassionate user states, any realistic prospect of receiving government-approved pot for medical necessity diminished, primarily for political reasons rooted in the program's obvious contradiction of official government policy.

Even the truncated compassionate user program, however, continued to pose the issue of consistency for federal officials. On December 14,

1999, on the campaign trail in New Hampshire, Vice President Al Gore admitted to reporters that his sister had received medical marijuana under the Tennessee program while undergoing cancer chemotherapy in 1984. "It came in a prescription container with a label on it," he admitted, adding that "the government in the past had given some patients undergoing chemotherapy permission to use marijuana for dealing with the side effects of chemotherapy." The vice president's sister's experience thus contradicted the pronouncements of her brother's administration: if she used medical marijuana under a government-approved program, the government itself necessarily must have acknowledged that pot offered some useful medical benefits, notwithstanding subsequent statements to the contrary.

The Tennessee law was repealed in 1992. Similar laws expired or were repealed in ten other states. As of 2000, such laws remained on the books in varying ways in thirteen states: Alabama, Georgia, Illinois, Massachusetts, Minnesota, New Jersey, New Mexico, New York, Rhode Island, South Carolina, Texas, Washington, and West Virginia. The explanation for their demise lies not only in political embarrassment but also in the fact that the marijuana had to come exclusively from the federal government's pot farm in Mississippi.

Due to the difficulty of access to marijuana, only seven state public health departments ever managed to get enough to get their minimal programs up and running. All eventually gave up after dealing with numerous federal obstacles. Buried under the red tape lay a message: federal and state compassionate pot programs belied the official line on reefer by acknowledging the very opposite of government anti–medical marijuana pronouncements.

THE INITIATIVE MOVEMENT

Goaded in part by the closure of the government's self-described compassionate user program and more so by a desire to remove draconian penalties from all pot use, the marijuana reform movement of the late 1990s found its impetus in 1996 in the unlikely states of California and Arizona. One of the most surprising results of that election was the passage in California and Arizona of ballot initiatives to permit sick people to use reefer. The result countered the apparent mood of those electorates, a center-right complacency suspicious of anything visionary. The initiatives passed resoundingly by 56 to 44 percent in California and by two to one in Arizona. These two seminal initiatives deserve detailed discussion, at least because they illustrate how frustrated segments of the electorate can effect change against explicit political opposition.

CALIFORNIA

California's Proposition 215[3]—the Compassionate Use Act of 1996—
stemmed in part from the experience of semitolerated buyers' clubs providing marijuana to patients on chemotherapy or suffering from AIDS,
glaucoma, and chronic pain. One of the guiding forces in the mid-'90s
propelling California Proposition 215 was Dennis Perron, director of the
San Francisco Cannabis Buyers Club, then with over 6,000 registered
patient-members. Coauthor of the California initiative, Perron also headed
Californians for Compassionate Use, which, along with Californians for
Medical Rights, coordinated the 1996 campaign.

Support for the initiative concentrated in urban areas such as San Francisco, Los Angeles, and San Diego. Proposition 215 polled well among
groups other than Republicans and voters over the age of sixty-five. Whites
and blacks voted overwhelmingly in favor of it; Latinos and Asians barely
opposed it, 49 percent to 51 percent. The pro-215 campaign spent about
$2 million. Much of it came from out-of-state contributors, notably bil-
lionaire George Soros and Cleveland auto insurance magnate Peter Lewis,
both convinced that politicians lacked the will to correct counterproductive drug policies.

Their contribution of substantial personal assets to change government
policy introduced another major theme to the drug war potpourri: when
lawmakers for reasons of political insecurity will not change counter-
productive laws, their default leaves correction of the problem to public-
spirited private citizens who may be willing, at great personal expense,
to initiate the corrections from which elected lawmakers shrink.

Six days before the vote on the California initiative, Clinton's drug czar
General McCaffrey arrived in Los Angeles brandishing a letter signed by
three former presidents saying the California initiative would send "the
erroneous message that dangerous and addictive drugs such as heroin,
LSD, marijuana, and methamphetamines are safe." Public officials from
Washington to Sacramento vilified the proposal with dark warnings about
a hidden agenda for universal legalization.

Overlooking the experience of Vice President Gore's sister, McCaffrey
asserted that "not a shred of scientific evidence" showed smoked marijuana to be medically useful. "This is not science," he asserted, adding,
"this is not medicine, this is a cruel hoax." Asked if marijuana might be
medically useful, as it seemed to be for Gore's sister, McCaffrey's categorical answer was "No, there are hundreds of studies that indicate that it
isn't." He ridiculed such medical claims as "Cheech 'n' Chong medicine."[4]

Despite opposition from politicians and law enforcement officials, the
California initiative passed easily. It resembled laws twice passed by the

state legislature and twice vetoed by Republican Governor Pete Wilson. The initiative allowed patients to possess, grow, and consume pot on a doctor's recommendation that marijuana would help the user combat "illnesses such as cancer, chronic pain, or any other illness for which marijuana provides relief." Proposition 215 required that a patient's primary caregiver—the individual who has "consistently assumed responsibility for the housing, health, or safety" of the patient—face no criminal sanctions. Doctors recommending pot as medicine were similarly exempt from punishment. The statute encouraged federal and state governments to provide for the safe and affordable distribution of marijuana to all patients in medical need.

Opposition to California Proposition 215 came from the governor and most elected district attorneys, plus some police chiefs and sheriffs fearing loss of turf and manpower. Bill Zimmerman, head of Californians for Medical Rights, repeated his opposition to legalization of drugs and emphasized that the initiative's provisions applied only to patients under the care of certified physicians.[5]

After passage of Proposition 215, an informal network of cannabis buyer cooperatives sprang up throughout the state to provide pot for qualified patients. One such was the Los Angeles Cannabis Resource Center, providing marijuana priced on a sliding scale. A paid staff of patients ran the privately funded center. After the center opened, the FBI tried, under cover, to obtain a registry card but it was turned down because its fictitious "treating physician" did not appear as a licensed California doctor. Drug Enforcement Administration officials also made an on-site visit to the center but did not shut it down—at least not at that time.[6]

ARIZONA'S FIRST INITIATIVE

The other seminal and unlikely impetus for the marijuana medicalization movement appeared in the more conservative state of Arizona. At its 1996 general election, voters approved Proposition 200, the "Drug Medicalization, Prevention and Control Act of 1996," permitting the prescription and use of any Schedule I drug. Schedule I drugs include alpha-methylfentanyl (china white), cocaine, heroin, lysergic acid diethylamide (LSD), marijuana, mecloqualone (qualudes), mescaline, and methcathinone (cat).

Arizona's initiative offered comparisons and differences with the California initiative. Like California, Arizona required no registry of patients. Arizona's initiative reached a broader audience. Proposition. 200 recognized drug abuse as "a public health problem" and abuse as "a disease."

Its drafters maintained that drug treatment and prevention "must be expanded" particularly to help persons suffering from debilitating diseases such as glaucoma, cancer, and AIDS by reducing "the pain and suffering of the seriously ill and terminally ill."

Proposition 200 permitted any licensed Arizona physician to prescribe a Schedule I drug "to treat a disease, or to relieve the pain and suffering of a seriously ill . . . or terminally ill patient." Before prescribing a Schedule I drug, the doctor must (1) document that scientific research supports the use of the Schedule I drug, (2) obtain the written opinion of a second medical doctor, and (3) receive the written consent of the patient.

Proposition 200 reduced the criminal penalties for first-time drug offenses. A person convicted of first-time personal possession or use would receive probation, without jail or prison, with the obligation to participate in a drug treatment program. The initiative directed the Board of Executive Clemency to release or parole from the Arizona prison system those inmates who had been serving sentences for personal possession or use of drugs prior to the initiative and who were not serving a concurrent sentence, unless the Board determined the prisoner a public danger. As a condition of release, the releasee had to participate in a drug treatment or education program and pay for it if able. The proposition also created a drug treatment and education fund for the costs of placing offenders in drug treatment and education programs and established a parents' commission on drug education and prevention to encourage parental involvement in drug education.[7] Like the California initiative, the Arizona medicalization movement attracted a coterie of prominent citizens dissatisfied with the government's pot policy and politicians' timidity about modifying its harshness.

The point man behind Arizona's act was Phoenix millionaire John Sperling, the head of the Apollo Group, a consortium of for-profit educational institutions associated with the University of Phoenix. An academic economist more than a political player in the criminal justice system, Sperling, like his cohorts Soros and Lewis, felt the need to "medicalize drug use to get it out of the hands of the criminal justice community and put it into the hands of the public health and medical community."

To Sperling, his strategist Sam Vagenas and his reformers, Arizona lawmakers, for reasons of image protection, had become impotent for considering "a more enlightened approach to drugs" for fear of being seen as "soft" on drugs and crime. Sperling also maintained that drug policy followed the dictates of a "criminal justice–industrial complex" that he considered "more dangerous to American liberties than Eisenhower's military-industrial complex."[8] He accordingly created "Arizonans for

Drug Policy Reform," a high-profile board of similar-minded local citizens. The centerpiece in their public relations effort was enlisting former Senators Barry Goldwater and Dennis DeConcini to publicly back Proposition 200.

Goldwater's support for the proposition was particularly ironic. Some twenty years before, at the time of the 1972 report of President Nixon's Commission on Marijuana and Drug Abuse, he had opined that any public initiative to decriminalize pot had no chance on his state's ballot. "Pot is like gambling. People in my state," he then said, "have voted down legalized gambling at least six times, even though most people like to gamble. I think the only chance for new marijuana laws is through the legislatures."[9]

Sperling's backers employed focus groups and polling techniques to assess public attitudes toward drugs, medical marijuana, and the wording of the initiative. As with the California initiative, proponents focused on the inviolability of the doctor-patient relationship, the nausea that accompanies cancer chemotherapy and radiation treatments, and the loss of appetite in AIDS patients. Focus groups chose "medicalization" over "decriminalization" for its health and compassion connotations. The message resonated with virtually every demographic group. Personal visits helped neutralize suspected political opponents in advance. Spending ran to just under $2 million, most of it from Sperling, Soros, and Lewis, each of whom contributed roughly a half million dollars from their personal funds.

REACTIONS TO CALIFORNIA AND ARIZONA INITIATIVES

Government reactions to the successful initiatives in California and Arizona were bombastic. Reeling from the *Murphy Brown* CBS program about medical marijuana, the Clinton administration attacked Arizona's Proposition 200 as a "dangerous heresy" and threatened to prosecute any physician recommending marijuana to patients.

General McCaffrey labeled both initiatives part of "a national strategy to legalize drugs." Secretary of Health and Human Services Donna Shalala, a former marijuana user who, as chancellor of the University of Wisconsin, had told *Time* in 1990 that alcohol was a greater problem than pot, complained that the California and Arizona initiatives reinforced the belief that marijuana was harmless. The Clinton administration, she avowed, remained "opposed to the legalization of marijuana," because, in her words, "all available research has concluded that marijuana is dangerous to our health."[10] No such dangers or research were mentioned. Nor did she mention tobacco, then killing over 400,000 Americans each year.

On December 30, 1996, one month after the California and Arizona initiatives passed, Shalala threatened to punish doctors prescribing marijuana with loss of their prescription licenses, a penalty obviously impairing their ability to practice medicine.[11] "Our health care professionals need to understand that federal law has not changed," she warned, noting that "It continues to be illegal in the United States to prescribe marijuana."[12]

In a statement lamenting the new California and Arizona initiatives, General McCaffrey complained that his office's opposition to the California and Arizona propositions "had support from former Presidents Ford, Carter, and Bush." Indeed, the three had signed his joint letter condemning both propositions as a "hoax." "Most parents," he added, "do not want their kids smoking dope. The problem is, there will be a small group of doctors recommending marijuana to people." He regretted that there "could not be a worse message to young people than the provisions of these referenda. Just when the nation is trying its hardest to educate teenagers not to use psychoactive drugs, now they are being told that marijuana and other drugs are good, they are medicine." He threatened that "the hoax" perpetrated on the nation "will be exposed." "By our judgment," he added, "increased drug abuse in every category will be the inevitable result of the referenda." He asserted:

> This is not medicine. This is a Cheech and Chong show. And now what we are committed to doing is to look in a scientific way at any proposition that would bring a new medicine to the assistance of the American medical establishment.[13]

McCaffrey saw the two state initiatives as "a stalking horse for legalization." His complaints became a script for hoax mongers. California's initiative, warned Orange County Sheriff Brad Gates, unconcerned about its real content, "wouldn't just legalize marijuana for medical use—it would legalize marijuana, period, with absolutely no controls on quality, or dosage, or who can get it." To Maricopa County (Phoenix) Attorney Richard Romley, a former teenage pot user, the initiative designers used the sick and terminally ill as "pawns in their drug-legalization strategy."

California's top law enforcement official was more upset. "What we have here," declared California Attorney General Dan Lungren, a gubernatorial hopeful, "is a law flying under false colors." Having led his state's unsuccessful battle against Proposition 215, Lungren was apoplectic at misjudging the electorate. "This thing is a disaster. What's going to happen? We're going to have an unprecedented mess." The situation fell far short of his predicted "legal anarchy."[14] On November 6, 1996, he issued guidelines on how state law enforcement officers should deal with the law, simply advising the obvious: officers should verify whether the suspect was using marijuana under a doctor's recommendation. These guidelines represented a significant policy reversal. Lungren had himself previously authorized a highly publicized raid on San Francisco's Cannabis Buyers Club.[15]

A DUPED ELECTORATE?

Hostile government officials' favorite explanation for the success of the two initiatives appeared in the condescending view that simple-minded California and Arizona voters had been "duped." "It's not the only mistake that was made in November," lamented virtue czar William Bennett. "That this initiative passed is a scandal. It's also understandable given the promotion and advertising that were used." Drug prohibition interests echoed the chorus. "A moneyed, out-of-state elite mounted a cynical and deceptive campaign to push its hidden agenda to legalize drugs," moaned former Secretary of Health Joe Califano Jr.

New York Times columnist A. M. Rosenthal named names. At the top of his enemies list was financier George Soros whose "gobs of money" Rosenthal likened to "the fortunes manipulated by drug criminals." He accused Soros and his ilk of "preaching the benefits of slavery."[16]

A 1996 phone conversation between McCaffrey and Rosenthal after the California and Arizona initiatives provides insight into both journalism and government policy:

ROSENTHAL: I'm calling because I know you have been watching this thing in California and Arizona as carefully as I should have, but, ah, it's really worrisome. Did Clinton campaign against it?

McCAFFREY: Both Clinton and Dole made statements, and Clinton obviously empowered all of us to get out there and try and educate the people. And I went and got three former presidents to sign a letter. We had Justice put out a legal opinion that didn't refer to the referendums but did refer to medical use of marijuana. And then we . . .

ROSENTHAL: You mean, saying it's not legal?

McCAFFREY: Yeah, saying, look, we've been through this before, federal law and federal directives will remain unaffected by any referendum, and federal law will remain operative and dominant over any state law. So now, finally, the problem was getting the facts out in front of the people in California and Arizona, but unfortunately, at that point, we had this bizarre situation where there was a lot of money, millions of dollars, pushing a referendum from out-of-state individuals, and not many of them. I think it was essentially six people who bankrolled the whole thing . . .

ROSENTHAL: The heart and soul of what, the initiatives?

McCAFFREY: This is not paranoia on my part; this is a national legalization of drugs strategy. It's not paranoia on my part. In other words I see this not as two medical initiatives dealing with the terminally ill; I see this as part of a national effort to legalize drugs, starting with marijuana, all over the United States.

ROSENTHAL: So do I.

McCAFFREY: It was absolutely cunning. It's worth a graduate-school paper to examine how they did it. They did polling, they determined what initiatives will work with the people, the voters in those states. The one in Arizona was even more Byzantine than the one in California. California is a little bit Cheech and Chong, but the one in Arizona, if you read that initiative. . . .

ROSENTHAL: Well, we got caught off base in California . . .

McCAFFREY: I agree, Abe. I've gone a long time in life not getting killed in combat because I pay attention to details. And you do what you're supposed to do, and if you do it regularly, you don't get caught off guard. We don't want to go back to 1979 when we had 25 million Americans regularly using drugs, when we had a third of the armed forces using drugs and the NYPD using drugs and we had the faculty of universities using drugs.

ROSENTHAL: You know, I wouldn't let a pornographer in my house, I wouldn't, I really will not allow—I'm just saying this to you—George Soros in my house.

McCAFFREY: I absolutely agree. He ought to be ashamed. . . .

Rosenthal: I really have this deep-bone feeling that if somebody like the president or you or somebody said that people like Soros should be ashamed of themselves—I'm not going to put his name in because you didn't say so—but people who give large amounts of money ought to be ashamed of themselves.

McCAFFREY: Yeah, I think that.[17]

SENATE HEARINGS

After absorbing the initial shock of the two referenda, congressional drug warriors regrouped. Republican Senator Orrin Hatch, chairman of the Senate judiciary committee, immediately called for a congressional investigation. "We can't let this go without a response," he warned. Echoing the same theme, Arizona Senator Jon Kyl told the judiciary committee his view of his own constituency: "I am extraordinarily embarrassed," he said, lamenting that his own constituency—the one that elected him—had been so easily "deceived."

In December 1996, Hatch's Senate judiciary committee arranged for a hearing whose title—"A Prescription for Addiction? The Arizona and California Medical Drug Use Initiatives"—dispensed with the burden of evenhandedness. The witness list consisted of five opponents of medical use and one proponent, Marvin Cohen, a supportive lawyer from Arizona's campaign. A former CAB official in the Carter administration, Cohen recited the history of Proposition 200, asserted that the federal drug war was a failure, and stated, in response to opening salvos from Senators Kyl and Hatch, that the contention the voters were duped was "absurd." He added, "Former Senator DeConcini is not soft-headed; Barry Goldwater is not soft-headed."

Chairman Hatch read a summary of his antipot convictions: the initiatives passed because voters were bamboozled; the "No" side was overwhelmed by the big money of sinister George Soros; and, anyhow, marijuana had no medical use. He made no mention of Al Gore's sister's use of medical pot or of the government's still-functioning Compassionate User Program. To Hatch "the philanthropists of the drug legalization movement pumped millions of dollars in out-of-state soft money into stealth campaigns designed to conceal their real objective: the legalization of drugs."

Hatch was only minimally correct. Some of the supporters of the medical-use initiatives did favor legalization, but most, including Soros, did not. Hatch's logic was also faulty: Permitting sick people to use marijuana to relieve their discomfort, just as with morphine, cocaine, Demerol, and many other powerful drugs, could be a first step toward legalization only in the sense that the federal government's own Compassionate User Program had impelled the same movement long before the 1996 state initiatives.

Hatch was entirely wrong about Soros. Indeed, Soros was a billionaire financier but, in quantitative terms, he was by 1996 one of the most generous people in the world, a true internationalist who had contributed $1.1 billion since 1989 to transform the former Soviet bloc into capitalist democracies. True, he was from "out of state" just like anyone else inescapably born outside this country, a "foreigner" indeed, just like many of this nation's outcast pot users in the 1930s. Born in Hungary, he suffered as a refugee from both Nazism and Communism. But he did not support broad drug legalization. His letter to the *Times* summarized his true views: "I am not for legalization but for a saner drug policy."[18]

Hatch's judiciary hearings echoed the Marijuana Tax Act hearings of 1937. He cited the origins of the debate with a bit of incorrect history.

"Between 1987 and 1988," he said, "the DEA and NORML, under the guidance of an administrative law judge, collected all relevant information on the alleged medical benefits of marijuana." He added:

> The DEA then conducted a comprehensive examination of that data in order to determine whether those allegations had merit. At the end of that study, the DEA concluded that there was no legitimate medical use for marijuana.[19]

Hatch failed to mention that the judge hearing the evidence, Francis L. Young, actually had come to a contrary conclusion. "The evidence in this record clearly shows that marijuana has been accepted as capable of relieving the distress of great numbers of very ill people, and doing so with safety under medical supervision," is what Judge Young actually wrote in 1988. "It would be unreasonable, arbitrary and capricious," Young had added, "for the DEA to continue to stand between those sufferers and the benefits in light of the evidence."[20]

The Young ruling, which Hatch got 180 degrees backward, had an eventful if unsightly history. In 1972, glaucoma patient Robert Randall and NORML had petitioned the Bureau of Narcotics and Dangerous Drugs (now the Drug Enforcement Agency) to reschedule marijuana as a Schedule II drug in order to recognize that, like other Schedule II drugs, it had an accepted medical use, particularly to treat Randall's serious glaucoma, for which no other drug offered relief. On September 6, 1988, after sixteen years of legal maneuvering about marijuana's medical benefits and public hearings on that subject, including extensive evidence and testimony, Young—an employee of the DEA—ruled in part that

> Marijuana, in its natural form, is one of the safest therapeutically active substances known to man. . . . One must reasonably conclude that there is safety for use of marijuana under medical supervision. To conclude otherwise, on the record, would be unreasonable, arbitrary, and capricious.[21]

Given Washington's existing ideology, such a ruling by the DEA's own chief administrative judge came as an unwelcome surprise. For political reasons unrelated to the evidence, the DEA could tolerate no such impartial finding. In December 1989, echoing Nixon's reaction to his 1972 marijuana commission, DEA administrator John Lawn, who had heard none of the evidence, overruled Young's opinion after sitting on it for fifteen months, calling Young's findings on pot's medical utility a "dangerous and cruel hoax." The doctors who testified before Young, according to Lawn, were all "in favor of legalizing marijuana." As for the patients who testified, they had "used marijuana recreationally prior to discovery of their illness." Therefore, Lawn, who had heard none of the testimony, overruled the judge who had. On February 18, 1994, twenty-two years after Randall began his legal odyssey, the Court of Appeals for the District of Columbia, untroubled by this unusual judicial putsch, upheld both Lawn and the DEA's continued placement of marijuana in the Schedule I listing.[22]

The Senate hearings convened in 1997 by Senator Hatch began with Sperling and Cohen sharing news stories favorable to the Arizona and California initiatives. Drug czar McCaffrey, Arizona Senator Jon Kyl, and Utah Senator Hatch referred repeatedly to the "crisis" engendered by those two initiatives. Several times in the hearings, these three spoke in barely veiled terms of the prospect of trying to prosecute Soros, Lewis, and Sperling under federal RICO ("racketeering and organized crime") statutes for funding the successful initiatives. The hearings ended with official hand wringing and proclamations of regret and amazement about how the voters of California and Arizona could be so easily duped into voting for initiatives they must have failed to understand.

CONCLUSION

The Arizona Supreme Court has twice studied the Arizona medicalization initiative of 1996. In its two reports, the Court found that Arizona saved about $2.5 million in annual prison costs through its 1996 initiative by requiring some drug offenders to be placed on probation rather than incarcerated. The pattern has been consistent. In 1999, Arizona spent $1 million on treatment and supervision of 390 inmates kept out of prison because of the 1996 law, while incarceration of those potheads would have cost the state $7.7 million.[23] Similar proportionate savings have been found in California.

Unaware of these costs savings or indifferent to them, Senator Hatch and his judiciary colleagues continued to speak of the parade of horrors supposedly flowing from the California and Arizona initiatives. The stage was thus set: Would the electorate cave in and join the chorus of hand-wringers?

6

THE PEOPLE'S COUNTERATTACK

After the explosion of comments by federal and state officials about the horrors expected from the marijuana initiatives, a compliant citizenry might have accepted its government's admonitions and disavowed any further marijuana innovations. Such was not the case, though the message is mixed.

Within two years of the 1996 California and Arizona referenda, voters approved medical marijuana proposals in Alaska, Nevada, Oregon, Washington state, Washington, D.C., Maine, and, legislatively, in Hawaii, along with a renewed enactment in Arizona. Voters in these states showed not timid compliance with government warnings but instead an air of incredulity at government policy.

ARIZONA REDUX

The Arizona experience illustrates the credibility issue facing many jurisdictions that have entertained med-pot laws. After passage of Proposition 200 in the November 5, 1996, general election, the Arizona legislature responded by invoking its assumed authority to amend popular initiatives. It sought to modify the voter-approved language of Proposition 200. The legislature faced intense federal political pressure to gut the new law. Under a four-month high-level blitz from Washington, with President Clinton himself leaning on holdouts, Arizona lawmakers passed a bill requiring federal approval of marijuana before having it medically prescribed in the state. This legislation gutted Arizona's Proposition 200 and put the ball back on Washington's side of the net.[1]

Legislators explained to the public that they were not really repealing the initiative but only "fine tuning" and "implementing" it. Arizona

Maricopa County Attorney Rick Romley and General McCaffrey devised a poll they hoped would show that the Arizona voters were "duped," that they would have voted against Proposition 200 if only they had been able to grasp its true meaning. In response, John Sperling hired pollster Rick Maslin to conduct a more accurate poll showing that the majority of the Arizona electorate knew well what it had voted for.[2] Arizona citizens calling themselves "The People Have Spoken" began a signature drive to let voters determine if these reactionary legislative bills should become law. Supporters of the "People" filed 200,000 signatures, twice the needed number, to ensure a rematch with the legislature. The 1998 general election thus placed two referenda on the ballot. The voters had a choice either to affirm their 1996 vote for medical marijuana in Proposition 200 or to disavow it as the mistake of a "duped" electorate. If they defeated the referendum, Proposition 200's proponents would repeal the legislature's efforts to gut the enactment. A yes vote meant support for the legislature's nullification of the 1996 initiative; a no vote meant rejection of the legislature's repeal and reinstatement of the original form of Proposition 200 as passed in 1996.

The result of the November 1998 Arizona election surprised both sides: 57 percent of the voters voted no and thus rejected their legislature's repeal of Proposition 200. The percentage repudiating the legislature's nullification approximated the percentage supporting the original 1996 initiative, suggesting that the electorate knew exactly what it intended in 1996, that it was not "duped," and that it disbelieved its lawmakers' doomsday forecasts.

In short order, Oregon, Washington, and Alaska, followed by Washington, D.C., Colorado, and Maine enacted clear preferences for medical marijuana. The Hawaii and Nevada legislatures passed similar measures in 2000 and 2001. The major features of these new laws are summarized here.

OREGON

In 1998, Oregonians for Medical Rights submitted 97,648 signatures to the secretary of state, well beyond the minimum of 73,261. The initiative—"Measure 67"—qualified for the ballot on July 10, 1998. It passed in November by a strong majority. Leaders in the initiative drive were Dr. Rick Bayer, Jeff Sugarman, and David Smigelski, who also helped organize "Oregonians for Medical Rights."

The Oregon initiative allows patients with a registry identification card to possess, deliver, or produce marijuana for medical purposes. A patient's designated primary caregiver can possess, deliver, or produce marijuana for the patient. The 1998 law allows patients to possess up to seven plants or three ounces.

Patients with the following debilitating medical conditions may receive a registry identification card: cancer, glaucoma, HIV/AIDS, cachexia, severe pain, severe nausea, seizures, or persistent muscle spasms, including multiple sclerosis. Patients seeking a registry identification card must provide the Oregon Department of Human Resources with a $150 fee and (1) valid, written documentation from a physician showing an approved debilitating medical condition and that marijuana should be used in treatment; (2) name, address, and date of birth; (3) name, address, and telephone number of their physician; and (4) name and address of their designated primary caregiver. Patients under 18 must have a parent or guardian approve the medical marijuana use and agree to control its use.

Pursuant to the referendum, the Oregon Department of Human Resources maintains a confidential list of registered medical marijuana patients and designated primary caregivers. Names on the list can be released to state and local law enforcement agents to verify that a person meets the definitions of registered patient or designated caregiver. Patients with a debilitating medical condition without a registry card can use an affirmative medical necessity defense if they have been criminally charged for possessing or growing marijuana. A patient-defendant possessing a physician's recommendation to use marijuana for medical purposes can also use an affirmative defense. Notwithstanding the affirmative defense, the patient is are also entitled to assert the common law "choice of evils" necessity defense, the same issue raised to the U.S. Supreme Court in the Oakland Cannabis buyers' case.[3]

A year after Oregon's Measure 67, law enforcement's anticipated horrors failed to appear. Opponents had claimed that pot dealers would use the law to legitimize all drugs. Police officers, they feared, would be forced to make hasty judgments distinguishing real patients from impostors, and snake-oil "pot doctors" would liberally recommend marijuana to all patients; citizens would openly smoke marijuana on the streets; children seeing this flaunting of authority would begin the steep descent into the hell of drug addiction. With the exception of tightening the prescription rules to restrain one doctor who signed 40 percent of the pot applications, none of these political predictions came to pass.

One of the most outspoken opponents of the Oregon law, Multnomah County Sheriff Dan Noelle, changed his view. After the election, as he saw the measure being implemented, he conceded that "so far" in the year 2001 things were "going well." "We assumed we would see a lot of abuses and we haven't seen it." Multnomah County District Attorney

Mike Schrunk, who did not oppose the measure, agreed that from a law enforcement perspective, "Oregonians are acting responsibly."

Oregon began issuing registration cards on May 1, 1999. More than 300 physicians participated in the program. A network of Oregon patients created an active support system where veteran pot activists welcomed neophytes into the fold. Grow rooms sprouted in the basements and spare bedrooms of some homes. The Oregon Medical Association issued guidelines for physicians to prescribe pot for patients wanting to use marijuana.[4] Oregon's medical panel added Alzheimer's disease to the list of recognized qualifying illnesses in 2001. The only difficulty with the law appeared to be financial—some disabled Oregonians wanting to use marijuana could not afford the $150 annual fee charged by the state or the costs related to growing plants.[5] By 1999, 594 persons had sought cards. By the end of 2002, nearly four thousand Oregonians were requesting cards for med-pot, with about 70 percent of them males over the age of forty, seeking to use it to treat severe pain and persistent muscle spasms.

WASHINGTON STATE

The state of Washington witnessed two separate medical marijuana initiatives, both sponsored by Washington Citizens for Medical Rights led by physician Rob Killian. The first initiative, I-685, modeled on Arizona Proposition 200, would have allowed doctors to recommend Schedule I drugs such as marijuana, heroin, and LSD if scientific research supported such use. Voters rejected this version by a 60 to 40 percent vote in 1997.

On July 10, 1998, the I-692 campaign submitted over 250,000 signatures to the secretary of state for a new version of the original referendum. This version appeared on the November 1998 ballot and passed by a substantial majority, taking effect December 3, 1998. Under its key provisions, growing, selling, purchasing, and using marijuana for nonmedical purposes remained illegal. Fraudulently producing or tampering with records to receive medical marijuana remained a class C felony. Any qualifying patient or primary caregiver received an affirmative legal defense against charges of violating the state's marijuana laws.

Qualifying patients included persons with cancer, HIV, multiple sclerosis, epilepsy, seizure disorders, spasticity disorders, intractable pain, glaucoma, or "[a]ny other medical condition duly approved by the Washington state medical quality assurance board." Patients cannot possess more than a sixty-day supply of marijuana. They must be Washington state residents with a statement signed by a physician or have a copy of a relevant medical record stating that the benefits of medical marijuana outweigh its health risks.

Unlike Arizona and California, Washington's press supported I-692. The *Seattle Times* editorialized strongly in favor of the initiative, urged lawmakers to refrain from gutting it, and suggested ways the legislature could improve on the voters' mandate.[6] Support for I-692 came from unexpected sources. In 1999, the State Medical Quality Assurance Board added Crohn's disease, an intestinal ailment, to the list of approved diseases. In 2000, the board added Hepatitis C to the list and thereafter approved a list of symptoms rather than illnesses to standardize the qualifying process. The Washington Medical Association distributed detailed guidelines to its membership specifying the illnesses permitting marijuana use.[7]

United States Attorney Kate Pflaumer, the federal government's top prosecutor in the state, promised that her office had no interest in prosecuting caregivers or patients possessing the permitted sixty-day supply of marijuana:

> Speaking for this office, we do not intend to alter our declination policies on marijuana which preclude our charging any federal offense for the quantities legalized by the new medical marijuana initiative. (I am assuming an authorized 60 day supply would be fewer than 250 plants.) Given our limited funding and overwhelming responsibilities to enforce an ever larger number of federal offenses, we simply cannot afford to devote prosecution resources to cases of this magnitude. In short, we anticipate maintaining our present declination standards.[8]

ALASKA

Alaska had been more tolerant of marijuana than many of the lower states. In the 1998 initiatives, the pattern held true. "Alaskans for Medical Rights," with David Finkelstein as a chief spokesman, placed before voters "Proposition 8" that paralleled many provisions in Oregon's and Washington's initiatives. It passed by a strong majority. The new medical marijuana law took effect in June 1999 when ID cards became available. Under the new law, the Department of Health and Social Services established a confidential registry of medical marijuana patients. Authorized state and local law enforcement agents have access to the registry for verifying possession of a registration card. Authorized employees of the Department of Health and Social Services (DHSS) also have access to the registry.

Patients with the following debilitating medical conditions qualify for medical pot with a doctor's approval: cancer, glaucoma, HIV/AIDS, cachexia, severe pain, severe nausea, seizure disorders, spasticity disorders, or conditions later approved by DHSS. These patients must submit written documentation confirming that their condition may benefit from marijuana; the name, address, date of birth, and social security number of the patient; the physician; and the patient's caregiver.

After verifying all information submitted by a patient within thirty days, the DHSS must issue to the patient within five days a serially numbered registry identification, with the following information: the patient's name, address, date of birth, and social security number; a statement that the patient has a debilitating medical condition that can be treated with medicinal marijuana; the issuance and expiration date; and the name and address of the patient's primary caregiver.

If the DHSS does not issue a patient a registry card within thirty-five days of application, the patient's application is deemed approved until otherwise notified. Patients must submit annual updated written documentation on their medical condition to retain their registration status. Patients may possess no more than one ounce of marijuana and may grow no more than six marijuana plants, with no more than three flowering plants at a time. A patient or caregiver with more than these amounts must prove that the greater amount is necessary to treat the patient's medical condition.

Physicians cannot be penalized for advising a patient or providing written documentation to a patient informing the patient of possible benefit from the medical marijuana. No person, including a patient or primary caregiver, may possess, buy, cultivate, or sell marijuana for nonmedical purposes. Property associated with the medical use of marijuana cannot be forfeited or otherwise harmed while in possession of state and local law enforcement. As of the end of 2002, nearly a thousand Alaskans were registered for medical pot, over two-thirds of them males over the age of forty.

MAINE

On November 2, 1999, following their governor's 1994 veto of similar legislation, voters in Maine approved "Question 2," a controversial plan for marijuana usage by sick patients. The vote was 61 percent in favor, 39 percent opposed. Maine thereby became the first state in the East to approve medical marijuana and the sixth in the nation since 1996 to enact a medical marijuana law.

General McCaffrey again saw the Maine med-marijuana movement as a smokescreen for universal legalization. He wrote in the *Maine Sunday Telegram* that the proposed law was "unnecessary and dangerous." He pointed out that the psychoactive component of marijuana (THC) had long been available as an approved drug under the brand name Marinol, thus admitting in principle that marijuana *did* possess medical benefits. "Just as people who are ill don't grow their own penicillin from moldy bread," said McCaffrey, "individuals can't guarantee the purity and dosage of THC by growing crude marijuana." Local police and sheriffs associations also opposed the referendum. Their position was undermined when Mark Dion, the sheriff of Cumberland County, came out publicly in favor of it, calling the new law a "humanitarian ceasefire."

The Maine Medical Marijuana Act, effective December 22, 1999, contained increased treatment options for seriously or terminally ill patients. It protected physicians from criminal and professional sanctions if they recommended medical marijuana to a patient and provided patients with a legal defense if arrested for using medical marijuana recommended by a physician.

The new law exempted patients from state laws against personal use of marijuana. The initiative did not exempt patients from federal law, nor could it help those who had to buy marijuana from suppliers who, by definition, remained criminals. The law allowed an individual diagnosed with one of a specified list of illnesses, or that person's caregiver, to possess up to six marijuana plants and one and a fourth ounce of dried marijuana to combat nausea, vomiting, and wasting syndrome from chemotherapy, AIDS, persistent muscle spasms from multiple sclerosis or other spasticity disorders, eye pressure from glaucoma, and epilepsy and other seizure disorders. To qualify for marijuana use, a patient needed to cooperate with a doctor who, in turn, needed to discuss the risks and benefits of marijuana with the patient, give an opinion as to its utility, and to provide continuing care if the patient chose to use marijuana.[9]

Jay McCloskey, the U.S. Attorney for Maine, affirmed he would only pursue dealers, not small-time users: "We don't go after the people with three plants or six plants or even sixty plants." In early 2000, the Maine Attorney General formed a task force to examine the issues surrounding passage of the initiative. By a majority vote, the report endorsed the medical use of marijuana pursuant to the initiative.

DISTRICT OF COLUMBIA

The checkered saga of medical marijuana in the District of Columbia differed from that in the states because of the intervention of Congress.

In 1998, after a successful but tumultuous signature campaign, "Washingtonians for the Legalization of Medical Marijuana" with Wayne Turner as spokesperson, succeeded in placing Initiative 59 on the November 1998 ballot. Its key parts included many provisions found in other states using medicinal marijuana. The D.C. initiative would affirm the right of patients with HIV/AIDS, glaucoma, muscle spasms, cancer, and other serious or chronic illnesses to obtain and use marijuana for medical purposes if a licensed physician recommended its use. Patients could designate or appoint a licensed healthcare practitioner, parent, sibling, spouse, child, or other close relative, domestic partner, case manager/worker, or best friend to be their primary caregiver. Up to four persons could be designated as primary caregivers.

Patients and caregivers could not be prosecuted for possessing, obtaining, or cultivating medical marijuana if the patient had the recommendation of a licensed physician. Patients or caregivers could grow a sufficient quantity of marijuana to ensure a patient's medical supply without interruption in treatment. Medical marijuana use could not be a defense in crimes of violence, of operating a motor vehicle while impaired or intoxicated, or crimes involving danger to another person or to the public.

Distributing marijuana intended for medical use to persons who were not true medical marijuana patients would remain illegal. Physicians could not be punished or denied any right, privilege, or registration for recommending use of medical marijuana to their patients. Residents of the District of Columbia could operate nonprofit corporations to cultivate, purchase, and distribute medical marijuana to patients and their caregivers. Nonprofit corporations would have to comply with the District's nonprofit corporation laws and pay any applicable fees to the Department of Consumer and Regulatory Affairs.

The capital's initiative apparently passed by 69 percent in November 1998—"apparently," that is, because the Republican Congress, also a vocal resident in Washington, D.C., adopted a provision inserted into the District's budget bill by Georgia Republican Bob Barr to suppress the vote count and ordering, further, that the results of the vote never be counted.

Convinced that they had not only a First Amendment right to vote but also a right to have their votes counted and publicized, the initiative's proponents filed suit in federal court on First Amendment grounds and succeeded in getting a court order forcing disclosure of the results, which were 69 percent in favor and 31 percent opposed.

The next response by the same Congress in September 1999 resembled the earlier one: Led by Barr and other conservative Republicans, Congress adopted a district budget with a rider overturning the initiative and specifying that the district's initiative "shall not take effect," thus disenfranchising in this instance the residents of the nation's capital, once touted as a showcase of democracy. This congressional action represented the first time in the nation's history that Congress overturned a ballot initiative passed by a majority of the voters in a legal election.[10] In December 2001, medical pot advocates filed suit to place the marijuana initiative back on the ballot in the capital.[11]

HAWAII

On June 15, 2000, Hawaii became the first state to use standard legislation to approve marijuana for medical purposes. Its provisions paralleled the common features of those described above.

While signing the bill into law, Governor Benjamin J. Cayetano said it was part of his effort to make Hawaii the healthcare center of the Pacific. "I'm glad to see this bill before me," Cayetano said, adding that his own feeling was that "more states are going to come on." Hawaii became the eighth state to legalize medical marijuana. Under the new law, people with marijuana who are stopped by the police would have to prove they are exempt from the state's criminal laws by some form of medical authorization. Criminal laws remain in effect for all citizens not registered for medical marijuana. Patients with qualifying illnesses must obtain a doctor's recommendation to use marijuana and must register with the state Department of Public Safety to avoid prosecution under state law.[12]

CALIFORNIA REDUX

California witnessed two further major referenda on its November 2000 ballot. Proposition 36, modeled explicitly on Arizona's Proposition 200, replaced the criminal justice model with a modified medical approach to crimes of possession and use of all drugs, including pot. Those convicted of drug offenses would receive probation with required treatment, without jail or prison except for repeated violations of probation. The measure was supported by the California Medical Association and social work groups of all kinds; it was opposed by Governor Gray Davis, by prison guards fearing loss of jobs, and by some drug court judges fearing loss of a penal hammer over recalcitrant offenders.

California's new initiative reached even further. In the Emerald Triangle north of San Francisco, Proposition G authorized liberal growing and diminished enforcement of pot. Passed by 58.3 percent of the electorate, the measure instructed the county sheriff and district attorney to give marijuana enforcement the "lowest priority with respect to other crimes" and to "remove the fear of prosecution and the stigma of criminality from people who harmlessly cultivate and/or use marijuana." The law allowed residents of this area to grow up to twenty-five plants, at a street value of about $100,000, without fear of arrest. Transporting and selling pot remained criminal. On June 6, 2001, the California senate approved legislation legalizing marijuana cooperatives for the sick. In the Emerald Triangle area—the same area where California's CAMP pot eradication program occurred—the local sheriff began issuing medical marijuana licenses to residents with a doctor's recommendation and to people who provide pot for them.

"This is a 180-degree change in our drug policy. It's revolutionary," said Dave Fratello, campaign manager for Prop. 36. "California has a reputation as a tough-on-crime state, and now I think we're showing we can be smart on crime too." Proposition 36 expected to keep 25,000 nonviolent drug offenders out of prison each year, saving the state some $125 million in annual prison costs and $475 million in new prison construction. Another $40 million savings was expected for local governments, mostly from saved prison expenses.

NEVADA

A constitutional amendment on Nevada's November 2000 ballot approved medical marijuana by a majority of 67 percent. Sponsored by "Nevadans for Medical Rights," with Dan Hart as campaign manager, Nevada's "Question 9" let doctors prescribe marijuana for severe illness and cancer, AIDS, glaucoma, and other painful and potentially terminal illnesses. Voters had approved the concept by 59 percent in 1998, but adding it to the state's constitution required another yes vote in November 2000.

Nevada had unusually strict antipot laws, with a felony for simple pot possession, yet an early Las Vegas *Review Journal* poll found 63 percent of likely voters backed the measure, with 28 percent opposed, the approximate voter tally. The state's policy-making drug commission, which fought the measure previously, was silent in the November 2000 election. Out-of-state money pushed both measures. The chief backer was "Americans for Medical Rights," bankrolled by New York financier and philanthropist George Soros, Cleveland insurance mogul Peter Lewis, and University of Phoenix founder John Sperling. The initiative did not limit the legal amount of marijuana a patient could possess. As in other medical marijuana jurisdictions, Nevada patients needed to register with the state in order to be protected from possible prosecution.

On May 23, 2001, Nevada's state assembly voted 30 to 12 to set up a state registry of patients to grow up to seven plants. Much of Nevada's pot law followed the Oregon model. Nevada also planned under the initiative to implement a specific mode of distribution of marijuana. As of 2001, it remained the only state to require the legislature to devise a scheme for marijuana distribution. On June 15, 2001, Nevada governor Kenny Guinn signed the new law. Entrepreneurs soon emerged to satisfy the new market. Assistant director of the state's department of agriculture Don Henderson said it would present no law enforcement problem as long as patients kept their plants at their homes and did not hire others to grow them.[13]

COLORADO

Colorado's Amendment 20, approved in November 2000 by a 53 percent to 47 percent majority, legalized the medical use of marijuana under strict controls. Its sponsor was "Coloradans for Medical Rights," with Luther Symons as chief campaign manager.

The amendment was first proposed in 1998, but then-secretary of state Vikki Buckley removed it from the ballot in an administrative decision quickly overturned in court. Advance polls showed the amendment passing by a strong majority. A *Rocky Mountain News* poll showed support by 71 percent of registered voters. Like the Nevada initiative, the amendment, effective June 1, 2001, permitted patients suffering from cancer, glaucoma, HIV/AIDS, multiple sclerosis, and chronic nervous system disorders to use pot with a physician's recommendation. Patients could possess up to two ounces of marijuana or cultivate six plants.

Supporters argued that the therapeutic effect of pot on pain and nausea would help patients put on weight and take the edge off chronic pain. To withhold this option for lessening their suffering, they argued, would constitute a cruel side effect of the drug war. Opponents called the initiative "medicine by popular vote." U.S. Attorney Thomas Strickland issued a November 7, 2000, statement that his office would continue to "aggressively enforce federal drug laws, including the prohibition of marijuana." Governor Bill Owens and Attorney General Ken Salazar, both opposed to medical pot, then urged federal prosecutors to pursue anyone selling, distributing, or growing pot, even if such a person qualified for medical use under the new program. The subsequent U.S. Attorney, Richard Spriggs, declined the invitation, saying his office did not exist to provide solutions to such state controversies.

General McCaffrey's response to these state initiatives matched his earlier reactions. "A crock" he called each of the successful initiatives. He called again for still "more research" to discover, for the last time, some harm in marijuana use.[14]

INITIATIVES IN 2002

The results of marijuana-related initiatives in 2002 showed less uniformity than the preceding pictures, including some reversals or at least holding patterns regarding previous strong propot sentiment.

ARIZONA

An original instigator of the pot liberalization movement, Arizona witnessed its far-reaching Proposition 203 go down to defeat in November 2002. That proposition, supported again by George Soros, Peter Lewis, and John Sperling, would have effectively decriminalized pot possession by reducing possession of two ounces or less from a criminal to a civil violation. The proposal also would have required probation instead of incarceration for reefer possession and use. In addition to changing marijuana's status from a criminal to a petty civil violation, Proposition 203's most controversial provision required the Arizona Department of Public Safety, a statewide law enforcement agency, to maintain and distribute marijuana to qualified patients.

The proposal would have caused some negative financial changes. Arizona's Joint Legislative Budget Committee estimated that 1,100 patients would be eligible for medicinal marijuana in the state, with the cost of a patient registry at $165,000, offset by an estimated $55,000 in revenues from fees. Even such a minimal shortfall was unattractive to a cash-strapped state.

The provision for the state Department of Public Safety—a government law enforcement agency—to dispense marijuana to qualified patients generated much more attention and scorn. State law enforcement and prosecutors' offices teamed up with Arizona Diamondbacks vice president Joe Garagiola Jr. in a public relations campaign against the proposition. President Reagan's former drug czar Bill Bennett circulated his view that marijuana distribution by an Arizona law enforcement agency would grossly clash with its statutory role, making invidious comparisons of dispensing marijuana even more profligately than tobacco.

Despite early polls showing enthusiasm for it, Proposition 203 went down to defeat by a 2 to 1 margin. The defeat most likely reflected a generally conservative turn in the mind-set of voters coupled with the seeming implausibility of a law enforcement agency doling out to citizens the same marijuana that it had recently confiscated from criminals.

NEVADA

An ambitious effort to decriminalize and tax marijuana appeared for the first time on the November 2002 ballot in Nevada. In 2000, Nevada voters had approved the use of medical marijuana. The legislature voted in 2001 to make possession of less than an ounce of pot a misdemeanor punishable by up to six months in jail and a $1,000 fine. Nevadans for Responsible Law Enforcement gathered the necessary 75,000 signatures to put a broader proposal before the voters as "Question 9" to allow adults, without any legal risk, to possess up to three ounces of taxed marijuana, roughly enough to make 100 joints.

Unlike initiatives in other states, Question 9 was not limited to medical pot but would have legalized and taxed marijuana and all potential users regardless of medical need. The plan offered some financial advantages. According to a study by the University of Nevada at Las Vegas, the state would receive $28 million a year in additional revenue if voters approved Question 9 and implemented the plan statewide.

Law enforcement and federal drug officials opposed the measure. Under-sheriff Richard Winger of Las Vegas told voters that three ounces would produce enough joints to transform users into small-time dealers. Asa Hutchinson, the federal drug enforcement administration chief, and federal drug czar John Walters both visited the state just before the election to campaign against it and to underscore the Bush administration's official opposition. Walters arranged for a $3 million grant to Nevada to help defeat the initiative. In his repeated forays across the state, one of Walters's primary arguments was that Las Vegas should resist the temptation to become "the center of drug tourism," a veiled suggestion that pot legalization would harm the state's gaming industries and its effort to become "family friendly." Another factor in the election was the presence on the same ballot of a "same-sex" marriage proposal generating much opposition. Seemingly due to the marriage proposition coupled with the prospect of Las Vegas becoming the nation's drug capital, Question 9 was soundly defeated at the polls.

Thereafter, Nevada Attorney General Brian Sandoval sent a letter to Walters complaining about his "excessive" and "disturbing" interference in the state's marijuana initiative. When the Nevada Secretary of State demanded Walters disclose the monies he spent campaigning against the initiative, as required by Nevada law, Walters simply shrugged off the request and refused to comply with the law, claiming immunity from all state law as a federal official.[15]

WASHINGTON, D.C.

Late in 2001, the Marijuana Policy Project sued the federal government to conduct a medical marijuana initiative. After succeeding in this legal battle, supporters began to collect the 40,000 signatures needed to place medical marijuana on a future November ballot.

One of the notable successes in 2002 was treatment initiative Measure 62, sponsored by the Drug Policy Alliance, overwhelmingly approved and requiring addicts, including pot users, to receive treatment, not jail. The measure, modeled on Arizona's successful 1996 anti-incarceration initiative, passed with 78 percent of the vote. As of early 2003, there was no indication that the Congress intended to gut the provision as it had done in the district's 1999 vote.

SAN FRANCISCO

Local ballot measures in 2002 fared better than some statewide initiatives. In San Francisco, adjacent to the fertile Emerald Triangle, voters passed proposition S by a 2 to 1 margin. That vote required city officials to explore means for growing and distributing medical marijuana to qualified patients. Because of law enforcement raids on cannabis user clubs just months before the election, voters had been outraged by the federal government's harassing raids on medical marijuana providers. After the vote, Bay-area officials named a three-member committee to hold hearings and bring in professional expertise to explore legal and medical avenues for providing medical marijuana to qualified patients, a process well underway by 2004.

2003 INITIATIVES

Some state developments in 2003 suggested that the medical marijuana movement remained on track. In September, citizens of Seattle voted to make marijuana offenses the lowest priority for city law enforcement. Despite opposition from drug czar John Walters about the medical evils of marijuana and the need for enforcement efforts to stamp out those evils, Initiative 75 passed by a comfortable 59% to 41% margin. Pursuant to the initiative, Seattle law enforcement agencies will only prosecute marijuana offenses, including medical marijuana, as a last resort.

CONCLUSION

Though the defeats of medical marijuana propositions in Arizona and Nevada in 2002 conflicted with some earlier approvals of a more relaxed penal approach to pot, explanations for the defeats, in addition to those mentioned, focused on the World Trade Center attacks on September 11, 2001, and the country's resulting conservative swing. Law enforcement suddenly became popular again. In some quarters, attacks on police, fire, political figures, and existing drug policies appeared unpatriotic. The electoral mood after September 11 in many quarters reflected a desire to maintain the security of the status quo rather than venture down innovative and uncharted paths.

But not all the electoral moods were conservative. In the spring of 2003, medicinal pot supporters joined the citizens of Maryland to encourage Governor Bob Ehrlich to allow a legislatively approved medical marijuana bill, like the Hawaii legislation, to become law. President Bush's drug czar John Walters again traveled from Washington, D.C., to campaign within the state on what seemed to be a local states-rights issue. He pressured the governor to veto the medical marijuana bill overwhelmingly passed by the Maryland legislature, campaigning in Maryland as he had in Nevada in 2002 to influence local law.

On May 3, 2003, Governor Ehrlich responded to the federal pressure by signing the bill into law, thereby becoming the first Republican governor to sign a medical marijuana bill. The Maryland legislation tracks new laws in western states by providing for medical authorization for marijuana. Patients on an approved list have the right to receive, possess, and use marijuana for their defined medical problems. Anyone arrested for using marijuana for such approved purposes can avoid prosecution by showing medical need and authorization for possessing and using medical marijuana. Maryland thus became the ninth state in the country to remove the state threat of jail for medical marijuana-use patients.

7

THE MEDICAL-LEGAL CONFLICT

Following approval of California's Proposition 215 in 1998, the Clinton administration announced that passage of such measures would not diminish enforcement of federal marijuana laws. In August 2000, the Department of Justice announced that the federal government would penalize all doctors recommending medical pot by revoking their ability to write prescriptions. Department lawyer Joseph Lobue said in particular that federal officials did not recognize California law or any other state reefer law: "It doesn't matter what California says," he announced.

Through drug czar McCaffrey, President Clinton also threatened that the Department of Justice would begin to prosecute physicians recommending marijuana to their patients as well as patients caught using marijuana as medicine. Possible penalties for doctors included exclusion from federally funded Medicaid and Medicare programs, federal criminal charges, and loss of DEA certification to prescribe controlled substances. The administration's response sought to intimidate pot users and caregivers while maintaining a hard line against pot for political purposes,[1] all the while making no mention of the pot experiences of the president, the use of medical marijuana by the sister of Vice President Gore, and the history of the government's still-continuing Compassionate User Program.

Energized by the government's threats to prosecute physicians and patients, Senator Lauch Faircloth of North Carolina, a major tobacco supporter, introduced a bill in Congress to provide federal sanctions for medical practitioners who administered, dispensed, or recommended medical marijuana.[2] The bill was referred to the Senate Judiciary Committee but not carried over after the 1998 congressional session. The

House of Representatives also resolved that marijuana was a dangerous and addictive drug, never to be legalized for medicinal use.[3]

MEDICAL ASSOCIATION RESPONSES

The 6,100-member California Academy of Family Physicians termed the Clinton administration's response to the California pot initiatives "draconian" and complained that its policy presented physicians with a "moral dilemma." The parent California Medical Association expressed fears that doctors prescribing marijuana would be labeled drug traffickers and lose their prescribing privileges or be prosecuted.

The California Medical Association, the California Academy of Family Physicians, and the San Francisco Medical Society, totaling some 100,000 physicians, warned their members not to recommend medical marijuana for fear of government prosecution and incarceration for felonies potentially carrying ten-year sentences.[4] Along with other medical associations, the Oregon Medical Association issued similar warnings to its membership. Several physicians announced that the risks of prosecution forced them to abandon medical marijuana as a viable treatment for suitable patients, thus generating an ethical conflict with patients as well as a potential legal conflict with the government and new ballot initiatives.[5]

PATIENT LIABILITY UNDER FEDERAL LAW

Pot-using patients faced a similar dilemma. As of 1998, patients risked federal liability for using marijuana for medical purposes. A patient possessing even a small amount faced the same penalties as someone possessing the drug for recreational use: up to one year in federal prison and a $10,000 fine.[6] A patient cultivating even one marijuana plant faced up to five years in prison and a $250,000 fine.[7] Cultivating 100 or more plants, including seedlings, could bring a mandatory five years and a maximum of forty years in federal prison as well as a $2 million fine.[8] The severity of these penalties could make qualified patients face the uncertainty of arrest each time they obtained and used medical marijuana.

PATIENT LIABILITY UNDER STATE LAW

Though state scheduling schemes for marijuana regulation largely mirror the federal scheme, new laws in Arizona and California and other initiative states in the late 1990s removed some or all state penalties for medical use of pot.[9] Although patients still break federal law by using marijuana, state officials have no grounds for arrest because such conduct became legal under the new state initiatives. Because most arrests are made by state and local law enforcement officials rather than by federal law enforcement officers, discreet marijuana-use patients had a good chance of avoiding arrest. By comparison with state law officials, not enough federal drug agents existed to hunt down and arrest most patients using marijuana for medical purposes.[10] State law, in effect, provided a sanctuary from federal law—but only if federal officers elected to ignore federal violations.

CAREGIVER RISK UNDER FEDERAL AND STATE LAW

After successful med-pot initiatives, caregivers faced the same legal dilemma as doctors and patients. Under federal law, primary caregivers growing or distributing medical marijuana faced even stiffer fines and jail sentences than did the patients they were supplying.[11] Anyone distributing marijuana to patients, even a registered pharmacist or official of the state government, outside the auspices of a federally approved research program, could be tried as a common drug dealer. Depending on the amount of medical marijuana involved, the penal possibilities extended to life in prison and the death penalty. Caregivers thus faced substantially more risk for liability than either patients or physicians.

Primary caregivers also faced a criminal risk under some state laws. Arizona's Proposition 200, for example, only relieved pot-using patients from criminal prosecution; it offered no protection to suppliers.[12] California's Proposition 215 defined a primary caregiver as someone who consistently assumed responsibility for the housing, health, or safety of the patient.[13] Under various standards adopted by the different cities and counties in California,[14] localities used widely varying criteria, such as who grows the marijuana plants, where they are grown, and what constitutes a reasonable number of plants,[15] leading to an even wider range of disparate enforcement of pot laws.[16]

RESPONSES OF MEDICAL ASSOCIATIONS

The response of state medical associations varied from caution to outrage at the Clinton administration's threat to prosecute pot-prescribing doctors. In April 1999, Oregon's Medical Association offered guidelines to its physician members similar to those in California, cautioning its members to be especially careful in discussing medical marijuana with patients and to leave no written documentation reflecting such conversations.[17]

California and Oregon physicians faced a further dilemma. The physicians' choice on the subject of medical marijuana became whether to fulfill their obligation to provide beneficial health care to patients or risk their personal freedom by tempting criminal prosecution. From the patient's perspective, the choice focused on enduring chronic pain and discomfort on the one hand and the risk of prosecution and incarceration on the other. Aware of these polarities, the *New England Journal of Medicine*, in a 1997 editorial entitled "Federal Foolishness and Marijuana," castigated governmental insensitivity both to doctors and to their patients.[18]

THE RISE OF BUYERS' CLUBS

The spread of "buyers' clubs," illegal under federal law, in California after its successful pot initiatives illustrated the medical-legal dilemma. After the passage of Proposition 215, new buyers' clubs arose throughout the state, most blatantly in San Francisco, Oakland, and Los Angeles, to fill the expected demand for medical marijuana. While many clubs adopted strict protocols for acquiring marijuana, such as requiring a doctor's signed recommendation, a detailed health questionnaire, and follow-up visits with a doctor, other clubs required only verification of a doctor's legitimacy without any medical recommendation for marijuana or any medical indication of the nature of the illness. Still other clubs operated under the guiding principle of unquestioning deference to the patient's wishes.

Two club distribution models became dominant. One model reflected a conventional, pharmacy-like delivery system where a patient visiting the club would present a note from a doctor. The proprietor of the club would then fill the prescription, with the patient returning home to use it. Oakland's Cannabis Buyers' Club exemplified this model.

A second pattern resembled the conduct of a Dutch social club more than the procedures of a pharmacy. Under this format the club offered a set menu of various types and grades of pot similar to the format found in a Dutch coffee house. Patients—commonly called "guests"—would order from the menu and remain on the premises to smoke and converse. Pot buyers' clubs in San Francisco and Los Angeles resembled this model. The Clinton Department of Justice sought to close down both models on the grounds that they violated federal prohibitions against pot.

THE CONANT LITIGATION

As doctors and patients struggled to make sense of the medical-legal conflicts over marijuana, a major California court case in 1997 provided some clarity.

Dr. Marcus Conant, a professor at the University of California Medical Center in San Francisco, had practiced medicine for about thirty-three years in the San Francisco area. Author or coauthor of over seventy publications addressing the treatment of AIDS/HIV, he had served as the medical director of the Conant Medical Group, the largest private AIDS practice in the United States, providing primary care for over 5,000 HIV-infected patients, including approximately 2,000 patients with AIDS. Dr. Conant had prescribed Marinol for many of his patients, but he had found that medical marijuana offered a better and in some cases the only viable treatment option.

In 1997, along with other California health providers, Conant sued the federal government for permission to use medical marijuana in his practice without government interference. The defendants included several top federal government officials, including drug czar McCaffrey, Attorney General Janet Reno, and Secretary of Health and Human Services Donna Shalala. According to the Conant complaint, the federal government neither had punished nor threatened physicians for recommending medical use of marijuana to treat terminally ill patients prior to passage of Proposition 215. Before that date, physician-patient discussions concerning medical marijuana attracted no government interest. However, following the passage of Proposition 215, General McCaffrey and other officials had suggested, for the first time, that the federal government might act against pot-prescribing physicians via criminal prosecutions. The Conant litigation intended in part to head off the threat of such prosecutions.

On February 14, 1997, the Conant plaintiffs, through their private attorneys and attorneys for the American Civil Liberties Union and The Drug Policy Alliance, filed suit in federal district court in California against the defendants in their official capacities to enjoin prosecution of all physicians recommending medical marijuana under Proposition 215. They claimed that the federal government's medical marijuana policy, as outlined by McCaffrey after passage of Proposition 215, was both inconsistent and threatened their First Amendment rights to free speech.

As the Conant case was being filed, Dr. Jerome Kassirer, editor-in-chief of the *New England Journal of Medicine*, published an editorial lambasting the government's prosecution threats as "misguided, heavy-handed and inhumane."[19] In the editor's view, the Clinton administration hypocritically allowed prescriptions of more dangerous morphine and Demerol while forbidding prescriptions of marijuana.[20] Kassirer also argued against the government's policy of requiring documented evidence of pot's medical benefits before loosening restrictions on research,[21] and he urged that marijuana be rescheduled to acknowledge its recognized medical benefits.[22] The article and its critiques became central features of the Conant litigation.

The Justice Department's initial responses to both the editorial and to the Conant suit were sharp.[23] "Smoke is not a medicine," scolded McCaffrey.[24] The government rejected a settlement proposal with Conant that would have avoided prosecution of physicians for using their best medical judgment in recommending medical marijuana in a bona fide doctor-patient relationship.[25] Health and Human Services Secretary Donna Shalala stated that healthcare professionals "need to understand that federal law has not changed."[26]

Judge Fern Smith, who first presided over the case, noted that the government persisted in issuing ambiguous and conflicting interpretations of its medical marijuana policy and that its attorneys could not clearly articulate the "contours" of federal policy on the subject. The judge certified the plaintiff class to include all California physicians discussing medical marijuana with patients, plus all patients with serious, debilitating diseases seeking medical advice about treatment by marijuana.

Although the First Amendment allowed physicians to advocate medical marijuana despite its illegality, physicians could not do so where such advocacy would incite imminent lawless action. However, because the government persisted in issuing conflicting interpretations of its marijuana policy, the plaintiffs argued that the government's decision to sanction physicians violated First Amendment protections.

On September 7, 2000, Judge William Alsup, who had taken over the case, issued a permanent injunction against the government's effort to prosecute physicians for recommending medical marijuana. He enjoined the Department of Justice from revoking licenses "merely because the doctor recommends medical marijuana to a patient based on a sincere medical judgment and from initiating any investigation solely on that ground." He added that the injunction would apply even if "the physician anticipates that the recommendation will, in turn, be used by the patient to obtain marijuana in violation of federal law."[27] The federal government indicated it would appeal.

THE MEDICAL NECESSITY CASE

A second major federal case, also originating in California, went a step further—for a while—in recognizing a federal "medical necessity" defense to the effect that no other remedy could achieve the medical benefits of marijuana. In *U.S. v. Oakland Cannabis Buyers' Cooperative*,[28] the trial court initially denied a medical necessity defense to patrons of the Oakland Buyers' Club. Then, on appeal, the Ninth Circuit Court of Appeals reversed the trial court ruling that had held that a buyers' club distribution of marijuana violated the Comprehensive Drug Abuse Prevention and Control Act of 1970.[29] Under the Ninth Circuit's view, a federal court could legally use the "medical necessity" defense to prevent prosecution of both caregivers and patients for using or recommending medical pot.[30] On March 2, 2000, the Ninth Circuit, en banc, denied the government's petition for a rehearing.

The medical necessity defense at issue in the case had a long history. The first successful use of that defense in a pot-related case occurred in *United States v. Randall* in 1976,[31] where the District of Columbia Superior Court recognized the medical necessity defense to the point of finding Robert Randall not guilty of using marijuana cigarettes to relieve his glaucoma. The court balanced Randall's interest in relief from pain against the government's interest in enforcing pot laws and concluded that his right to preserve his health outweighed the governmental interest in prosecution.

Though some variation existed, the Randall decision squared with decisions elsewhere. In 1991, in *Jenks v. State*, the Florida Court of Appeals held that a state statute making marijuana possession a crime did not prevent use of the medical necessity defense in court.[32] Jenks, a hemophiliac who contracted AIDS through a blood transfusion, unknowingly passed AIDS to his wife. Suffering severe nausea and weight loss, the couple began using pot to maintain appetite and general health. They also grew two marijuana plants for which they were arrested and prosecuted. The Florida Court of Appeals held that the Jenks met the burden of proving the elements of medical necessity as set forth in *Randall* and concluded that the trial court had erred in denying them a medical necessity defense.

SUPREME COURT ACTION

On November 27, 2000, in response to a petition from the Clinton Justice Department, the United States Supreme Court agreed to review the Oakland Buyers' Club case and, in particular, the viability in federal courts of the medical necessity defense for use of medical marijuana. The Clinton administration's legal briefs told the court that the medical necessity defense was "directly at odds" with federal law and "threatened the government's ability to enforce federal drug laws." The Department of Justice argued that the common law defense of medical necessity had disappeared when Congress placed pot in Schedule I of the federal Controlled Substances Act of 1970, which defined that category as including drugs "with no accepted medical use."

When the medical necessity case was argued on March 29, 2001, before the Supreme Court, a number of conservative lawmakers assembled at the court to spar with supporters of medical marijuana. "What's really going on here," announced Representative Dave Weldon (R-Fla.), "is people are trying to legalize smoking marijuana and they're using cancer and AIDS patients as a prop." Representative Bob Barr (R-Ga.), the same person who had prevented counting and implementation of the District of Columbia medical marijuana initiative, also came in person to weigh in with his conservative views. "This is really an effort by the druggies," he announced, "to legalize marijuana."

Earlier, this proponent of free market tobacco had observed that "all civilized countries in the world are under assault by drug proponents seeking to enslave citizens." Speaking of Rob Kampia, the executive director of the Marijuana Policy Project, Barr added, "I don't respect Mr. Kampia." To his face he asserted, "You're not a wonderful person. You're doing something despicable, and you're putting a nice face on it." Subcommittee chairman Mark Souder (R-Ind.), added to the compliments, telling Kampia, "You are an articulate advocate for an evil position."

The next day a crowded Supreme Court heard the medical necessity arguments. Outside the court, demonstrators on both sides marched with banners supporting their positions. The pot side included signs saying "Let My People Grow." Santa Clara University law professor and former dean Gerald Uelmen argued for the cannabis buyers' clubs. Acting Solicitor General Barbara Underwood argued for the government.

California Attorney General Bill Lockyer supported the position of the buyers' clubs with a brief on their behalf, arguing that the federal government invaded state sovereignty by interfering with his state's right to regulate the health and welfare of its own citizens. The California Medical Association also supported the Oakland Buyers' Club, as did civil liberties and drug policy organizations plus a group of local sheriffs and law enforcement officials from other states that had adopted medical marijuana initiatives.

Members of the court quickly dispelled any pretense of uncertainty. A good part of its collective mind appeared to have been well made up before the arguments. Justice Anthony Kennedy quickly stated to Uelmen: "You've got non-medical people deciding what's a medical necessity— that's a huge rewriting," he said, of the federal law listing marijuana as a banned substance. In lieu of questions, Justice Sandra O'Connor made conclusory statements: "The Ninth Circuit," she stated, had "erred when it created this blanket defense." Chief Justice William Rehnquist observed that Uelmen's case law support for the medical necessity defense was "far off the point."

Ms. Underwood faced little questioning, most of it sympathetic. It was thus no surprise when the Court handed down its ruling, in May 2001, that the medical necessity defense would be unavailable in federal courts to create any legal exception for club-related medical marijuana distribution.[33] Given the dismissive treatment of Uelmen by some of the justices at oral arguments, the 8 to 0 holding came as no surprise. Justice Thomas's decision skirted the states' rights issue at the heart of the case, namely, whether the state of California had the right to legalize med-pot within its borders. A concurring opinion from Justice Stevens chided the conservative majority for "overbroad language . . . given the importance of showing respect for sovereign states."

Conservative Republican Bob Barr of Georgia, a proponent of wide-open tobacco laws, waxed ecstatic at the court's decision: "Marijuana is a dangerous, mind altering substance that should not be legalized for whatever contrived reason," he decreed.[34] Attorney General John Ashcroft, also a states' rights advocate, praised the Supreme Court decision: "We can't function well as a country if each state makes its own rules about what's available healthcare wise."[35]

BROAD OR NARROW?

The court's decision was narrow. It read the Schedule I provision of the Controlled Substances Act and found, correctly, no specific recognition of a medical necessity defense. Its ruling meant only that the federal government could prosecute pot distributors in federal court without them having the benefit of the medical necessity defense. Given the difficulty of securing a criminal conviction against doctors and patients from sympathetic jurors, coupled with the reality that well over 95 percent of drug prosecutions occur in state rather than federal courts, the demise of the medical necessity defense in federal courts probably would cause little impact either on the streets or in state courts.

While agreeing with the majority, Justice Stevens's separate opinion supported by two other justices hinted at a direction for future legal action. To his mind, the public interest in letting individuals find their own relief from suffering prevailed over federal law. The explicit case dealt, he suggested, not with individuals but with distribution of marijuana by a commercial supplier like the Oakland Buyers' Club. Individuals, he implied, might be exempt from the court's holding.

The decision had no impact on state courts where the majority of drug cases are prosecuted and where the defense remained viable, even in those states lacking medical marijuana laws. Nor did the decision affect any established state medical marijuana initiatives. It also had no effect on a state allowing its citizen-patients to grow, possess, and use medical marijuana short of distribution, nor did it prevent individuals from obtaining medical marijuana. Its scope encompassed only federal prosecutions of persons or clubs distributing pot to member patients prosecuted in federal courts.

One effect of the decision was to force distribution systems to go underground, by growing their own supply to avoid distribution through more public channels. Not the least of the decision's ironies lay in the fact that when he was governor of Texas, President George W. Bush, a committed advocate of states' rights, had asserted that states enjoy the right to decide for themselves about medical marijuana. "I believe each state can choose that decision as they so choose," he said in October 1999, in an article in *The Dallas Morning News* cited by Justice Stevens in the Supreme Court's decision, a view exactly matching that of California Attorney General Bill Lockyer in his unsuccessful amicus brief to the Supreme Court.[36]

CONANT ON APPEAL

The legal news from the courts in 2002 was not all negative for medpot crusaders. The Conant case, decided in their favor by the federal trial court in California, was appealed to the Ninth Circuit Court of Appeals. On October 29, 2002, that court ruled in *Conant v. Walters* that the federal government may not revoke the licenses of doctors who recommend marijuana to their patients. The decision upheld the five-year-old district court ruling blocking the government's efforts to frustrate California's 1996 initiative.[37]

The court accepted every major argument from the California physicians. Where drug czar John Walters, Attorney General John Ashcroft, and DEA administrator Asa Hutchison had tried to revoke doctors' licenses for recommending marijuana to their patients, the court instead stated that "Physicians must be able to speak frankly and openly to their patients." Chief Judge Mary Schroeder, quoting Justice John Paul Stevens of the Supreme Court, added that federal courts should defer to the states in "situations in which the citizens of a state have chosen to serve as a laboratory in the trial of novel social and economic experiments." Sue Rusche of Families in Action, though dismayed at the ruling, predicted that it would be reversed because in her words, "The Supreme Court doesn't like the Ninth Circuit." Although the Bush administration immediately petitioned the Supreme Court to reverse the Ninth Circuit's decision, the Supreme Court declined to review the case, meaning that the Ninth Circuit's decision remained in effect.

THE CALIFORNIA RAIDS

None of these decisions invalidated the federal prohibition on use of marijuana, medical or otherwise. The newly elected Bush administration sought to stamp its mark against what it considered the spreading morass of permissiveness regarding marijuana, especially the expanding medicalization of pot under the guise of legitimate medical treatment.

In October 2001, armed with the favorable May ruling from the U.S. Supreme Court in the Oakland Cannabis Buyers' Club case, thirty federal drug enforcement agents raided the Los Angeles Marijuana Resource Center. An organization supplying pot to 960 sick members with chronic health problems, three-fourths with AIDS, the center had been operating with the cooperation of the county sheriff's department and under a mortgage cosigned by the city of West Hollywood. Federal agents uprooted 400 marijuana plants, removed growing equipment, and seized computers and files with the names and records of all the center's 960 patients.

The DEA cited the Supreme Court decision in its search warrant, saying "illegal conduct permeates the organization's activities and that all documents, records, and equipment seized constitute the fruits of federal criminal offenses." All the patients possessed doctors' prescriptions for use of pot as a painkiller. No arrest warrants were issued, but the center's pharmacy was closed, leaving the patients to look for medical pot from drug dealers on the streets in the black market.

More raids were forthcoming. On September 5, 2002, federal agents armed with automatic weapons raided the WoMen's Alliance for Medical Marijuana, another marijuana hospice near Santa Cruz, California, that had been providing medical marijuana to its 150 members. Agents arrested its owners, including the persons who helped write California Proposition 215, the state's 1996 successful medical marijuana initiative. Officers seized more than 100 marijuana plants, cut down another 150 with chain saws, and confiscated three rifles and a shotgun. Owners Valerie and Michael Corral were arrested on federal charges of intent to distribute marijuana.

Valerie Corral used marijuana to control seizures resulting from head trauma following a car accident. She was driven away in her pajamas. Suzanne Pfeil, a paraplegic patient suffering from polio, was told to stand up to be handcuffed; when she could not do so, she was handcuffed to her bed.

The raid infuriated local California officials who had cooperated closely with the Corrals for six years to devise a system to define medical users and issue identification cards, and provide organically grown pot free of charge. California Attorney General Bill Lockyer condemned the bust as a waste of law enforcement resources and a cruel step against a group presenting no danger to the public. He fired off a letter to Attorney General John Ashcroft asking for a personal meeting to "discuss the federal government's unprecedented attacks on locally authorized medical marijuana operations."

The following week, the Santa Cruz city council staged its own version of the Boston Tea Party: It allowed the co-op to hand out marijuana publicly to its patients in the city hall courtyard. In an effort to protect the Corrals from federal prosecution, the city deputized the founders of the Santa Cruz pot farm, enabling them under state and local law to "cultivate, distribute and possess medical marijuana." San Jose police chief William Lansdowne then removed his officers from the DEA's task force, saying that his police officers had more important things to do than harass pot clubs operating under state law.

Richard Meyer, a spokesperson for DEA drug administrator Asa Hutchinson, responded to California's outrage by saying "No one in the United States is allowed to distribute illegal drugs, period." At the same time of his comments, the federal government was continuing to distribute medical marijuana to the seven surviving patients grandfathered into the government's Compassionate User Program dating from the early 1970s. Three days after the Santa Cruz raid, the DEA raided a similar med-pot operation in Sonoma County. On February 14, 2003, other federal agents raided Los Angeles pot clubs and related businesses in ten states as part of a nationwide "Operation Pipe Dream," searching hundreds of private homes and businesses and arresting fifty-five people for possessing bongs and roach clips.[38] Tommy Chong of "Cheech and Chong" fame was arrested on February 24, 2003, for manufacturing a line of bongs. In a laudatory press conference with drug czar John Walters, Attorney General John Ashcroft proclaimed that the pot paraphernalia industry had "invaded the homes of families across the country without their knowledge," and John Walters added his support for such operations against persons who "poison our children."[39]

One of the saddest such home invasions occurred in fall 2002 when federal agents raided just such a private home in Wisconsin and arrested Dennis and Denise Schilling for selling $120 worth of marijuana to undercover agents. Evicted, their house subject to forfeiture, the Schillings resided in a run-down motel. There, late one evening, they hanged themselves.[40] "Perhaps someday people like me will not be so persecuted," wrote Denise Schilling in her suicide note.[41]

CONVERSION

Late in 2002, Representatives Barney Frank of Massachusetts and Ron Paul of Texas introduced legislation to permit states to allow the use of marijuana for medical purposes. One of its supporters was Lyn Nofziger, who worked closely with President Reagan and then supported his aggressive antimarijuana policies.[42] Nofziger became convinced of the benefits of medical pot when his oldest daughter died from lymphoma at the age of thirty-eight. "Before she died she underwent heavy chemotherapy that caused nausea, diarrhea, and loss of appetite." When neither Marinol nor Demerol helped, Nofziger and his family found that "marijuana best helped reduce the effects of the chemotherapy to the point where she regained her appetite and actually began putting on weight." According to Nofziger, taking medical pot "made her life more bearable to her and to her family."

By the time of the Conant litigation, Nofziger had abandoned the Reagan party line regarding pot: "I have learned that marijuana can also help persons with glaucoma, the wasting symptoms of AIDS, multiple sclerosis and other afflictions." He wrote that he had become "an avid supporter of efforts to legalize marijuana for medicinal purposes."[43]

CONCLUSION

Advocates of states' rights sometimes appear exempt from consistency in behavior. In 1998, Attorney General John Ashcroft, who organized and approved the California raids on its buyers' clubs and acted as an ardent supporter of state's rights, had praised a proconfederacy magazine for defending "Southern patriots" like states-rightist Jefferson Davis.[44] "Order and liberty go together like love and marriage," Ashcroft once told a group of judges, "you can't have one without the other."[45] During the presidential campaign, his boss, President George W. Bush, regularly told campaign audiences that the federal government was too big and too active outside its own sphere and that states should decide for themselves whether to legalize medical marijuana.[46] Obviously, these convictions admit of major exceptions for marijuana threats.

8

Conclusion: Lessons in Political Unscience

The art of war is all that is expected of a ruler.

Machiavelli, *The Prince*

Drug czar William Bennett liked to stress law's modeling powers for the citizenry. He once did so more eloquently than Machiavelli: "The law is the witness and external deposit of our moral life," said Bennett, because it inescapably teaches its citizens by modeling expected standards of behavior.[1] By that standard, what does our nation's pot campaign model? Although our government's marijuana crusade certainly teaches lessons and models behaviors, the lessons and the models come more from Machiavelli and the Three Stooges than from any principled policy inspiring citizen allegiance. Many of these lessons policy makers neither intend nor want to acknowledge, not even the basic Moms Mambly proposition that "if you always do what you've always done, you'll get what you always got."

Here, in a political science retrospective, appear some of the uncomfortable lessons of our government's sixty-year-long campaign against marijuana.

EX ANTE CRIMINALIZATION

Beginning with the marijuana prohibitions of the 1920s and 1930s, including the 1937 Marijuana Tax Act and culminating in the Controlled Substances Act of 1970 and universal state prohibitions, our federal and state governments have criminalized pot without any accurate knowledge about its harmful effects. This cart-before-the-horse criminalization explains the fervid demand, notably in the Nixon, Reagan, and first Bush administrations, to find something provably, medically wrong with marijuana in order to shore up the criminal prohibition. Before his late-in-life conversion, Reagan's czar Charles Schuster often expressed wonder at his administration's dogged demand to "find something wrong with marijuana."

The urgency reflects the evidentiary vacuum at the heart of marijuana criminalization. As Schuster, Nofziger, and others in the Reagan administration then realized, criminalization of marijuana badly needs the discovery of verifiable medical harm to give credibility to the prohibition. None has been forthcoming. In 2002, Schuster himself, like Nofziger, switched sides by endorsing the Rand Institute's 2002 study showing lack of evidence for the same gateway hypothesis Schuster advocated during his tenure with Reagan.

Despite repeated medical data showing pot's worst effects slightly less severe than those of legal tobacco, the desperate search for the Holy Grail of demonstrable medical harm continues without any clues to date suggesting the existence of such harm. The strongest medical damnation drug czar John Walters could invoke against the 2002 Nevada state initiative was that marijuana's harms resemble those of tobacco and alcohol, both of which remain legal and easily accessible, even to minors.

In the absence of any medically provable harm, government officials fill up the pot prohibition's spacious vacuum with all sorts of ersatz justifications: first, Anslinger's racial justifications, followed by reefer madness warnings, followed by threats of amotivational syndrome, plus disheveled and long-haired hippies undermining patriotism, and culminating in drug czars like Bennett, Turner, and Walters urging severe prohibition lest the entire nation succumb to cultural and moral disarray, all because of marijuana.

In the absence of hard medical data showing pot's harm, officials like Anslinger and his heirs resort to fictional causality pronouncements about its effects: homosexuality, jazz, laziness, insanity, long hair, antiauthoritarianism, manic and amotivational behavior, and Keith Schuchard's "male breasts," all said to result from the same evil weed. These fictions proliferate in the void of objective causal evidence about marijuana's medical harm. Pot prohibitions constitute an anomaly in how lawmakers typically enact criminal prohibitions: Usually, it is prior verifiable harm that justifies the prohibition; not so with pot.

RESEARCH YIELDS TO IDEOLOGY

A second anomaly in our government's marijuana crusade offers an epistemological novelty no less striking: government officials' consistent pattern of convening expert research commissions to investigate pot, mandating their objectivity and impartiality, and then repudiating their unwelcome findings.

The last half-century witnesses a veritable parade of such independent expert commissions producing objective marijuana studies: The New York Academy of Medicine (1944); President Kennedy's White House Commission on Narcotics and Drug Abuse (1962); President Nixon's National Commission on Marijuana and Drug Abuse (1972); the National Academy of Sciences Substance Abuse report (1982); the United Nation's World Health Organization report (1999); and, not least of all, the National Institute of Medicine report (1999), this last commissioned by drug czar General McCaffrey himself.

With only minor differences, these expert bodies, composed of leading figures in law, medicine, and social policy, have recommended either decriminalization or at least diminished law enforcement energies against reefer. Two of these groups—the National Academy of Sciences (1982) and the National Institute of Medicine (1999)—recognized real medical benefits from marijuana.

Presidents and highly visible drug policy wonks have almost uniformly denounced these careful recommendations and their underlying research. Sometimes drug czars and other demonizers have hurled calumny at the researchers personally, as though their assumed moral depravity generated scientific bad faith. Is the bad faith in the researchers who generate the findings or in the politicians who reject them? It is, after all, the latter group who chose the researchers, anointed them, and mandated their independence, only in the end to repudiate their unwelcome findings.

This pattern of convening expert research commissions and then repudiating their findings reflects nothing more than political timidity. Presidents and drug czars repudiate the recommendations of their experts, some they themselves appointed, not on scientific but on political grounds: It might hurt political careers to accept untimely truths.

Objective research on pot's medical effects thus joins different levels of discourse. Objective scientific conclusions are found lacking not on scientific grounds but for reasons of political expediency. When political expediency is threatened, some officials defend the status quo by subjecting their appointed researchers to cruel ad hominem invective. "All on the stuff themselves," is how Nixon described his marijuana commission experts for their unwelcome findings. The objective findings—and sometimes the researchers—are relegated to the waste bin, and the marijuana campaign continues as the same anti-intellectual exercise as it was before the objective research findings.

As the Baan Commission in Holland and the Wootton Commission in England show, few other civilized countries establish independent research bodies, endow them with sizeable staffs and budgets, empower them to conduct wide-ranging, nonpartisan research, mandate courageous and independent inquiry, and then, when the results arrive, castigate the researchers for reaching conclusions contradicting the comfort of the status quo.

Beyond its anti-intellectualism, this pattern of official rejection of officially sponsored research puts political self-image ahead of national enlightenment. Rejection of impartial scientific findings transforms political leadership into an oxymoron, for such head-in-the-sand practices prolong the citizenry's dogmatic slumber. Politicians enhance their careers on the backs of citizen ignorance. Government officials pander to public opinion rather than shaping it with accurate information. This new "dark age" rewards official pandering at the expense of an unenlightened citizenry. Worse than teaching to the slowest students in the class, this kind of know-nothing dogmatism encourages the unenlightened to stay that way.

Near the peak of this disdain of correct information, independent research itself becomes feared. After Surgeon General Joycelyn Elders suggested studying even modest marijuana legalization, President Clinton declared his personal opposition to any new marijuana research. His fear was that any more independent research results would upset his politically useful but erroneous assumptions about pot. If the safest policy regarding ignorance is simply to perpetuate it, the comfort of the uninformed status quo becomes the arbiter of the acceptability of scientific research.

Drug policy abhors a vacuum. As they reject scientific research, officials seeking to buttress our ill-founded pot policy adopt paternalism, hysteria, and censorship of opposing views—witness Congress's surrender to Anslinger's parade of imagined horrors in the 1937 Tax Act hearings and the DEA's 1979 acquiescence to Keith Schuchard's medical fictions in *Parents, Peers and Pot*. Rejection of unwelcome research can also bring a related rejection of unwelcome legal findings—witness Congress's 1998 refusal to honor the District of Columbia's medical marijuana initiative vote and DEA administrator John Lawn's 1988 reversal of Judge Francis Young's courtroom findings about pot's health benefits. Unlike most enlightened countries, our pot warriors discount information able to enlighten the electorate while controlling information in a way to serve political popularity, with the citizenry's enlightenment subordinate to political gain.

COUNTERCULTURAL CRIME

The official war on pot shows repugnance at the cultural by-products of its users: long hair, hippie lifestyles, jazz, pacifism, and a closet full of other antiestablishment discomforts annoying the religious and cultural right. For Commissioner Anslinger, the worst of pot's threats resided not in its medical harm but in its assumed incentive to the violence, jazz, and sexual misconduct he generously ascribed to pot-using minorities, especially Hispanics, blacks, and other "foreigners." His greatest fear, it turns out, resided not in marijuana but in "The Other."

More subtly perhaps, but certainly no less patriotically, Presidents Nixon and Reagan and their drug czars repeatedly denounced marijuana's assumed ability to spawn antiauthoritarian, unpatriotic free-thinking liberals—"all the Jews," Nixon collectively termed them. Similar consternation over pot's cultural mystique appears in the *National Review* articles by Hart and Oberdeck cited in Chapter 2 and in the repeated diatribes of drug czars Turner, Bennett, McCaffrey, and Walters about marijuana's imagined propensity to unravel the nation's entire moral fabric.

Unable to change weed users' music, dress, politics, bathing, or hair practices, and faced with the First Amendment Attorney General John Mitchell found so annoying, reefer warriors have sought to combat the subtleties of cultural dissonance with the bluntness of harsh penal prohibitions. Morality can react to the motivation of harsh punishment—witness the doctrine of Hell. In his tenure with the first President Bush, Bill Bennett liked to say that coercion could provide the best route to moral virtue. In his denunciations of disheveled hippie lifestyles, pot becomes seen as directly causing national disarray and thus deserving such hellish sanctions. Politicians aiming to shore up establishment values readily conclude that pot users must be dissuaded by force or, failing that, in Bill Bennett's words, by "beheading." The possibility of confusing cause and effect escapes these policy makers. They perhaps forget the alliance of this philosophy with the Lenin who wrote: "With an iron fist we will lead humanity to happiness."[2]

An unintended consequence of official pot hysteria soon appears: the canonization of deviance. The scorned deviants now become empowered to profess to see through government propaganda. In liberal quarters, the pot crusade has resulted in encouraging the one central feature its warriors wish to exorcise: the unpatriotic, antigovernment, long-haired, free-thinking liberal lifestyle. The marijuana crusade boomerangs when it legitimizes deviance by enrolling articulate potheads in the sainted company of nonconformists like Henry David Thoreau and Martin Luther

King Jr.—thinkers who also rallied the country away from status quo repression and toward openness to change.

In youthful watering holes, pot thus has become a powerful rallying symbol for antigovernment attitudes. Jerry Rubin acknowledged it squarely in his 1970 speech at the University of Virginia: smoking pot, he then boasted, makes the smoker "an enemy of society," neither curse nor shame but, instead, the badge of honor of a percipient critic staring down government paternalism. In 1970, President Johnson's commission on campus unrest found that pot had then created a mocking counterculture on college campuses that, by the millennium, had spread beyond the campus to mainstream America. It is still there and increasingly clothed like an angry Old Testament prophet denouncing government proclamations of doom.

If forbidden fruit tastes better precisely because it is forbidden, the more it is forbidden, the more nonconformists sing about its charms. The marijuana war has bred a new generation of antigovernment music, as the 2001 top radio hit "Because I Got High." The song appeared on the sound track of the movie *Jay and Silent Bob Strike Back* and on Afroman's 2001 hit album.[3] Thanks to the pot counterculture, the comedians Cheech and Chong move to the forefront of a new stoner culture unmasking official nonsense. Forbidden fruit can be sung about in ways more dissonant than ever heard in Anslinger's detested jazz. For the skeptical counterculture, pot has become a musical *felix culpa* (fortunate fault).

ENFORCEMENT LIKE "BEING STRUCK BY LIGHTNING"

Unlike serious crimes such as murder and robbery that police pursue with something approaching uniformity, pot prohibitions reveal highly uneven enforcement to the point of rank caprice. The presence of statutory prohibitions in law books hardly ensures their enforcement. As the third chapter suggests, local officials typically make their own decisions about whether marijuana deserves time, money, and diversion of resources. Many officials enforce pot laws only for open and notorious flaunting, with the result that discreet violations escape attention. As west coast communities discovered in federal raids in 2003, cannabis buyers' clubs supported by some local governments within a state thrive while other clubs in other parts of the same state suffer law enforcement raids.

The caprice of law enforcement extends to persons and relationships as well as to places. Favored classes of users appear by default rather than design. Especially notable is the cabal of exempt high-profile politicians using reefer with impunity—a bulging group populated by Presidents Clinton and George W. Bush, plus Al Gore, Clarence Thomas, Newt Gingrich, Bruce Babbitt, Donna Shalala, Bill Bradley, and a host of other high officials whose acknowledged marijuana indiscretions have escaped the penal results and raids inflicted on less famous users.

Another favored group in this enforcement checkerboard includes politically connected family offenders whose pot use has merited mitigated punishment—scions and icons of high-profile politicians like Richard Riley, Dan Burton, and former Secretary of State James Baker. Another exempt group consists of the artistic icons before whom the criminal law cowers: professional athletes like the pot users on the 2002 New York Mets and high-profile divas like singer Whitney Houston who, when found at a Hawaii airport with pot and told to stay put, simply boarded her plane and flew away from the problem.

Another capricious group includes political hypocrites who say one thing regarding marijuana and do another, well exemplified by Commissioner Anslinger's pot warnings while simultaneously providing morphine—far more dangerous than pot—to his addicted friend Senator Joseph McCarthy. In the same den of hypocrisy sits virtue czar Bill Bennett and his $8 million gambling habit, an addiction seemingly greater than that of many pot addicts he consigned to jail time. This same gallery also includes the smiling image of President Clinton arresting over four million pot users just before announcing at the end of his second term that pot should be decriminalized—small comfort to those thousands who, unlike the president, had the misfortune to have inhaled in earnest before decriminalization could take effect.[4]

Given this high-level caprice, the dregs of concerted pot enforcement fall arbitrarily on visible street corners randomly chosen by local enforcers. Arrests predominate in the parks, playgrounds, and streets of our inner cities, where struggling neighborhoods sacrifice their minorities to a punishment more privileged suburban users escape. Pot enforcement reveals one nation divisible by political geography and favoritism. What the Supreme Court once said about the likelihood of the death penalty applies equally to pot liability: It is as unpredictable as being struck by lightning. Perceptive citizens cannot avoid asking that if marijuana law is so haphazard and subject to whim, is the rest of the law the same?

FAILINGS OF LOGIC

The gateway theory constitutes a modern example of the classic Aristotelian fallacy of *post hoc ergo propter hoc*, the assumption that a preceding event causes whatever follows. The gateway theory asserts that reefer must be prohibited because it leads inescapably to hard drugs like heroin and cocaine.

Several things can be said about this gateway theory. The first is that, as indicated in the third chapter's discussion of the Columbia University gateway study, though some 17 percent of pot users have tried heroin or cocaine, the remaining 83 percent did not; that is, five of six did not pass through the gateway. The stepping-stone assertion has been debunked by every independent research body that has carefully considered it, from Nixon's 1972 marijuana commission through General McCaffrey's 1999 National Institute of Medicine study to the 2002 Rand study.

The gateway theory naively assumes that whatever precedes an evil causes it. Gateway advocates equate temporal precedence with causality. However, correlation does not constitute causality. If policy makers honestly implemented it, the gateway theory would require penalizing beer because it precedes hard liquor, and candy because it precedes cigarettes. All hard-drug addicts ate peanut butter and jelly sandwiches in their youth and, earlier, suckled their mother's milk, which by this logic must become the mother gateway to all drugs.

Apart from the logical fallacies, careful research does not support the gateway theory. The 1999 Institute of Medicine report found that of those who used marijuana, 75 percent never used any other illicit drug. The rates of hard-drug use relate more to their fashion status than to any connection to marijuana. In 1986, near the peak of the cocaine epidemic, 33 percent of high school seniors using marijuana also had tried cocaine, but by 1994 only 14 percent of pot users had progressed to cocaine.

Some drug warriors like Carleton Turner see marijuana acting on the brain similarly to cocaine and heroin by plugging the same receptors and thereby priming them for increased stimulation. But alcohol and many over-the-counter drugs cause this same result, often with a stronger impact both on the user and the user's companions. Yet no one seriously argues that tobacco leaves are the gateway to LSD or that Budweiser is the gateway to Chivas Regal or Lowenbrau the dark path to Jack Daniels.

"There is no evidence," concluded the 1998 Institute of Medicine report commissioned by the drug czar's own office, that marijuana serves as a stepping stone to hard drugs. The same result appears in the 2002 Rand Institute study showing that the hard-drug use can be fully explained without recourse to the gateway theory.

MISPLACED PRIORITIES

Invidious comparisons between pot on the one hand and alcohol and tobacco on the other create an Alice in Wonderland world of topsy-turvy priorities where the greater evil becomes the lesser and the lesser the greater. Alcohol and tobacco cause many times more harm to personal health, safety, and social cohesion than marijuana. To take only the latest of these consistent annual statistical comparisons:

Annual Causes of Deaths in the U.S.:
Tobacco: 430,700
Poor diet and overeating: 400,000
Alcohol: 110,640
Adverse reactions to prescription drugs: 32,000
Suicide: 30,575
Homicide: 18,272
Anti-inflammatory drugs such as aspirin: 7,600
Marijuana: 0
(*Time*, 22 March 2004, p. 19)

Pro-tobacco politicians like former Georgia Republican Representative Bob Barr cannot accept statistics such as these. But to an objective viewer our legal prohibitions are inconsistent with our drug harms. Anti-pot politicians simply will not ban alcohol or tobacco even though each generates harms vastly greater than reefer.

One explanation for the inconsistency, of course, lies in the embarrassing futility of any further alcohol prohibition—it has been tried, we well know, and it failed. Another lies in the myopia of tobacco enthusiasts like Barr who, for economic reasons, would rather exterminate pot than suffer the loss of one carcinogenic cigarette.

The alcohol and tobacco industries' generous donations to both major political parties calm any impulse to criminalize these drugs proportionate to their health threats. In 1998, Common Cause estimated that the alcohol industry distributed $8.6 million in PAC and soft money in the 1995–96 election cycle. Generosity from tobacco companies causes similar legislative paralysis. The tobacco industry promotes its drug so aggressively as to drown out the government's antismoking messages. Restrictions on minors are lax; they have at least as much free access to tobacco and alcohol as to marijuana.

Smoking appears in 21 percent of deaths involving heart disease and most deaths from lung disease. While cigarettes cause more than 400,000 deaths annually, pot has yet to cause a single one. A year before President Bush's 1989 contrived alarm about drug dealing directly across from the White House, the United States Surgeon General released studies showing that cigarettes addict upwards of 80 percent of lengthy users, while less than a third of those who try crack become addicted, compared to the very few who become addicted from marijuana. While the vast majority of pot users abandon marijuana by their early thirties, especially after marriage, the one drug that users abandon least in early adulthood is tobacco. Of those who smoked half a pack or more a day as high school seniors, seven of ten continued to smoke at age thirty-two.[5]

Our government's selective myopia about alcohol, tobacco, and pot betrays conscious disregard of these blatant inconsistencies. If alcohol and tobacco enjoy nearly free distribution despite their statistically more severe social and medical harms, it becomes an exercise in boundless imagination to discern how by those standards marijuana deserves any criminalization at all.

MEDICAL DOUBLESPEAK

The right-hand-not-knowing-what-the-left-hand-is-doing idiom squarely fits Washington's repeated denials of any medical benefit from marijuana. "Smoking is not medicine," General McCaffrey and John Walters repeatedly assert. But it *is* a medicine, and its medical utility emanates from the same federal government that also asserts the exact opposite.

The same government that issues repeated denials of pot's medical benefits conceived the Compassionate Investigational New Drug Program in 1975 to allow sick people to use government-grown and supplied marijuana precisely for its medical benefits. As many as twenty states, beginning with New York in 1980, followed this federal model to enact similar state medical marijuana programs. Al Gore's sister participated in the same approved government program in Tennessee in the 1980s. She received government-grown and -delivered marijuana to combat her cancer. The fact that in the last decade these government programs have forcibly declined in numbers of patients reflects only the first President Bush's embarrassment born of this inconsistency. The seven patients still receiving medical marijuana in 2004 testify not to any change in the government's recognition of pot's medical benefits but to this continuing inconsistency.

An honest inquiry into the authenticity of medical pot need not stop at the Compassionate User Program. Numerous government commissions have found medical benefit from marijuana, beginning with Nixon's 1972 marijuana commission, continuing with the 1982 National Academy of Science's Report, and most explicitly in the 1999 National Institute of

Medicine report. The last body found enough benefit in smoked marijuana to recommend marketing an inhaler to expedite THC directly to the lungs.

The same government that incarcerated some 21,000 pot possessors during the two Clinton terms previously approved, via its Food and Drug Administration, the prescription drug Marinol containing the same active THC found in marijuana. The government's condemnatory policy thus approximates right-eye, left-eye, dyslexia: The government denies the very medical benefits of the same THC approved by its own Food and Drug Administration's endorsement of Marinol and dronabinol. As the first President Bush said about the compassionate user program, it "sends the wrong message." But the entire pattern of government conduct regarding marijuana suggests that it is the government itself that is on the receiving end of its own wrong message.

STRONGER POT

One of the more pungent ironies of the past two decades' war on reefer lies in an unexpected counterpoint to eradication plans. Government efforts in the 1980s and 1990s to eradicate reefer, particularly in western states, nurtured a powerful new species now grown in safer national forests, private residences, backyard greenhouses, and in California's Emerald Triangle. Presidents Reagan and Bush deserve much of the credit for this new species. How it developed is a lesson in the unintended consequences of pot eradication.

Until the mid-1970s, almost all the pot used in the United States came from Mexico. Prior to the Reagan administration, the Mexican government humored our nation's demands for eradication by spraying Mexican reefer with the herbicide paraquat. As Mexican supplies diminished, a new market developed within the United States where American growers began producing an initially inferior product known as *cannabis sativa*, a low-potency plant susceptible to frost damage.

Foreign potheads soon introduced to this country a new strain known as *cannabis indica*, a more potent, freeze-resistant strain from central Asia. Soon entrepreneurial American geneticists achieved a blend of *sativa* and *indica*. This new blend, first grown outdoors, soon moved to the national forests and eventually into private homes and greenhouses as the Reagan pot war escalated. Indoors, secure from police observation and arrest, pot growers could use bright lights, powerful nutrients, and loving care to breed a more powerful strain of the weed than had existed under previous moderate enforcement.

Much of the innovative cultivation for the new strains came in California and the northwest. There growers succeeded in blending *sativa* and *indica* into hybrids with flowers as big as fists and concentrations of THC as high as 20 percent, roughly ten times the potency of the typical *sativa* prior to Reagan's reefer war. As the Reagan-Bush extermination policies hindered the market for Mexican pot, they simultaneously bred a more powerful homegrown hybrid harder to eradicate than Mexican weed. "Northern Lights," "Skunk #1," "Big Bud," and "California Orange" now sell as ironic symbols of our government's counterproductive extermination goals. The irony includes the fact that many of the most potent hybrids grow on federal lands dedicated to national forests and national parks where local law enforcement has no jurisdiction. Any two of the new strains could well be named for Presidents Reagan and Bush whose policies nursed them into being.

PETTY ISOLATIONISM

Conservative drug demonizers regularly excoriate other countries, notably Holland, for its liberal pot policies. These countries—which include not only Holland but England and most of western Europe and Canada—crafted their present tolerant pot policies not from a momentary political whim or from playing to their Religious Right but instead from simply following the recommendations of their nonpartisan research commissions. Holland's present policy toward marijuana, which makes small amounts available on request in licensed coffee shops, resulted from following the recommendations of the Baan Working Group in 1974. The Dutch adopted these recommendations two years after President Nixon condemned the more modest recommendations of his National Commission on Marijuana and Drug Abuse.

Canada's move to legalize pot in 2003 reflected a Dutch-like policy shift among other Western nations. Canada's legalization reveals a trend away from the reefer madness of demonizers like Anslinger toward a more liberal, practical view focusing on harm reduction and medical compassion. Canada is only the most recent player in this continuing international trend. Spain and Italy decriminalized marijuana in the 1990s. Portugal decriminalized it in 2001, Luxembourg and Belgium, the next year.

As of 2004, western European countries do not try, as we do, to stamp out all drug use, nor do they employ the heavy machinery of the criminal law, as we do, to exterminate pot. Instead, they follow a pattern of either limited legalization, as in Holland and Belgium, or harm reduction, as in France and Switzerland, so that the enforcement effort falls not on the causal user but, instead, on drug lords' large-scale importation. The Dutch again best illustrate this pattern. Amsterdam's famous coffee shops sell no hard drugs, avoid selling to minors, create no nuisances, possess no more than 500 grams (18 ounces) on the premises, and sell no more than five grams at a time. The Dutch have signed the 1988 UN convention that prevents total deregulation of pot.

Compared to Canada, Holland, and other European countries, including their drug and crime rates,[6] our nation's scorched-earth reefer policy strikes the rest of the world as petty and haughty. We display an insular cultural superiority as we profess a better and blunter course of penal repression for the same problems. The politically uncomfortable reality for us is that Holland, Belgium, Spain, Canada, and Jamaica, as of 2004, have seen no increase in pot use as a result of their moderated policies.[7]

Holland again offers the best example because it is the most researched. As of 2000, cannabis use among Dutch school kids ages ten to eighteen had fallen to the point that about one in five of this group used pot at some time in their lives, but less than a tenth used it in the prior month. In the United States, as of February 2001, 41 percent of tenth graders had smoked marijuana compared with 17 percent throughout all European countries. Young Dutch teens remain less likely to sample marijuana than their American peers. From 1992 to 1994, only 7.2 percent of Dutch youths between twelve and fifteen reported having tried pot, compared to 13 percent of Americans of the same age. Far fewer Dutch youth experiment with cocaine, showing the Dutch government's success in separating hard from soft drugs. To many Dutch citizens, our nation's reefer madness campaigns seem naive and destructive.[8]

Similar reforms have begun in England. In the fall of 2001, Stockport, England, became the home of England's first "pot café," providing marijuana cigarettes to chronically ill patrons in this Manchester suburb along the lines of the Dutch practice. It has fast become a battleground for Britain's growing pot smokers' rights movement. Saying that police should direct their efforts at hard drugs rather than at pot, Home Secretary David Plunkett simultaneously proposed that England downgrade pot to a Class C drug, from Class B, making pot possession no longer an arrestable offense.

Whether the Stockport experiment survives or not, England appears poised to follow the liberalization patterns of Canada and the European mainland. When that happens, the United States's policies toward marijuana will become totally isolated from the apolitical policies of the countries we like to think of as our allies.

CRYING WOLF

Our nation's marijuana campaign exemplifies the political science philosophy of famed political philosopher Leo Strauss. Teaching for many decades at the University of Chicago, Strauss developed the idea that political success is closely linked to citizen deception. He found that successful statesmen capitalize on people's vulnerabilities by relying on advisors to detect these vulnerabilities and whisper them in their ears, sometimes keeping the vulnerabilities secret even from their possessors. The advisor who whispers in the ear of the king is in this sense as important as the king, because through his advisors the king discovers how best to manipulate his subjects by playing on their vulnerabilities.

Strauss's idea, originating in Plato, is that politicians' success requires them to tell compelling lies to their citizenry as well as to each other. Deception becomes a powerful lever to increase power by discrediting citizen perceptions and suggesting vulnerabilities. The key to political success lies in identifying and exploiting citizen fears.

Strauss's ideas about the advantages of deception work well until the deceptions are discovered. Then the electorate becomes neurotic, divided between a sunny, whitewashed group of believers and an angry, betrayed group of unbelievers. Our nation's marijuana war has fostered this neurotic personality split. As national pot policy has usurped pragmatism, objectivity, logic, and raw statistics, its deceptions encourage skeptical citizens to lose credibility about other government policies.

As President Vaclav Havel found in the Czech Republic, loss of government credibility easily stimulates a theater of exaggeration and ridicule among skeptics. Our marijuana policies regularly illustrate government as theater of the absurd—witness President Bush's staged display in 1989 of confiscated dope on TV following his contrived drug bust across from the White House or drug czar Lee Brown peering through chopped down marijuana plants to warn a national TV audience that pot could send them to the emergency room—this last at a rate, we now know, far below the emergency admission rate for abused over-the-counter drugs like aspirin and sleeping pills.

Government-as-theater regularly sends triumphal messages to naïve listeners. When drug enforcers' triumphant press conferences appear only as staged propaganda, the skeptics in the electorate treat the rehearsed script as playacting rather than real life. The gullible listeners wind up missing truly serious messages that do deserve obedience, such as government warnings about alcohol, tobacco, abuse of prescription drugs, and a host of harmful eating habits.

Our government's past quarter-century's theatrical approach to pot reenacts the fable of the boy who cried wolf so repeatedly that no one responded when the real wolf appeared. Much of the literate and skeptical citizenry no longer believes the scripted hysteria coming from government drug czars. As of 2004, the nation's nine successful state medical marijuana initiatives and two legislative enactments show that a majority of ordinary citizens in these states (some quite conservative), have decided that, at least on the medical marijuana front, the federal government's warnings about the wolf at the door—or at overflowing emergency rooms—cannot be believed any longer.

With a conventional nondrug social issue where government policy clashes with social mores and medicine, corrective legislation eventually solves the disharmony. This obvious remedy appears too drastic to American lawmakers. Any moderation of the marijuana prohibition, no matter how timid, raises the specter of appearing soft on crime. The result is legislative paralysis. On drug issues lawmakers can move only on a one-way street, only toward more penal repression, not the reverse. The same political opportunism that generates this repression makes it difficult to roll back because two established conservative groups—law enforcement and the religious right—will not support change, the former on empire-retention grounds, the latter on grounds of moral salvation. Ironically, policymakers' inability to moderate policy excess in the legislative arena exemplifies the same "amotivational syndrome" drug warriors formerly attributed to potheads.

A CULTURE OF FEAR

The English poet Samuel Taylor Coleridge once wrote that in politics "what begins in fear ends in folly." Though Coleridge, an opium user, was not speaking of America's drug war, Richard Nixon probably was when he wrote "People react to fear, not love. They don't teach that in Sunday school but it's true."

Fear provides the clue for understanding the political motivations making our marijuana war beneficial for politicians. The marijuana war continues because it brings political benefits to fearmongers who can present themselves as heroic giants able to save the fearful public from a dreaded enemy. One of the clearest indicia of the messianic approach to drugs appears in the frequent, staged, self-laudatory press conferences after the Department of Justice or a drug czar succeed in confiscating great numbers of pot plants or cigarettes. Inconsistencies abound even for these messiah figures. The nation's pot war serves the interests of chest-thumping officials simultaneously wanting their virtues and vices—wanting, that is, to enjoy some harmful legal drugs like alcohol and tobacco while remaining able to inveigh against lower-class drugs like marijuana. Politicians thus can maintain their habits of tobacco, alcohol, and gambling while rescuing the electorate from trumped-up evils like marijuana. One need only recall the salvific proclamations from drug czar

Carleton Turner: "I am here to clean up society," and from czar John Walters in 2002, "It is my job to protect Americans from dangerous threats." Bill Bennett's *Body Count* engendered similar fear by proclaiming that "America's beleaguered cities are about to be victimized by a paradigm-shattering wave of ultra-violent, morally vacuous young people some call the 'superpredators'" who, the book added, contribute to the vast numbers of potheads admitted to emergency rooms.[9] Such doomsday predictions create a messianic image by generating votes from citizens seeking to rid themselves of government-sponsored fear.

As these quotations suggest, painting reefer as a feared enemy allows the political warrior to appear as the people's savior offering salvation from such a "Devil's Harvest." By creating fear around popular drugs like marijuana, politicians masquerade as Sir Galahads shielding the fearful public from an imagined evil. The greater the fear among the unenlightened, the more votes for the rescuer. Leo Strauss's politics of government deception are at work.

During Anslinger's reign, little opposition countered his assertions about reefer as the "killer weed." He spoke of moral threats in an era of feared foreigners unlike the WASP establishment. His bureau developed the idea that marijuana causes crime among foreigners and leads to harder drugs like cocaine and heroin. Countering fears of "The Other" requires criminal rather than civil sanctions, a "tough on drugs" policy that continues more than five decades after Anslinger to make this nation, as of 2004, the most prison prone of all the countries of the world.[10] Nixon and Reagan continued the culture of fear so aggressively that they portrayed the marijuana and drug problem as the greatest threat facing the country from 1986 to 1992.

President Clinton also discovered the advantages of fear. When his reelection prospects were in jeopardy, he upped the punitive ante against marijuana directly contrary to his personal beliefs, in order to avoid the accusation of being soft on drugs. So strident became his drug condemnation that ABC television devoted a March 1997 monthlong campaign—its "March Against Drugs"—in each of its major programs, including newscasts, to highlighting the horrors of all drugs, marijuana included. ABC News reporters bemoaned to prime-time audiences how teenagers could "get marijuana faster than a popsicle." The campaign culminated in a March 31 interview with President Clinton goading parents into warning their children to avoid all drugs, including the marijuana the president himself had smoked, without mention of the greater harms of the alcohol and tobacco these youngsters were indulging in in greater quantities.

For the half-century since Anslinger, successive American presidents and their drug czars, sometimes allied with media like ABC and the Hearst newspaper chain, have combined to fan the nation's fears about marijuana and to suppress objective information about its medicinal qualities. As marijuana becomes a public fear, the alarmed populace succumbs to a "rescue-me" mentality seeking succor from paternalist leaders. Politicians who rail against the "evil weed" offer themselves as saviors to a threatened people praying for relief not on their knees but in their ballot boxes. The marijuana prohibition thereby reenacts a secular Garden of Eden, with forbidden fruit causing banishment to a lesser place where evangelical, on-guard politicians rescue the fearful by stamping on the enemy. Marijuana has become the new apple, requiring a new exile into jails outside the nation's Eden.

WHAT TO DO?

> The Definition of insanity is doing the same old thing over and over and expecting a different result.
>
> Candidate Bill Clinton, July 1992

In the face of government inaction, citizens themselves may need to take into their own hands the future shape of marijuana policy. As political theorists from Herbert Marcuse to Eric Schlosser have shown, the engineers of social and penal change are rarely those at the top but rather those constituting the underground. Political repression comes from above; liberation comes from below.

A developing national consensus now favors the sick and dying and their caregivers whose messages about medical marijuana appear more compassionate and plausible than those coming from frowning, bony-fingered politicians. Yale law professor Steven Duke has observed that a public this incredulous about official predictions of doom may well conclude that the same government is also lying about other and greater harms like alcohol, tobacco, heroin, cocaine, guns, and unprotected sex.[11]

Our pot policy achieves no social good and causes much harm. It defines many good people as criminal, discriminates selectively against lower-class users, and denies pot's medical benefits to the sick, all in the name of a capricious demonizing whose enormous operatic costs increase the very problem it dramatises. Authoritarian lawmakers march out of step with the public as well as with empirical data. Polls consistently show that the public favors marijuana for health purposes. Many jurisdictions have now gone on record requiring marijuana enforcement to be the lowest police priority.

If they had political courage, federal authorities could begin marijuana reform by rescinding the prohibition on medical marijuana for ill patients and eliminating marijuana's status as a Schedule I drug. An enlightened marijuana policy could rest on nothing more sensational that the scientific research of repeated government bodies calling for more tolerance and openness. One of the first places to focus official attention is on the spreading incredulity of government-created moral panic. When a law is overextended to the point of disbelief, it becomes an enemy rather than a catalyst for consensus. The utility of our criminal law rests not in popular votes but in shared values. When upward of two-thirds of the electorate supports at least some recognition of medical marijuana, continued official prohibition generates only disrespect for serious official condemnations like highway speeding, gambling, tobacco, and alcohol abuse.

The policy choice need not be the stark alternatives of continued prohibition and wholesale legalization. A step-by-step process is available. We would begin a graduated process by legalizing medical marijuana across the board in federal as well as state jurisdictions. Then we could move to the legalization of small amounts of nonmedical pot for personal use, as has effectively been done for pornography in private homes. Assuming no disasters appear, we could advance to a policy that has worked well in Holland: allow pot to be bought, sold, and used in licensed coffee houses.

If no social disasters such as "male breasts" result from these graduated steps, outright legalization could be the next and final step, to put pot in the same broad category as our far more detrimental but legal drugs, alcohol and tobacco. If the camel's nose appears safely under this tent, we ought then to welcome the entire camel. In the process of doing so, we would abandon the upside-down process of first prohibiting a drug and then desperately trying afterward, at great financial and credibility costs, to discover a reason for doing so.

Whether politicians have the courage to inaugurate even such a modest graduated approach raises considerable doubt. If our officials are unable to lead rather than pander to votes from sunny pockets of conformity, there remains the remedy of another Boston tea party like that of Santa Cruz, California, and the initiative efforts described in earlier pages. When politicians will not make the right legislative decisions for reasons of protecting personal image, an enlightened electorate can only resort to the tools of initiative and referendum to fashion the changes that paralyze their leaders. As a first step in addressing this paralysis, changing the offices of judges and prosecutors from elective to appointive would greatly diminish their penchant for vote-pandering to gullible parts of the electorate.

Some lawmakers and enforcement officials have regularly described the medical marijuana movement as a "hoax." Like the boy who cried "wolf" in its absence, hoax mongers can find themselves done-in by the very hoaxes now clawing at their door. The poet Allen Ginsberg once put the paradox this way:

> When the citizens of this country see that such an old-time, taken-for-granted, flag-waving, reactionary truism of policy, press, and law as the "reefer menace" is in fact a creepy hoax, a scarecrow, a national scarecrow, a national hallucination emanating from the perverted brain of a single man (perhaps) such as Anslinger, what will they begin to think of the whole taken-for-granted public REALITY? What of the other issues filled with the same threatening hysteria? The specter of communism? Respect for the police and courts? Respect for the Treasury Department? If marijuana is a hoax, what is Money?[12]

NOTES

CHAPTER 1

1. NORML website, http://www.mapinc.org, last visited January 8, 2001. See also E. Schlosser, "More Reefer Madness," *Atlantic Monthly*, April 1997, p. 90.

2. *Arizona Republic*, May 24, 2000, p. B7.

3. Id. See also Drug Policy Alliance website, http://www.drugpolicy.org, last visited January 8, 2001.

4. E. Schlosser, "Reefer Madness," *Atlantic Monthly*, August 1994, at 46.

5. D. Kunitz, "On Drugs," *Harpers*, October 2001, at 92. For the DEA's prosecution of hemp users, see *The Public Interest*, January 30, 2002.

6. E. Schlosser, supra note 4 at 48.

7. Id. at 49.

8. Id. See also J. McWilliams, *The Protectors: Harry Anslinger and the Federal Bureau of Narcotics* (University of Delaware Press, 1990) and R. Bonnie and C. Whitebread, *The Marihuana Conviction* (Charlottesville: University Press of Virginia, 1974) at 100, 149.

9. H. Anslinger and F. Oursler, *The Murderers* (New York: Farrar, Straus, Cudahy, 1961) at 38.

10. Bonnie and Whitebread, supra note 8 at 143–144.

11. *The Murderers*, supra note 9 at 38.

12. "Marijuana or Indian Hemp and Its Preparations," issued by the International Narcotic Education Association (1936) at 3.

13. *The Murderers*, supra note 9 at 38. See also "Comments on Narcotic Drugs," Interim Report of the Joint Committee of the ABA-AMA on Narcotic Drugs, by the Federal Bureau of Narcotics, U.S. Treasury Department, 1958. See also J. Rublowsky, *The Stoned Age* (Putnam, N.Y., 1974) at 107. The paraphrased quotes are taken from "Marijuana Menaces Youth," *American Magazine*, March 1936, pp. 150–151, "Marijuana: Assassin of Youth," *American*

Magazine, July 1937, at 18, and "Marijuana as a Developer of Criminals," *American Journal of Police Science* 2 (1931) at 252 and 256.

14. *Chicago Herald Examiner* (1926), reprinted in M. Hayes and L. Bowery, "Marihuana," 23 *Journal of Criminal Law and Criminology* 1086–1094 (1932). See also *The Marihuana Conviction*, supra note 8 at 74. See also Drug Policy Alliance website, http://www.drugpolicy.org, last visited January 8, 2001.

15. Anslinger file "Arrests and Convictions," AP, box 8, file 10 of his personal collection. See also J. McWilliams, supra note 8 at 53.

16. E. Schlosser, supra note 1 at 90.

17. "Summary of the Licata case," 17 October 1933, AP, box 5, file "Scrapbook," vol. 7, 1931–1949.

18. *New York Times*, September 16, 1934, Sec. 4, p. 6.

19. "Marijuana or Indian Hemp," supra note 12 at 3.

20. *New York Daily Worker*, December 28, 1940, at B8.

21. Speech to Women's National Exposition of Arts and Industry, March, 1935, AP file "Speeches of HA," 1930–1938. See also M. Gray, *Drug Crazy* (New York: Routledge, 2000) at 77 and J. McWilliams, supra note 8 at 51.

22. *The Washington Herald*, 12 April 1937. See also *The Marihuana Conviction*, supra note 8 at 117.

23. Hearings, House of Representatives, Committee on Ways and Means, Control of Narcotics and Marijuana, 82nd Cong., lst sess., 1951, at 40.

24. Hearings, On Improvements in the Federal Criminal Code, Senate Judiciary Committee, S. Res. 67, 84th Cong., lst sess., Part I, 1955, at 17.

25. Circular Letter #324, from H.A. Anslinger, December 4, 1934, F.D. Roosevelt Library, box 19, file OVF 21–X.

26. National Committee on Law Observance and Enforcement, "Crime and the Foreign Born" (Washington, D.C.: Government Printing Office, 1931) at 154 et seq.

27. E. Schlosser, supra note 4 at 49. For the McCarthy information, see T.C. Reeves, *The Life and Times of Joseph McCarthy: A Biography* (New York: Stein and Day, l982) at 671.

28. *Rocky Mt. News*, 27 September 1931.

29. C.H. Whitebread, "A History of Non-Medical Drugs," Speech to California Judges Association, 1995 conference. See also *The Marihuana Conviction*, supra note 8 at 29–39.

30. Letter from F. Baskette to Federal Bureau of Narcotics, 4 September 1936. AP, box 6, file "Clippings 1934–1939."

31. Bonnie and Whitehead, supra note 8, 34, 37.

32. "The Need for Narcotic Education," NBC Speech, 24 March 1936.

33. "Marijuana Users—Musicians, 1933–1937," AP, box 9, and text at p. 12.

34. Taxation of Marijuana, House of Representatives, Ways and Means Committee, Hearings, May 4, 1937, at 107–113.

35. House of Representatives, Ways and Means Committee, Hearings on Taxation of Marijuana on H.R. 6385, 75th Cong., lst sess., 1937, at 20.

36. Id at 6.

37. Id. See also *The Marihuana Conviction*, supra note 8 at 28.

38. Hearings, supra note 34 at 20.

39. Id, hearings of May 11, 1937, at 1–2.

40. Id.

41. J.M. Pholen, "The Marijuana Bugaboo," *Military Surgeon* 93 at 94–95 (1943).

42. "Sociological, Medical, Psychological and Pharmacological Studies by the Mayor's Committee on Marihuana," (The LaGuardia Report), in D. Soloman, *The Marijuana Papers* (New York: Signet, 1968) at 297–307.

43. Id.

44. H. Anslinger, "The Psychiatric Effects of Marijuana Intoxication," 101 *JAMA* (1943) at 212–213.

45. Robert Kampia and Chuck Thomas, Marijuana Policy Project Foundation, "How Can a State Legislature Enable Patients to Use Medicinal Marijuana Despite Federal Prohibition?" (1996). See also 21 U.S.C.A. Sec. 812(a)–(b) (West Supp. 1998). Congress established five schedules of controlled substances placing drugs in each schedule according to its potential for abuse and accepted medical use.

46. 21 U.S.C. Sec. 812(b)(1)(A)(1994).

47. Id. Sec. 812(b)(1)(B).

48. Id. Sec. 812(b)(1)(C).

49. See Kampia and Thomas, supra note 45 at 6.

50. D. Musto, *The American Disease* (New Haven: Yale University Press, 1973).

CHAPTER 2

1. President Kennedy's Ad Hoc Panel on Drug Abuse in 1962 concluded: "It is the opinion of the panel that the hazards of marijuana per se have been exaggerated and that long criminal sentences imposed on an occasional user or possessor of the drug are in poor social perspective." White House Conference on Narcotics and Drug Abuse, Progress Report, Washington, D.C., Government Printing Office, p. 286.

2. W.B. Eldridge, *Narcotics and the Law* (New York: New York University Press, 1962) at 140–141.

3. J. Himmelstein, *The Strange Career of Marijuana* (Westport, CT: Greenwood Press, 1983) at 145.

4. Giordano testimony before a subcommittee of the Committee on Appropriations, 90th Cong., 1st sess., 1967, at 484–485.

5. For use of pot by war protesters, see *Time*, October 10, 1970, quoting the President's Commission on Campus Unrest. See also D. Baum, *Smoke and Mirrors* (Boston: Little Brown, 1997) at 7.

6. CBS Evening News, August 6, 1970.

7. *Time*, March 12, 1965, at 49.

8. T. Humes, "The Crisis in Drugs," pamphlet, St. Francis College, Summer 1969, at 8–9.

9. C. Parks, "H. Anslinger, Distinguished Citizen," *Town and Gown*, September 1968 at 47.

10. P. Anderson, *High in America* (New York: Viking Press, 1981) at 54.

11. M. Mauer, "Why Are Our Tough Crime Policies So Popular?" 11 *Stan. L. and Policy* R. 9 (1999).

12. "Text of Nixon Message on Plan to Attack Drug Abuse," *Congressional Quarterly Almanac* 24 (1969) at 57A. See also K. Beckett, *Making Crime Pay* (New York: Oxford University Press, 1997) at 38.

13. Id.

14. S.K. Oberdeck, "Problems of Pot," *National Review*, June 1, 1971, at 597.

15. R. Nixon, *Richard Nixon* (New York: Simon & Schuster, 1978) 491.

16. *Newsweek*, September 7, 1970, at 22.

17. *New Yorker*, April 15, 2002, 43.

18. Presidential Commission on Campus Unrest, Government Printing Office, Washington, D.C., 1970 at 11.

19. Text of Nixon "Message on Drug Abuse," *Congressional Quarterly Almanac* 24 (1969) at 57A. Mitchell's speech is in Vital Speeches, June 15, 1970, and quoted at length in Baum, supra note 54 at 35.

20. R. Haldeman, *The Haldeman Diaries: Inside the White House* (New York: Putnam's Sons, 1994) at 291–292. See also Baum, supra note 5 at 54. See also "Nixon on Tape," *New Yorker*, April 15, 2002, at 43.

21. *Washington Post*, June 6, 1971.

22. *Washington Post*, June 8, 1971, at A1.

23. First Report of the National Commission on Marijuana and Drug Abuse, *Marijuana: A Signal of Misunderstanding* (Washington, D.C.: Government Printing Office, 1972), 132.

24. Press Conference, *Washington Post*, March 25, 1972, at A1.

25. *Santa Barbara News Press*, March 26, 1972.

26. *Philadelphia Bulletin*, March 23, 1972, at 3.

27. *Birmingham News*, March 23, 1972, at A1.

28. J. Hart, "Marijuana and the Counter Culture," *National Review*, December 8, 1972, at 1348.

29. *Washington Post* L1, March 1973, at A4, quoting an address of the president on crime and drug abuse, broadcast on radio from Camp David, October 15, 1972 (White House Press release of this date).

30. E. Schlosser, "Reefer Madness," *Atlantic Monthly*, August 1994, at 52. See also text infra at pp. 35–36.

31. M. Massing, *The Fix* (New York: Simon and Schuster, 1988) at 271.

32. "A Report to the President," White Paper on Drug Abuse, Domestic Council Drug Abuse Task Force, Washington, D.C., Government Printing Office, 1975, at 5.

33. Id.

34. "Drug Law Revision," *Congressional Quarterly Almanac* 32, 1977, at 41E.

35. Carter's presidential message, August 2, 1977, on file at the Carter Library and reported in the *Congressional Quarterly Almanac*, supra note 34. See also *The Fix*, supra note 31 at 142.

36. Hints of drug enforcement blackmail against Carter appear in *Politics Today*, May 1977.

37. Du Pont's original remarks appear in *U.S. News & World Report* interview, August 7, 1978. See also Baum, supra note 5 at 122. *The Fix*, supra note 31 at 156.

38. *The Fix* at 148.

39. *Washington Post*, July 21, 1978, at A9.

40. "Pot, Privacy and Power," *The New Republic*, August 5, 1978. See also Baum, supra note 5 at 126.

41. *New York Times*, November 27, 1978, at A1.

42. "White House Prepares War on Marijuana," *U.S. News & World Report*, May 21, 1978.

43. *The Fix*, supra note 31 at 150.

44. M. Manatt, *Parents, Peers, and Pot*, Department of Health, Education and Welfare, Washington D.C., 1978, 1979, at 1–24.

45. Johnston, O'Malley, and Bachman, "Monitoring the Future: National Survey of Drug Abuse," University of Michigan, Ann Arbor, 1978.

46. "Excessive use of tobacco" and similar attacks on tobacco appear in early Carter drafts on drug strategy, but these references are deleted by an unknown hand. The documents are on file at the Carter Library in Atlanta. See also Baum, supra note 5 at 97.

47. E. Sutherland, "The Diffusion of Sexual Psychopath Laws," 56 *American Journal of Sociology* (1950), 142, 148. K. Gantatz, *Crime in the Modern Mind*, 1–17 (1955).

48. W. Kaminer, "Federal Offense: The Politics of Crime Control," *Atlantic*, June 1994, at 102.

49. S. Hall, *The Road to Ruin* (London: Verso Press, 1988) at 17; D. Garland, *The Culture of Control* (Chicago: University of Chicago Press, 2000) at 10.

50. Id., Garland.

51. W.F. Smith speech to the National Press Club, October 22, 1981.

52. Public Papers of the Presidents of the United States, R. Reagan, January 1–July 31, 1982, p. 813.

53. "Remarks of the President," September 28, 1981, on file in the Reagan Library.

54. "Major Crime Package," *Congressional Quarterly Almanac*, 40, 213–214, 1984.

55. S. Wisotsky, *Beyond the War on Drugs* (Buffalo: Prometheus Books, 1980) at 97–100.

56. National Research Council, "An Analysis of Marijuana Policy," Washing-

ton, D.C., National Academy Press, 1982. See also "The Potshot That Back-fired," *Time,* July 19, 1982.

57. Radio address, October 2, 1982.

58. See Hanna Rosin, "The Return of Pot," *New Republic,* February 17, 1997, at 22–23.

59. See Drug Enforcement Administration, U.S. Department of Justice, at 25: "Building on a Tradition of Excellence," http://www.usdoj.gov/dea/agency/press.htm (last visited January 5, 1999).

60. Baum, supra note 5 at 260.

61. "Health Consequences of Marijuana," Testimony before the Senate Judiciary Committee, January 16–17, 1980, at 102–110.

62. C. Turner, "Marijuana Research and Problems: An Overview," *Pharmacy International,* May 1980.

63. D. Baum Interview with Carlton Turner, described in Baum, supra note 5 at 355.

64. *New York Times,* May 5, 1981, at A16.

65. "White House Stop Drug Use Program—Why the Emphasis Is on Marijuana," *Government Executive,* October 1982. See also Baum, supra note 5 at 154.

66. Interview, Baum and Carleton Turner, supra note 5 at 151.

67. *Time,* January 19, 1987.

68. R. Serrano, "Police Board Won't Probe Gates Furor," *Los Angeles Times,* September 19, 1990.

69. *The Fix,* supra note 31 at 164 (Carleton Turner interview).

70. J. Brady, "Heavy Smoking Called Disorder," *New York Times,* June 5, 1975, at 34.

71. "The Texas Mission," *Washington Post,* February 17, 1982, at C1.

72. *Government Executive,* supra note 65.

73. M. Tonry, *Sentencing Matters* (New York: Oxford Press, 1996) at 72.

74. E. Meese, speech to the International Chamber of Commerce, reported in the *New York Times,* August 8, 1985, at 6.

75. *Newsweek,* October 27, 1986, at 95.

76. *The Fix,* supra note 31 at 186. See also text infra at p. 136.

77. M. Pollan, *The Botany of Desire* (New York: Random House, 2001) at 126. See also E. Blumenstein and E. Nilsen, "Policing for Profit," 65 *University of Chicago Law Review* 35 (1998) on forfeiture excesses.

78. Id. (Pollan).

79. *The Fix,* supra note 31 at 189.

80. Id at 190. See also "Cocaine Assessment," Unified Intelligence Division, Drug Enforcement Administration, October 1992, App. B.

81. M. Helmke, "Quayle in Support of Taking a Look at Legalized Pot," *Indianapolis Star,* March 6, 1977.

82. *Congressional Quarterly Almanac,* 44, 46–75A, 1989.

83. Id.

84. *Public Papers of the Presidents* (Washington, D.C.: Government Printing Office, book I, 1989) at 3. See also Baum, supra note 5 at 288.

85. W. Bennett, *The Devaluing of America* (New York: Simon and Schuster, 1992) at 24, 94–95.

86. W. Bennett, "Should Drugs Be Legalized?" *Readers Digest*, March 1990.

87. Pollan, supra note 77 at 128.

88. *The Devaluing of America*, supra note 85 at 27, 94–95.

89. Baum, supra note 54 at 266.

90. "Drugs, Consequences and Confrontation," Bennett's maiden speech to the United Hebrew Congregation, Washington, D.C., May 3, 1989.

91. W. Bennett, *Body Count* (New York: Simon & Schuster, 1996) at 206.

92. *Devaluing of America*, supra note 85 at 101. See also Baum, supra note 5 at 221, 298. Student suspension from federal student loans is found in 20 USC 1091 (v) and (b).

93. Bennett admits this beheading story without apology in his *Devaluing of America*, supra note 85 at 116. By 1990, Bennett had an office staff of 130, with a budget of $16.5 million ("Martinez to follow Bennett as Drug Czar," *Congressional Quarterly Almanac*, 44 at 503 [1990]). Baum supra note 5 at 298.

94. Bennett, *Body Count*, supra note 91 at 74–75.

95. P. Reuter, "Hawks Ascendant: The Punitive Trend in Drug Policy," Rand Corp., Santa Monica, 1992, quoting the 1992 University of Michigan "Monitoring the Future" student survey.

96. Baum, supra note 5 at 265, 298, 309.

97. W. Bennett, *The Book of Virtues* (New York: Simon & Schuster, 1993) at 107.

98. W. Bennett, *The Moral Compass* (New York: Simon & Schuster, 1999), at 363 ("Easing the Path").

99. N. Lewis, "Bennett to Resign as Chief of U.S. Anti-Drug Effort," *New York Times,* November 8, 1990, at A26.

100. Baum, supra note 5 at pp. 1–2.

101. E. Bertram et al., *Drug War Politics* (Berkeley: University of California Press, 1996) at 116.

102. Memo to U.S. Attorneys in U.S. Attorney Bulletin, Executive Office for U.S. Attorneys, Department of Justice, Washington, D.C., 1990, at 180.

103. M. Kramer, "Clinton's Drug Policy Is a Bust," *Time,* December 20, 1993, p. 35.

104. "Monitoring the Future," Annual Survey of Student Attitudes, University of Michigan, Ann Arbor, released December 18, 1993.

105. Id., for the year 1995, released December 15, 1995.

106. Press Release, U.S. House of Representatives, Committee on Government Programs, February 14, 1995.

107. CNN News, January 3, 1994.

108. "Monitoring the Future," supra note 104 at 7.

109. "Drug War Politics," Office of Drug Policy, Budget Summary, Washington, D.C., 1994, at 121, 132.

110. C. Connell, "Legalizing Drugs Would Reduce Crime Rate: Elders," Associated Press, December 7, 1993, and *L.A. Times*, December 10, 1994.

111. R. Sanchez, "Clinton Drug Chief Targets Marijuana," *Washington Post*, July 18, 1995, at A3.

112. M. Kramer, "Clinton's Drug Policy," *Time*, December 20, 1993.

113. J. Bennett and T. DiLorenzo, *Official Lies* (Alexandria, VA: Groom Books, 1992) at 241.

114. "Adolescent Drug Prevention Policy Recommendations," National Drug Control Policy Office, Washington, D.C., July 27, 1994.

115. J. Bovard, *Feeling Your Pain* (New York: St. Martins Press, 2000) at 86–107.

116. See Michael Tonry, *Malign Neglect: Race, Crime, and Punishment in America* 116–23 (1995); see also Eric Blumenson and Eval Nilsen, "Policing for Profit: The Drug War's Hidden Economic Agenda," 65 *University of Chicago Law Review* 35 (1998). As of 2002, we annually spend $15 billion in federal funds and $33 billion in state and local funds to finance [the war on drugs]. Id. at 36–37 (footnotes omitted). In 1995, there were almost 1.5 million drug arrests, of which 500,000 were for marijuana possession, and, as of 2002, nearly 60 percent of federal prisoners were incarcerated for drug offenses.

117. "In Drug War, Fantasy Beats Reality," *Chicago Tribune*, July 25, 1998, and K. Zeese, "Gen. McCaffrey's History of Misinformation," *Drug Scene Weekly*, October 15, 1999. See also C. Reinarman, "Why Dutch Drug Policy Threatens the U.S.," *Het Parool*, July 30, 1998.

118. Bovard, supra note 115 at 107.

119. *Washington Times*, July 15, 1998, A4.

120. See D. Cancar, "Suppressed Study Showed Marijuana Safer than Booze," *Cincinnati Enquirer*, March 8, 1998, as well as Bovard, supra note 115 at 88.

121. Department of Justice, Uniform Crime Reports (1999).

122. D. Broder, "Drug War Needs New Thinking," *Arizona Republic*, August 28, 2001, at B7.

123. *New York Times*, January 7, 2001, showing a young male of high school age saying: "I usually get stoned at school, after soccer practice, before piano lessons or at my friend's house."

124. Bovard, supra note 115. M. Earleywine, *Understanding Marijuana* (New York: Oxford, 2002) at 235.

125. "Cocaine Sentencing—Still Unjust" (editorial), *New York Times*, November 5, 1995, at A14.

126. N. Kristoff, "George Bush Used Drugs to '74," National Public Radio "Fresh Air," August 1, 2000. See also B. Press, "Was George Bush AWOL?" [to avoid military drug testing], World Net Commentary, February 6, 2004.

127. *Body Count*, supra note 91 at 155, 186.

128. Id. See also P. Stark, "Increased Regulations of Prescription Drugs Is Necessary," in D. Bender and B. Leone, *Drug Abuse: Opposing Viewpoints* (San Diego: Greenhaven, 1994) pp. 142–149.

129. *Weekly Standard*, March 5, 2001, p. 1.

130. CNN Interview, January 17, 2001; D. Broder, "DEA Marijuana Madness," *Washington Post*, November 11, 2000. See also A. Sullivan, "Nanny in Chief," *Time*, Februry 2, 2004.

131. W. Raspberry, "Likely Drug Czar Is Another Retread with Old Ideas," *Arizona Republic*, May 1, 2001, B7.

132. *Atlantic*, March 2004 at 50. See also R. Liccardo Pacula and Beau Kilmer, "Marijuana and Crime: Is There a Connection beyond Prohibition?" National Bureau of Economic Research, 2003.

133. M. Earleywine, *Understanding Marijuana* (New York: Oxford University Press, 2002) at 211 and *New Scientist*, March 19, 2002, reporting that a single glass of wine impairs driving more than smoking a joint.

134. See "Nanny in Chief," supra note 130. See also S. Talvi, "Reefer Madness Redux," *The Nation*, April 9, 2003.

135. Earleywine, supra note 133 at 227.

136. Id.

CHAPTER 3

1. R. MacCour and P. Reuter, *Drug War Heresies* (New York: Cambridge University Press, 2001) at 95, 305, 326. M. Earleywine, *Understanding Marijuana* (New York: Oxford, 2002) at 234–235.

2. E. Nadelmann, "Commonsense Drug Policy," 77 *Foreign Affairs* 111, 122 (January–February 1998). Baum, *Smoke and Mirrors* (Boston: Little Brown, 1997) at 223.

3. Earleywine, supra note 1 at 225.

4. Ariz. Rev. Stat. section 13-1105. Cf. also E. Schlosser, "Reefer Madness," *Atlantic Monthly*, August 1994, at 54.

5. E. Schlosser, "The Politics of Pot," *Rolling Stone*, March 4, 1999, at 47–52 and his *Reefer Madness* (New York: Houghlin Mufflin, 2003) at 50.

6. Id. at 55.

7. M. Frankel, *Criminal Sentences: Law without Order* (New York: Hill and Wang, 1972) at 3.

8. M. Mauer, *The Race to Incarcerate* (New York: New Press, 1999) at 134.

9. MacCour and Reuter, supra note 1 at 114.

10. *Arizona Republic*, July 2, 2000 at J1.

11. MacCour and Reuter, supra note 1 at 305, 326. Earleywine, supra note 1 at 234–235.

12. Baum, supra note 2 at 223.

13. M. Aldrich, T. Mikuriya, *Journal of Psychoactive Drugs*, Vol. 20 (January–March, 1988). See also J. Torruella, "One Judge's Attempt at a Rational Discussion of the So-Called War on Drugs," 6 *Public Interest Law Journal*, 1, 23 (1996). See also *Drug War Heresies*, supra note 1 at 303. See also text, infra, at pp. 146–147.

14. M. Lynch, "Battlefield Conversions," *Reason*, January 2002, at 39.

15. "Anti-Drug Misfire," *Christian Science Monitor*, May 18, 2001, at 10.

More than 120,000 students have been denied loans for drug-related convictions as of 2004, according to the Marijuana Policy Project Press Release of 13 February 2004.

16. *Drug War Heresies*, supra note 1 at 114.

17. Editorial, "A Bad Case of Déjà Vu," *New Scientist*, July 5, 1997, at 3. See also E. Schlosser, supra note 4 at 96.

18. Bovard, *Feeling Your Pain* (New York: St. Martins Press, 2000) at 103–104.

19. Id.

20. E. Schlosser, "The Politics of Pot," *Rolling Stone*, March 4, 1999, at 47–52 and his *Reefer Madness* (New York: Houghton Miffling, 2003) at 52–53.

21. Id., "The Politics," at 47–52.

22. M. Helmke, "Quayle in Support of Taking a Look at Legalized Pot," *Indianapolis Star*, March 6, 1977.

23. "Gingrich on Drug Dealers," *New York Times*, 15 July 1995. See also E. Schlosser, "More Reefer Madness," *Atlantic Monthly*, April 1997, p. 90.

24. "NBA's Uncontrolled Substance Abuse Policy," *New York Times*, October 26, 1997, p. A26.

25. Id.

26. *New York Times*, February 7, 2000, p. A1.

27. *New Yorker*, October 7, 2002 at 41.

28. "Reefer Madness," NORML website, May 6, 2003.

29. U.S. Sentencing Commission, Washington, D.C., 1998.

30. United States Sentencing Commission, 1997 Data file OPAF (1997). More than 25 percent of the 38.7 percent were marijuana-related cases. Id.

31. Id. See also Schlosser, supra note 23 at 92.

32. *Time*, April 6, 1998, p. 22.

33. *Arizona Republic*, June 20, 2001 at A11.

34. E. Nadelmann, "Commonsense Drug Policy," note 2 at 122.

35. J.W. Shenk, "America's Altered States," *Harpers*, May 1999, at 47.

36. *Time*, December 9, 1996, at 29.

37. Id.

38. *New York Times*, December 20, 1996, at B12.

39. J. Himmelstein, *The Strange Career of Marijuana* (Westport, CT: Greenwood Press, 1983) at 85.

40. W. Bennett, *Body Count* (New York: Simon & Schuster, 1996) at 164.

41. C. Wren, "Phantom Numbers Haunt the War on Drugs," *New York Times*, April 20, 1997, at 4E.

42. *The Economist*, July 28, 2000, at 9.

43. *New York Times*, April 20, 1997, p. E4. See also Office of National Drug Control Policy, Drugs and Crime Data, Drug Use Trends, June 1995 at p. 3.

44. Bennett, supra note 40 at pp. 43–47.

45. Id.

46. Earleywine, supra note 1 at 64.

47. P. Reuter and M. Kleiman, "Risks and Prices: An Economic Analysis of

Drug Enforcement," in N. Morris and M. Tonry (eds.), *Crime and Justice, Annual Review* (Chicago: University of Chicago Press, 1986) at 289–340.

48. "America's War on Marijuana," *Frontline*, PBS, April 28, 1998. See also "Marijuana's Mellow Image," *New York Times*, May 19, 2001, at A1.

49. Schlosser, "Reefer Madness," *Atlantic Monthly*, April 1997 at 46, and *Reefer Madness*, supra note 20 at 35–36.

50. "California Expects Bumper Pot Crop," *Arizona Republic*, September 6, 2001, at A5.

51. "Marijuana: Canada Moves to Decriminalize Small Amounts," *Arizona Republic*, May 28, 2003 at A10.

52. J. Ostrowski, "Thinking about Drug Legalization," Cato Institute, Public Policy Series No. 121, May 25, 1999. See also "Cartels Take over California Pot Gardens," *Arizona Republic*, November 3, 2002, A20.

53. M. Earleywine, supra note 1 at 234–235.

CHAPTER 4

1. "Pot Effects," *Arizona Republic*, December 22, 1996, p. B8.

2. G. Nahas, *Keep off the Grass* (Middlebury, VT: Paul Erickson, 1990).

3. M. Gray, *Drug Crazy* (New York: Routledge, 2000) at 178.

4. A. Trebach, *The Great Drug War* (New York: MacMillan, 1987) at 126–127.

5. Id. See also Earleywine, *Understanding Marijuana* (New York: Oxford, 2002) at 50.

6. Id. See also J. MacDonald and G. Chesher, "The Human Toxicity of Marijuana: A Critique of a Review by Nahas and Latour," *Drug and Alcohol Review* 13 (1994) at 209–216.

7. G. Nahas, *Marijuana: Deceptive Weed* (New York: Raven Press, 1973) at 319–320.

8. H. Jonas and P. Lovinger, *The Marijuana Question and Science's Search for Answers* (New York: Dodd and Mead, 1985) at 193.

9. "Pot's Effects," *Arizona Republic*, December 22, 1996 at B8.

10. "Pharmacopia," *Esquire*, October 1997 at 134. A 1999 study in the American Journal of Epidemiology reported "no significant differences between heavy users, light users, and nonusers of cannabis," as summarized also in M. Gray, *Busted* (New York: Thunder's Mouth, 2002) at 223.

11. R. MacCour and P. Reuter, *Drug War Heresies* (New York: Cambridge University Press, 2001) at 352.

12. Id at 252–258. See also Earleywine, supra note 5 at 140.

13. "Pot's Effects," supra note 1.

14. See L. Grinspoon, and J.B. Bakalar, "Marijuana as Medicine: A plea for Reconsideration," 273 *JAMA* 1875, 1876 (1996). See also L. Grinspoon, "Whither Medical Marijuana?" 27 *Contemporary Drug Problems* 3 (2000). See also *Marijuana and Medicine: Assessing the Science Base* 240 (Janet E. Joy et al. eds., 1999).

15. L. Zimmer and J. Morgan, *Marijuana Myths, Marijuana Facts: A Review of the Scientific Evidence*, Drug Policy Alliance, 1997. See also Earleywine, supra note 5 at 195.

16. R. Ostrow, "Forty-eight Percent of Cancer Specialists in Study Would Prescribe Pot," *L.A. Times*, May 1, 1981, at A12.

17. In the Matter of Marijuana Rescheduling Petition #86–22, Opinion September 6, 1988, recommended ruling by ALJ (Drug Enforcement Administration).

18. M. Gray, supra note 3. For further details see text infra at pp. 101–102.

19. As reported in *Arizona Republic*, October 27, 1997. See also Earleywine, supra note 5 at 95.

20. Id.

21. In the Matter of Marijuana Rescheduling Petition, Drug Enforcement Administration, Docket No. 86-22, September 6, 1988 (Opinion, Recommended Ruling, Findings of Fact, Conclusions of Law and Decision of Administrative Law Judge Francis L. Young).

22. See Greg A. Bilz, "The Medical Use of Marijuana: The Politics of Medicine," 13 *Hamline J. Pub. L. & Pol'y* 117, 117 (1992) (citing Ronald J. Ostrow, supra note 16. See also Richard E. Doblin and M. Kleiman, "Marijuana as Antiemetic Medicine: A Survey of Oncologists' Experiences and Attitudes," 9 *Journal of Clinical Oncology* 1314 (1991); W. Leary, "U.S. Panel Urges Study of Medical Marijuana," *New York Times*, February 21, 1997, at A27.

23. Doblin and Kleiman, supra note 22.

24. Id.

25. D. Baum, *Smoke and Mirrors* (Boston: Little Brown, 1997) at 111.

26. M. Gray, supra note 3 at 177.

27. L. Grinspoon, *Marijuana, the Forbidden Medicine* (Harvard, 1993).

28. J. Shenk, "America's Altered States," *Harpers*, May 1999, at 40.

29. Quoted in E. Schlosser, "Reefer Madness," *Atlantic Monthly*, August 1994, at 48.

30. "Deglamorizing Cannabis," (editorial) *Lancet* 346, at 8985 (1995). See also to same effect *Lancet*, November 14, 1998.

31. "Marijuana Successfully Treats Tourette's Syndrome," NORML Press Release, March 11, 1999, and Susan Gilbert, "Health Watch: Marijuana and Strokes," *New York Times*, July 28, 1998.

32. "Cannabis Helps MS Sufferers," BBC Online, March 2, 2000. Similar research shows beneficial effects on Parkinson's Disease, Drug Policy Alliance, Newsletter, November 14, 2002.

33. Doblin and Kleiman, supra note 22. To the same effect, see "Marijuana as Antiemetic Medicine: A Survey of Oncologists," summarized in *Washington Post*, June 22, 1991.

34. M. Pollan, *The Botany of Desire* (New York: Random House, 2001) at 153–154.

35. Editorial, *National Review*, August 20, 2001, at 38.

36. Drug Policy Alliance Newsletter, November 14, 2002, at 7.

37. *Lancet*, supra note 30.

38. E. Schlosser, "Politics of Pot," *Rolling Stone*, March 4, 1999, at 47–52.

39. *New Scientist*, March 19, 2002.

40. C. Williams, M. Peat, D. Crouch, "Drugs in fatally injured young male drivers," Public Health Reports, 100, 19–25.

41. J. Joy, S. Watson, J. Benson (Institute of Medicine), *Marijuana and Medicine: Assessing the Science Base* (Washington, D.C.: National Academy Press, 1999). For recent benefits to HIV patients, see "Marijuana Eases HIV-Related Nerve Pain," Reuters Health, February 12, 2004, at http://www.reuters.co.uk/newsarticle.jhtml, last visited that date.

42. Id.

43. Id.

44. *New York Times*, A19, March 19, 1999, summarizing the Institute of Medicine report and reaction.

45. National Institutes of Health, Announcement of the Department of Health and Human Services Guidance on Procedures for the Provision of Marijuana for Medical Research (1999) http://grants.nih.gov/grants/guide/notice-filesno99-091 (last visited March 29, 2000).

46. *New York Times* Online, December 15, 2001, at http://partners.nytimes.com, last visited that date.

47. Rand Institute News Release, December 2, 2002.

48. Addiction, December, 2002.

49. *Lancet*, supra note 30.

50. Earleywine, supra note 5 at 195.

51. Id.

CHAPTER 5

1. E. Schlosser, "More Reefer Madness," *Atlantic Monthly*, April 1997, p. 90.

2. J. Bovard, *Feeling Your Pain* (New York: St. Martins Press, 2000) at 88.

3. Codified at Cal. Health & Safety Code Sec. 11362.5 (b) (1) (a) (1999).

4. See White House Briefing conference, Fed. News Service, December 30, 1996.

5. "Prescription: Drugs," *Reason*, February 1997, at 36.

6. Schlosser, supra note 1 at 67–68.

7. Ariz. Rev. Stat. Ann. 13-901.01A and 41-1604.15.

8. J. Sperling, *Rebel with a Cause* (New York: John Wiley & Sons, 2000) at 205.

9. Goldwater Interview, *National Observer*, February 26, 1972.

10. E. Schlosser, "The Politics of Pot," *Rolling Stone*, March 4, 1999, at 48.

11. See "Clinton Opposes Rx Marijuana and Will Prosecute If Abuse Suspected," *Newsday*, December 31, 1996, at A20.

12. Id.

13. McCaffrey Interview with Carl Rochelle, CNN, December 30, 1996. See also J. Schaler (ed.), *Drugs* (New York: Prometheus Books, 1998) at 123.

14. *Los Angeles Times*, November 6, 1996, at A1.

15. "Prescription: Drugs," *Reason*, February 1997, at 36.

16. H. Hertzberg, "The Pot Perplex," *The New Yorker*, January 6, 1997, at 4.

17. "Dope Fiends," *Harpers*, November 2000 at 23–26, with permission.

18. G. Soros, "It's Time to Say No to Self-Destructive Prohibition," *Washington Post*, February 2, 1997.

19. "Prescription: Drugs," *Reason*, supra note 5.

20. In the Matter of Marijuana Rescheduling Petition, Drug Enforcement Administration, Docket No. 86-22, September 6, 1988 (Opinion, Recommended Ruling, Findings of Fact, Conclusions of Law and Decision of Administrative Law Judge Francis L. Young).

21. Id.

22. *Alliance for Cannabis Therapeutics v. Drug Enforcement Agency*, 15 F 3d 1131 (D.C. Cir. 1994).

23. "Study Says Drug Law Reduces Prison Costs," *Arizona Republic*, November 20, 2001, at B4.

CHAPTER 6

1. M. Gray, *Drug Crazy* (New York: Routledge, 2000) at 174.

2. J. Sperling, *Rebel With a Cause*, (New York: John Wiley & Sons, 2000) at 209.

3. *U.S. v. Oakland Cannabis Buyers' Cooperative*, 190 F3d 1109 (9th Cir 1999). See pp. 127–130.

4. "Tokin Gestures" *Willamette Week*, December 3, 1999.

5. *Arizona Republic*, March 22, 2000, p. A10.

6. "Don't Gut Marijuana Law," *The Seattle Times*, February 22, 1999, p. 1.

7. Washington State Medical Association facsimile from John Arveson to membership, February 2, 1999.

8. C. Ostrom, "Feds Clarify Medical Marijuana Guidelines: Reject Busting Patients," *The Seattle Times*, December 2, 1999, at B1.

9. *New York Times*, March 14, 2000, p. A12.

10. Marijuana Policy Project, "Rep. Barr's Move to Overturn D.C. Medical Marijuana Initiative," Press Release, September 20, 1999, http://www.mpp.org/nr092099.html, last visited March 29, 2000.

11. *Washington Post*, December 18, 2001.

12. *New York Times*, June 15, 2000, p. A12.

13. *Arizona Republic*, August 12, 2001, at A19.

14. Associated Press Interview, March 4, 2000.

15. S. Talvi, "Reefer Madness Redux," *The Nation*, April 9, 2003.

CHAPTER 7

1. See "Administration Response to Arizona Proposition 200 and California Proposition 215," 62 Fed. Reg. 6164, 6164–66 (1977) (notice signed Janu-

ary 15, 1997, by General Barry R. McCaffrey, Director, Office of National Drug Control Policy); Hearing on Examining the Newly Adopted Initiatives that Modify Arizona and California Law by Decriminalizing Drug Use in Some Circumstances Before the Senate Commision on the Judiciary, 104th Cong. 35 (1997) (prepared statement of Thomas A. Constantine, Administrator of the Drug Enforcement Administration); White House Briefing News Conference, Federal News Service, December 30, 1996; see also David G. Savage and Jennifer Warren, "U.S. Threatens Penalties If Doctors Prescribe Pot Drugs: Criminal Charges, Other Sanctions Are Possible, Officials Warn California and Arizona Physicians," *L.A. Times*, December 31, 1996, at A3; Drug Enforcement Administration, U.S. Department of Justice, Arizona Proposition 200 & California Proposition 2, http://www.usdoj.gov/dea/pubs/pressrel/pr961106.htm. (last visited January 5, 1999).

2. S. 40, 105th Cong. (1997).

3. H.R. Res. 372, 105th Cong. (1998); H.R. Rep. No. 105-451(I) (1998).

4. Herbert A. Sample, "Clinton May Punish Doctors Who Recommend Marijuana," *San Diego Union-Tribune*, December 30, 1996, at A1; Luz Villarreal, "Court Fight Looms on Pot Measure," *L.A. Daily News*, December 31, 1996, at N1.

5. See Grinspoon and Bakalar, "Marijuana as Medicine: A plea for Reconsideration," 273 *JAMA* 1875, 1876 (1996); "Supporters of Prop. 215 Smoldering: The Clinton Administration Is Accused of Intimidating Doctors," *Orange County Register*, December 31, 1996, at A4.

6. See 21 U.S.C. Sec. 844 (1998).

7. See id. Sec. 841(b)(1)(D).

8. See id. Sec. 841(b)(1)(B).

9. See Cal. Health & Safety Code Sec. 11362.5 (West Supp. 1998); see also Ariz. Rev. Stat. Ann. Sec. 13-3412.01 (West Supp. 1997).

10. Kampia and Thomas, Marijuana Policy Project Foundation, "How Can a State Legislature Enable Patients to Use Medicinal Marijuana Despite Federal Prohibition?" (1996) at 19.

11. Id.

12. See Ariz. Rev. Sta. Ann. Sec. 13-3412.01 (West 1997).

13. Cal. Health & Safety Code Sec. 11362.5(e)(West 1996).

14. See Grinspoon and Bakalar, supra note 5 at C1.

15. Id.

16. Id.

17. Oregon Medical Association guidelines adopted by the Oregon Medical Association, House of Delegates, April 25, 1999.

18. T. Monmaney and E. Bailey, "Journal Assails U.S. Stand on Medical Pot Use," *Los Angeles Times*, January 31, 1997, at B8.

19. "Federal Foolishness and Marijuana" (editorial), *New England Journal of Medicine*, January 1997. See also G. Martin, "Medical Journal Blasts U.S. on Marijuana for the Sick; Editorial Calls Drug Policy Misguided, *San Fransisco Chronicle*, January 30, 1997, at A1.

20. Id.

21. Id.

22. Monmaney and Bailey, supra note 18.

23. "Clinton Opposes Rx Marijuana and Will Prosecute If Abuse Suspected," *Newsday*, December 31, 1996, at A20; McCaffrey Interview with Carl Rochelle, CNN, December 30, 1996. See also J. Schaler (ed.), *Drugs* (New York: Prometheus Books, 1998) at 123 (describing the reaction of the federal government in response to the passage of the Compassionate Use Act and the *Conant* case).

24. Jodie Snyder, "Medical Journal Prescribes Pot," *Fresno Bee*, January 30, 1997, at A8.

25. Eric Brazil, "Drug Czar Won't Budge," *San Francisco Examiner*, February 9, 1997, at C2.

26. Christina Kent, "Feds: Prescribe Pot, Face Prosecution," *A.M. Med. News*, January 20, 1997, at 1. See also "Medical Marijuana," 30 McGeorge L R 1417 (1999).

27. *Conant et al v. McCaffrey et al*, C97-00139, 2000 WL 128174, fully published at 309 F 3d 629 (9th Cir 2000).

28. *U.S. v. Oakland Cannabis Buyers' Cooperative*, 190 F3d 1109 (9th Cir 1999).

29. Id. See also 21 USCA 885(d) (1970).

30. *U.S. v. Oakland Cannabis Buyers' Cooperative*, 190 F3d 1111 (9th Cir 1999).

31. *U.S. v. Randall*, No. 65923-75 (D.C. Superior Court, November 24, 1976) 104 Daily Wash. Law Record 2249 (D.C. Sup. Ct., Nov. 24, 1976) pp. 91–92.

32. *Jenks v. State*, 582 So 2d, 676, 679 (Fla D Ct App 1991).

33. Id. See also *U.S. v. Oakland Cannabis Buyers Cooperative* 532 U.S. 483 (2001) and *Raich v. Ashcroft* 352 F3d 1222 (9th Cir., 2003) (Controlled Substances Act inapplicable to cultivation of medical marijuana).

34. Id. See also *High Times*, October 2001, at 30.

35. *Time*, May 28, 2001, at 50.

36. D. Broder, "DEA Marijuana Madness," *Washington Post*, November 11, 2000, and Oakland Cannabis Buyers Cooperative, supra note 33.

37. *Conant et al v. Walters et al*, 309 F.3d 629 (2002) and *Raich*, supra note 33 (medical cultivation not for commercial use).

38. *Reason*, June 3, 2003, at 18.

39. Id.

40. *New Yorker*, April 14, 2003. See also *Reason*, supra note 38.

41. Common Sense for Drug Policy, at info@csdp.org., last visited May 18, 2001, reprinted in *Reason*, June 2001, at 30.

42. E. Schlosser, "More Reefer Madness," *Atlantic Monthly*, April 1997, p. 24–25. See also J. Bachman et al., *Drug Use in Young Adulthood* (Mahweh, N.J.: Lawrence Erlbaum, 1997).

43. CNS News Service, September 7, 2002

44. Id. See also National Law Journal, December 15, 2003 at 4 and *Reason*, supra note 38.

45. S. Talsi, "Reefer Madness," *The Nation*, April 9, 2003.

46. Dallas Morning News, quoted in D. Broder, "DEA Marijuana Madness," *Washington Post*, November 11, 2000.

CHAPTER 8

1. W. Bennett, *Body Count* (New York: Simon & Schuster, 1996) at 25–34.

2. *New Yorker*, April 14, 2003.

3. Common Sense for Drug Policy, at info@csdp.org.last visited May 18, 2001, reprinted in Reason, June, 2001, at 30.

4. "U.S. Leads World in Prison Population," *Arizona Republic*, June 8, 2003, at A14.

5. J. Bachman et al., *Drug Use in Young Adulthood* (Mahweh, NJ: Lawrence Erlbaum, 1997).

6. Heresies, R. MacCour and P. Reuter, *Drug War Heresies* (New York: Cambridge University Press, 2001) at 240, 26, 263 and Earleywine, Id.

7. Id.

8. Arizona Republic, February 21, 2001, at A6, and Tony Sheldon, "Cannabis Use Falls Among Dutch Youth," British Medical Journal, September 14, 2000, at 123. For U.S. and Dutch drug comparisons, see Royal Netherlands Embassy, "Drug Use Statistics: A Comparison" (2000), reporting 160 heroin addicts in the Netherlands and 430 per 100,000 in the U.S. That same report shows a rate of 1.8 murders per 100,000 in the Netherlands compared to 8.22 in the U.S. See also "U.S., Europe at Odds over Drug Problem," *Houston Chronicle*, November 12, 1995, at A34 and C. Reinarman, "Why Dutch Drug Policy Threatens the U.S.," in *Busted*, (New York: Thunder's Mouth, 2002) at 127.

9. Bennett, supra note 1 at 25–34.

10. "U.S. Leads World in Prison Population," *Arizona Republic*, June 8, 2003 at A14.

11. S. Duke, "Drug Prohibition: An Unnatural Disaster?" 27Conn. L. R. 38, 1995. See also S. Duke and A.C. Gross, *America's Longest War* (New York: Putnam and Sons, 1993).

12. A. Ginsberg, *The Deliberate Price: Selected Essays 1952–1955* (New York: Harper Collins, 2000), at 100.

BIBLIOGRAPHY

BOOKS

Anderson, P. *High in America*. New York: Viking Press, 1981.

Anslinger, H., and F. Oursler. *The Murderers*. New York: Farrar, Straus, Cudahy, 1961.

Baum, D. *Smoke and Mirrors*. Boston: Little Brown, 1996.

Beckett, K. *Making Crime Pay: Law and Order in Contemporary American Politics*. New York: Oxford University Press, 1997.

Bennett, J., and T. DiLorenzo. *Official Lies*. Alexandria, Va.: Groom Books, 1992.

Bennett, W. et al. *Body Count*. New York: Simon and Schuster, 1996.

Bennett, W. *The Moral Compass*. New York: Simon and Schuster, 1995.

Bennett, W. *The Book of Virtues*. New York: Simon and Schuster, 1993.

Bennett, W. *The Devaluing of America*. New York: Simon and Schuster, 1992.

Bertram, E., et al. *Drug War Politics*. Berkeley: University of California Press, 1996.

Bonnie, R., and C. Whitebread. *The Marihuana Conviction*. Charlottesville: University Press of Virginia, 1974.

Bovard, J. *Feeling Your Pain*. New York: St. Martin's Press, 2000.

Earleywine, M. *Understanding Marijuana: A New Look at the Scientific Evidence*. New York: Oxford University Press, 2002.

Eldridge, F. *Narcotics and the Law*. New York: New York University Press, 1962.

Frankel, M. *Criminal Sentences: Law without Order*. New York: Hill and Wang, 1972.

Garland, D. *The Culture of Control*. Chicago: University of Chicago Press, 2001.

Ginsberg, A. *The Deliberate Price: Selected Essays 1952–1955*. New York: Harper Collins, 2000.

Grinspoon, L. *Marijuana, Forbidden Medicine*. New Haven: Yale University Press, 1993.

Haldeman, R. *The Haldeman Diaries: Inside the White House.* New York: Putnam's Sons, 1994.

Himmelstein, J. *The Strange Career of Marijuana: Politics and Ideology of Drug Control.* Westport, Conn.: Greenwood Press, 1983.

Jonas, H., and P. Lovinger. *The Marijuana Question and Science's Search for Answers.* New York: Dodd and Mead, 1985.

Joy, J., S. Watson, and J. Benson. *Marijuana and Medicine: Assessing the Science Base.* (Institute of Medicine). Washington, D.C.: National Academy Press, 1999.

Joy, Janet E., et al. *Marijuana and Medicine: Assessing the Science Base.* Washington, D.C.: National Academy Press, 1999.

Kampia, Robert, and Chuck Thomas. *How Can a State Legislature Enable Patients to Use Medicinal Marijuana Despite Federal Prohibition?* Washington, D.C.: Marijuana Policy Project Foundation, 1996.

Lynch, T., ed. *After Prohibition: An Adult Approach to Drug Policies in the 21st Century.* Washington, D.C.: CATO Institute, 2000.

MacCour, R., and P. Reuter. *Drug War Heresies.* New York: Cambridge University Press, 2001.

Manatt, M. *Parents, Peers, and Pot.* Washington, D.C.: Dept. of Health, Education and Welfare, 1978, 1979.

Massing, M. *The Fix.* New York: Simon and Schuster, 1998.

Mauer, M. *The Race to Incarcerate.* New York: New Press, 1999.

McWilliams, J. *The Protectors: Harry Anslinger and the Federal Bureau of Narcotics.* Wilmington: University of Delaware Press, 1990.

Morris, N. and M. Tonry. *Crime and Justice, Annual Review.* Chicago: University of Chicago Press, 1986.

Musto, D. *The American Disease.* New Haven: Yale University Press, 1973.

Nahas, G. *Marijuana: Deceptive Weed.* New York: Raven Press, 1973.

Pollan, M. *The Botany of Desire.* New York: Random House, 2001.

Reeves, T.C. *The Life and Times of Joseph McCarthy: A Biography.* New York: Stein and Day, 1982.

Rublowsky, J. *The Stoned Age.* New York: Putnam, 1974.

Schaler, J. *Drugs: Should We Legalize, Decriminalize, or Deregulate?* New York: Prometheus Books, 1998.

Soloman, D. *The Marijuana Papers (The LaGuardia Report) Sociological, Medical, Psychological and Pharmacological Studies by the Mayor's Committee on Marihuana.* New York: Signet, 1968.

Sperling, J. *Rebel with a Cause.* New York: John Wiley & Sons, 2000.

Tonry, M. *Malign Neglect: Race, Crime, and Punishment in America.* New York: Oxford, 1995.

Tonry, M. *Sentencing Matters.* New York: Oxford, 1996.

Trebach, A. *The Great Drug War.* New York: MacMillan, 1987.

Wisotsky, S. *Beyond the War on Drugs.* Buffalo: Prometheus Books, 1960.

Zimmer, L., and J. Morgan. *Marijuana Myths, Marijuana Facts: A Review of the Scientific Evidence.* New York: Drug Policy Alliance, 1997.

MAGAZINES

Aldrich, M., and T. Mikuriya. "Marijuana." *Journal of Psychoactive Drugs* 20 (January–March 1988).

Anslinger, H. "The Psychiatric Effects of Marijuana Intoxication." *JAMA* 101 (1943).

"Anti-Drug Misfire." *Christian Science Monitor*, May 18, 2001.

Bennett, W. "Should Drugs Be Legalized?" *Readers Digest*, March 1990.

Bilz, Gregg A. "The Medical Use of Marijuana: The Politics of Medicine." *Hamline J. Pub. L. & Pol'y* 13 (1992).

Blumenson, Eric, and Eval Nilsen. "Policing for Profit: The Drug War's Hidden Economic Agenda." 65 *University of Chicago Law Review* 35 (1998).

"Clinton Opposes Rx Marijuana and Will Prosecute if Abuse Suspected." *Newsday*, December 31, 1996.

Doblin, R.E., and M.A. Kleiman. "Marijuana as Antiemetic Medicine: A Survey of Oncologists' Experiences and Attitudes." *Journal of Clinical Oncology* (1991).

"Dope Fiends." *Harpers*, November 2000, 23–26.

Duke, S. "Drug Prohibition: An Unnatural Disaster." *Connecticut Law Review* 27 (1995).

Editorial. "A Bad Case of Déjà vu." *New Scientist*, July 5, 1997.

Editorial. "Deglamorizing Cannabis." 346 *Lancet*, at 8985 (1995).

Editorial. "Federal Foolishness and Marijuana." *New England Journal of Medicine*, January 1997.

Editorial. *National Review*, August 20, 2001.

Goldwater Interview. *National Observer*, February 26, 1972.

Grinspoon, L., and J.B. Bakalar. "Marijuana as Medicine: A Plea for Reconsideration." 273 *JAMA* 1875, 1876 (1996).

Hart, J. "Marijuana and the Counter Culture." *National Review*, December 8, 1972.

"Hints of Drug Enforcement Blackmail against Carter." *Politics Today*, May, 1977.

Kaminer, W. "Federal Offense: The Politics of Crime Control." *Atlantic*, June 1994.

Kent, Christina. "Feds: Prescribe Pot, Face Prosecution." *AMA Medical News*, January 20, 1997.

Kramer, M. "Clinton's Drug Policy Is a Bust." *Time*, December 20, 1993.

Kunitz, D. "On Drugs." *Harpers*, October 2001.

Lynch, M. "Battlefield Conversions." *Reason*, January 2002.

MacDonald, S., and Chesher, G. "The Human Toxicity of Marijuana: A Critique of a Review by Nahas and Latour." *Drug and Alcohol Review* 13 (1994).

"Major Crime Package." *Congressional Quarterly Almanac*, 1984.

"Marijuana or Indian Hemp and Its Preparations," issued by the International Narcotic Education Association (1936) at 3.

Nadelmann, E. "Commonsense Drug Policy." 77 *Foreign Affairs* 111, 122 (January–February 1998).

Oberdeck, S.K. "Problems of Pot." *National Review*, June 1, 1971.

Ostrowski, J. "Thinking about Drug Legalization." Cato Institute, Public Policy Series No. 121, May 25, 1999.

"Parks, C. "H. Anslinger, Distinguished Citizen." *Town and Gown*, September 1968.

"Pharmacopia." *Esquire*, October 1997.

Pholen, J. M. "The Marijuana Bugaboo." *Military Surgeon*, 1943.

"Pot, Privacy and Power." *New Republic*, August 5, 1978.

"The Potshot That Backfired." *Time*, July 19, 1982.

"Prescription: Drugs." *Reason*, February 1997.

Reuter, P. "Hawks Ascendant: The Punitive Trend in Drug Policy." Rand Corporation, Santa Monica, 1992.

Rosin, Hanna. "The Return of Pot." *New Republic*, February 17, 1997, at 22–23.

Schlosser, E. "The Politics of Pot." *Rolling Stone*, March 4, 1999.

Schlosser, E. "Reefer Madness." *Atlantic Monthly*, August 1994.

Sheldon, T. "Cannabis Use Falls Among Dutch Youth." *British Medical Journal*, September 14, 2000.

Shenk, J. "America's Altered States." *Harpers*, May 1999.

Sutherland, E. "The Diffusion of Sexual Psychopath Laws." 56 *American Journal of Sociology* 142, 148, 1950.

"Text of Nixon Message on Plan to Attack Drug Abuse." *Congressional Quarterly Almanac* 24 (1969).

"Turner, C. "Marijuana Research and Problems, An Overview." *Pharmacy International*, May 1980.

"White House Prepares War on Marijuana." *U.S. News & World Report*, May 21, 1978.

"White House Stops Drug Use Program—Why the Emphasis Is on Marijuana." *Government Executive*, October 1982.

Zeese, K. "General McCaffrey's History of Misinformation." *Drug Scene Weekly*, October 15, 1999.

NEWS ARTICLES—PRIMARY SOURCES

Brady, J. "Heavy Smoking Called Disorder." *New York Times*, June 5, 1975, 34.

Brazil, E. "Drug Czar Won't Budge," *San Francisco Examiner*, February 9, 1997, at C2.

Broder, D. "DEA Marijuana Madness," *Washington Post*, November 11, 2001, at B7.

Broder, D. "Drug War Needs New Thinking." *Arizona Republic*, August 28, 2001, B7.

"California Expects Bumper Pot Crop." *Arizona Republic*, September 6, 2001, A5.

Cancar, D. "Suppressed Study Showed Marijuana Safer than Booze." *Cincinnati Enquirer*, March 8, 1998.

Chicago Herald Examiner (1926), reprinted in M. Hayes and L. Bowery, "Marihuana." 23 *Journal of Criminal Law and Criminology* 1086–1094 (1932).

"Don't Gut Marijuana Law," *The Seattle Times*, February 22, 1999, 1.

Editorial. "Cocaine Sentencing—Still Unjust." *New York Times*, November 5, 1995, A14.

Gilbert, Susan. "Health Watch: Marijuana and Strokes." *New York Times*, July 28, 1998.

"Gingrich on Drug Dealers." *New York Times*, July, 15 1995.

Helmke, M. "Quayle in Support of Taking a Look at Legalized Pot." *Indianapolis Star*, March 6, 1977.

Hertzberg, H. "The Pot Perplex." *The New Yorker*, January 6, 1997, 4.

"In Drug War, Fantasy Beats Reality." *Chicago Tribune*, July 25, 1998.

Leary, W. "U.S. Panel Urges Study of Medical Marijuana." *New York Times*, February 21, 1997, A27.

Lewis, N. "Bennett to Resign as Chief of U.S. Anti-Drug Effort." *New York Times*, November 8, 1990, A26.

"Marijuana's Mellow Image." *New York Times*, May 19, 2001, A1.

Martin, G. "Medical Journal Blasts U.S. on Marijuana for the Sick; Editorial Calls Drug Policy Misguided." *San Francisco Chronicle*, January 30, 1997, A1.

Monmaney, Terence, and Eric Bailey. "Journal Assails U.S. Stand on Medical Pot Use." *Los Angeles Times*, January 31, 1997, B8.

"NBA's Uncontrolled Substance Abuse Policy." *New York Times*, October 26, 1997, A26.

Nixon Press Conference. *Washington Post*, March 25, 1972, A1.

Ostrom, C. "Feds Clarify Medical Marijuana Guidelines: Reject Busting Patients," *Seattle Times*, December 2, 1999, B1.

Ostrow, R. "Forty-eight Percent of Cancer Specialists in Study Would Prescribe Pot." *Los Angeles Times*, May 1, 1981, A12.

"Pot Effects." *Arizona Republic*, December 22, 1996, B8.

Raspberry, William. "Likely Drug Czar Is Another Retread with Old Ideas." *Arizona Republic*, May 1, 2001, B7.

Sample, Herbert A. "Clinton May Punish Doctors Who Recommend Marijuana," *San Diego Union-Tribune*, December 30, 1996, A1.

Sanchez, R. "Clinton Drug Chief Targets Marijuana." *Washington Post*, July 18, 1995, A3.

Savage, David G., and Jennifer Warren. "U.S. Threatens Penalties If Doctors Prescribe Pot Drugs: Criminal Charges, Other Sanctions Are Possible, Officials Warn California and Arizona Physicians." *Los Angeles Times*, December 31, 1996, A3.

Serrano, R. "Police Board Won't Probe Gates Furor." *Los Angeles Times*, September 19, 1990.

Snyder, J. "Medical Journal Prescribes Pot." *Fresno Bee*, January 30, 1997, at A8.

Soros, G. "It's Time to Say No to Self-Destructive Prohibition." *Washington Post*, February 2, 1997.

"Study Says Drug Law Reduces Prison Costs." *Arizona Republic*, November 20, 2001, B4.

"Supporters of Prop. 215 Smoldering: The Clinton Administration Is Accused of Intimidating Doctors." *Orange County Register*, December 31, 1996, A4.

"The Texas Mission." *Washington Post*, February 17, 1982, C1.

"Tokin Gestures." *Willamette Week*, December 3, 1999.

"U.S. Europe at Odds over Drug Problem." *Houston Chronicle*, November 12, 1995, at A34.

Villarreal, Luz. "Court Fight Looms on Pot Measure." *L.A. Daily News*, December 31, 1996, N1.

Washington Post, 11 March 1973, at A4, quoting an address of the President on Crime and Drug Abuse, broadcast on radio from Camp David, October 15, 1972.

Wren, C. "Phantom Numbers Haunt the War on Drugs." *New York Times*, April 20, 1997.

NEWS ARTICLES—SECONDARY SOURCES

Arizona Republic, October 27, 1997.
Arizona Republic, March 22, 2000, A10.
Arizona Republic, May 2000, B7.
Arizona Republic, July 2, 2000, J1.
Arizona Republic, February 21, 2001 at A6.
Arizona Republic, June 20, 2001, A11.
Arizona Republic, August 12, 2001, at A19.
Birmingham News, March 23, 1972, A1.
The Economist, July 28, 2000, 9.
Los Angeles Times, November 6, 1996, A1.
New York Daily Worker, December 28, 1940, B8.
New York Times, September 16, 1934, sec. 4, p. 6.
New York Times, November 27, 1978, A1.
New York Times, May 5, 1981, A16.
New York Times, August 8, 1985, 6.
New York Times, December 20, 1996, B12.
New York Times, April 20, 1997, E4.
New York Times, March 19, 1999, A19.
New York Times, March 14, 2000, A12.
New York Times, June 15, 2000, A19.
New York Times, January 7, 2001.
New York Times, February 7, 2001, A1.
Philadelphia Bulletin, March 23, 1972, 3.
Rocky Mt. View, September 27, 1931.

Santa Barbara News Press, March 25, 1972, A1.
Washington Herald, April 12, 1937.
Washington Post, June 6, 1971.
Washington Post, June 8, 1971, A1.
Washington Post, July 21, 1978, A9.
Washington Post, December 18, 2001.

WEBSITES

"Cannabis Helps MS Sufferers," BBC Online, March 2, 2000.
Common Sense for Drug Policy, at info@csdp.org, last visited May 18, 2001.
Drug Enforcement Administration, U.S. Dept. of Justice, Arizona Proposition
    200 & California Proposition 2 (last visited January 5, 1999) http://
    www.usdoj.gov/dea/pubs/pressrel/pr961106.htm.
Drug Enforcement Administration, U.S. Dept. of Justice, at 25: "Building on a
    Tradition of Excellence," http://www.usdoj.gov/dea/agency/press.htm.
Drug Policy Alliance website, http:// www.drugpolicy.org.
Marijuana Policy Project, "Rep. Barr's Move to Overturn D.C. Medical
    Marijuana Initiative," Press Release, September 20, 1999, http://
    www.mpp.org/nr092099.html.
National Institutes of Health, Announcement of the Department of Health and
    Human Services Guidance on Procedures for the Provision of Marijuana
    for Medical Research (1999), http://grants.nih.gov/grants/guide/no-
    tice-files not99-091.
The New York Times Online, December 15, 2001, at http://partners.nytimes.com.

GOVERNMENTAL PUBLICATIONS AND COURT CASES

"Administration Response to Arizona Proposition 200 and California Proposi-
    tion 215," 62 Fed. Reg. 6164, 6164-66 (1977) (signed January 15, 1997,
    by General Barry R. McCaffrey, Director, Office of National Drug Con-
    trol Policy).
"Adolescent Drug Prevention Policy Recommendations." National Drug Con-
    trol Policy Office, Washington, D.C., July 27, 1994.
Alliance for Cannabis Therapeutics v. Drug Enforcement Agency, 15 F 3d 1131
    (D.C. Cir., 1994).
Ariz. Rev. Stat. Ann. 13-901.01A and 41-1604.15.
Ariz. Rev. Stat. Ann. Sec. 34-3412.01 (West 1997).
Ariz. Rev. Stat. Section 13-1105.
Cal. Health & Safety Code Sec. 11362.5(e) (West 1996).
Cal. Health & Safety Code Sec. 11362.5 (West Supp. 1998); see also Ariz. Rev.
    Stat. Ann. Sec. 13-3412.01 (West Supp. 1997).
Carter's presidential message, August 2, 1977, on file at the Carter Library.

"Cocaine Assessment." Unified Intelligence Division, Drug Enforcement Administration, October 1992, App B.

"Comments on Narcotic Drugs," Interim Report of the Joint Committee of the ABA-AMA on Narcotic Drugs, by the Federal Bureau of Narcotics, U.S. Treasury Department, 1958.

Conant et al. v. McCaffrey et al., 309 F 3d 629 (9th Cir. 2000)

Congressional Quarterly Almanac, 44, 46–75A, 1989.

Department of Justice, Uniform Crime Reports (1999).

"Drug Law Revision." *Congressional Quarterly Almanac* 32, 1977, at 41E.

"Drug War Politics." Office of Drug Policy, Budget Summary, Washington, D.C., 1994, at 121, 132.

Grinspoon, L. "Whither Medical Marijuana?" 27 *Contemp. Drug Probs* 3 (2000).

Hearing on Examining the Newly Adopted Initiatives that Modify Arizona and California Law by Decriminalizing Drug Use in Some Circumstances Before the Senate Committee on the Judiciary, 104th Cong. 35 (1997) (prepared statement of Thomas A. Constantine, Administrator of the Drug Enforcement Administration).

House of Representatives Ways and Means Committee. *Hearings on Taxation of Marijuana on H.R. 6385,* 75th Cong., 1st sess., 1937, at 20.

House of Representatives Ways and Means Committee. *Hearings on Control of Narcotics and Marijuana*, 82nd Cong., 1st sess., 1951, at 40.

H.R. Res. 372, 105th Cong. (1998); H.R. Rep. No. 105-451(I)(1998).

In the Matter of Marijuana Rescheduling Petition, Drug Enforcement Administration, Docket No. 86-22, September 6, 1988 (Opinion, Recommended Ruling, Findings of Fact, Conclusions of Law and Decision of Administrative Law Judge Francis L. Young).

In the Matter of Marijuana Rescheduling Petition #86-22, opinion September 6, 1988, recommended ruling by ALJ (Drug Enforcement Administration).

Jenks v. State, 582 So. 2d, 676,679 (Fla D.Ct. App. 1991).

"Medical Marijuana," 30 McGeorge L.R., 1999.

Memo to U.S. Attorneys in U.S. Attorney Bulletin, Executive Office for U.S. Attorneys, Department of Justice, Washington, D.C., 1990, at 180.

National Committee on Law Observance and Enforcement, "Crime and the Foreign Born" (Washington, D.C., Government Printing Office, 1931) at 154 et seq.

National Research Council, "An Analysis of Marijuana Policy" (Washington, D.C., National Academy Press, 1982).

Office of National Drug Control Policy, "Drugs and Crime Data, Drug Use Trends," June 1995 at p. 3.

Press Release, Public Information Office, Royal Netherlands Embassy "Drug Use Statistics: A Comparison" (2000).

Press Release, U.S. House of Representatives, Committee on Government Programs, February 14, 1995.

Public Papers of the Presidents of the United States, R. Reagan, January 1–July 31, 1982, p. 813.

Public Papers of the Presidents, Washington, D.C., Government Printing Office, book I, 1989, at 3.

"A Report to the President." White Paper on Drug Abuse, Domestic Council Drug Abuse Task Force, Washington, D.C., Government Printing Office, 1975, at 5.

Taxation of Marijuana, House of Representatives, Ways and Means Committee, Hearings, May 4, 1937 at 107–113.

Torruella, J. "One Judge's Attempt at a Rational Discussion of the So-Called War on Drugs." 6 *Public Interest Law Journal*, 1, 23 (1996).

United States Sentencing Commission, 1997 Data file OPAF (1997).

U.S. Senate Judiciary Committee. Hearings on Improvements in the Fed. Crim. Code, S. Res. 67, 84 Cong., 1st sess., Part I, 1955 at 17.

U.S. Sentencing Commission, Washington, 1998.

U. S. v. Oakland Cannabis Buyers' Cooperative, 190 F.3d 1109, 9th Cir., (1999).

U.S. v. Oakland Cannabis Buyers' Cooperative, 190 F3d 1111 (9th Cir., 1999 No. 65923-75 (D.C Superior Court, November 24, 1976).

White House Briefing News Conference, Federal News Service, December 30, 1996; S. 40, 105th Cong. (1997).

White House Briefing News Conference, Federal News Service, December 30, 1996.

White House Conference on Narcotics and Drug Abuse, Progress Report, Washington, D.C., Government Printing Office, p. 286.

MISCELLANEOUS

"America's War on Marijuana," *Frontline*, PBS, April 28, 1998.

Anslinger file, "Arrests and Convictions," AP, box 8, file 10 of his personal collection.

Associated Press Interview, March 4, 2000.

CBS Evening News, August 6, 1970.

Circular Letter #324, from H.A. Anslinger, December 4, 1934, F.D. Roosevelt Library, box 19, file OVF 21-X.

Connell, C. "Legalizing Drugs Would Reduce Crime Rate: Elders." Associated Press, December 7, 1993.

D. Baum Interview with Carlton Turner, described in Baum, *Smoke and Mirrors*, Boston: Little Brown, 1996.

"Drugs, Consequences and Confrontation." Bennett's maiden speech to the United Hebrew Congregation, Washington, D.C., May 3, 1989.

Du Pont's original remarks appear in *U.S. News and World Report* interview, August 7, 1978.

First Report of the National Commission on Marijuana and Drug Abuse. "Marijuana: A Signal of Misunderstanding," Government Printing Office, Washington, D.C., 132 (1972).

Giordano testimony before a subcommittee of the Committee on Appropriations, 90th Cong., lst sess., 1967, at 484–485.

"Health Consequences of Marijuana." Testimony before the Senate Judiciary Committee, January 16–17, 1980, at 102–110.

Humes, T. "The Crisis in Drugs," pamphlet, St. Francis College, Summer 1969, at 8–9.

Johnston, L.D., O'Malley, P.M., and Bachman, J.G. "Monitoring the Future: National Survey of Drug Abuse." University of Michigan, Ann Arbor, 1978.

Letter from F. Baskette to Federal Bureau of Narcotics, September 4, 1936.

"Marijuana Successfully Treats Tourette's Syndrome." NORML Press Release, March 11, 1999.

"Marijuana Users—Musicians, 1933–1937," AP, box 9, of Anslinger file.

McCaffrey interview with Carl Rochelle, CNN, December 30, 1996.

"Monitoring the Future," Annual Survey of Student Attitudes, University of Michigan, Ann Arbor, released December 18, 1993.

Oregon Medical Association guidelines adopted by the Oregon Medical Association. House of Delegates, April 25, 1999.

Presidential Commission on Campus Unrest, Government Printing Office, Washington, D.C., 1970, at 11.

Radio address of President Reagan, October 2, 1982.

"Remarks of the President," September 28, 1981, on file in the Reagan Library.

Speech to Women's National Exposition of Arts and Industry, March 1935, AP file, "Speeches of HA," 1930–1938.

"Summary of the Licata case," 17 October 1933, AP, box 5, file "Scrapbook," vol. 7, 1931–1949, of Anslinger file.

"The Need for Narcotic Education," Anslinger NBC Speech, 24 March 1936.

Text of Nixon "Message on Drug Abuse." *Congressional Quarterly* 24 (1969) at 57A.

Washington State Medical Association facsimile from John Arveson to membership, February 2, 1999.

W.F. Smith speech to the National Press Club, October 22, 1981.

Whitebread, C.H. "A History of Non-Medical Drugs." Speech to California Judges Association, 1995 conference.

INDEX

About the Author

RUDOLPH J. GERBER is a retired appellate judge who served on the Arizona Court of Appeals until 2001. Currently a practicing attorney in Phoenix, he is also on the faculty of the School of Justice Studies at Arizona State University.

HV
5822
.M3
G47
2004

Gerber, Rudolph
  Joseph, 1938-

Legalizing
  marijuana.

$35.00

036533

DATE			

BAKER & TAYLOR